Contagious Capitalism

GLOBALIZATION AND THE POLITICS OF LABOR IN CHINA

Mary Elizabeth Gallagher

PRINCETON UNIVERSITY PRESS

PRINCETON AND OXFORD

Third printing, and first paperback printing, 2007
Paperback ISBN-13: 978-0-691-13036-1
Paperback ISBN-10: 0-691-13036-1

The Library of Congress has cataloged the cloth edition of this book as follows

Gallagher, Mary Elizabeth, 1969–
Contagious capitalism : globalization and the politics of labor in China / Mary Elizabeth
Gallagher.
p. cm.
Revision of the author's thesis (Ph.D.)—Princeton University, 2001.
Includes bibliographical references and index.
ISBN 0-691-11761-6 (cloth : alk. paper)
1. Investments, Foreign—Government policy—China. 2. Investments, Foreign—
Political aspects—China. 3. China—Commercial policy. 4. Labor—China.
5. Capitalism—China. 6. Globalization—Economic aspects—China. 7. China—
Politics and government—1976– I. Title.
HG5782 .G35
330.951—dc22   2004054930

British Library Cataloging-in-Publication Data is available

This book has been composed in Sabon

Printed on acid-free paper. ∞

press.princeton.edu

Printed in the United States of America

10 9 8 7 6 5 4 3

To Magda and Elinor

Contents

List of Illustrations

Acknowledgments

THIS BOOK WOULD NOT have been possible without institutional and financial support from the following institutions: At Princeton University, the Department of Politics, the Center of International Studies at the Woodrow Wilson School of Public and International Affairs, and the Department of East Asian Studies all generously funded parts of the research. At the University of Michigan, the Department of Political Science, the Center for International Business Education, the Center for Chinese Studies, and the Institute for Industrial and Labor Relations all helped in one way or another to improve the research and the writing of this project. I also thank the Foreign Affairs College in Beijing and East China University of Politics and Law in Shanghai for hosting me at different times and supporting my research endeavors.

My undergraduate adviser at Smith College, Steve Goldstein, deserves thanks for first sparking my interest in Chinese politics. His enthusiasm for excellent teaching and scholarship encouraged me to pursue an academic career. My dissertation committee at Princeton, which included Lynn White, Atul Kohli, and Anna Seleny, all deserve much thanks and gratitude for encouraging me, for reading many drafts, and for generally being nice people and exemplary scholars. Lynn White deserves special thanks for his gentle impatience, which helped me to finish both the dissertation and the book. In addition to my committee at Princeton, I also thank the many other scholars and teachers who gave generously of their time and their ideas. They include Nancy Bermeo, Kathryn Stoner-Weiss, Sheri Berman, Michael Doyle, Gil Rozman, Jeff Kopstein, Gary Bass, and Kate McNamara. Monica Selinger and Edna Lloyd provided excellent administrative support and help for every conceivable problem. My fellow graduate students at Princeton were indispensable as colleagues and friends. We were all lucky to have each other. I would especially like to thank Michele Penner Angrist, Dietlind Stolle, Shinju Fujihira, Kimberly Morgan, Mark Stephan, Sharon Barrios, Vanya Krieckhaus, Susan Kannel, Marc Berenson, Xiaonong Cheng, Bell Kwok, Xu Wang, Phil Saunders, Jeannie Sowers, and Michael Ross.

As the project grew from a dissertation into a book many others helped by listening to my ideas or reading various chapters. They include especially the community studying China at the University of Michigan, especially Brad Farnesworth, Al Feuerwerker, Whit Gray, Ching Kwan Lee, Ken Lieberthal, Linda Lim, Jinyun Liu, Albert Park, Marty Powers, and

Wang Zheng. Many others commented on parts of the project and gave generously of their time and ideas. They include Eric Thun, Anita Chan, Marc Blecher, Elizabeth Perry, Iain Johnston, Merle Goldman, Mark Selden, Ruth Collier, Elizabeth Remick, Dorothy Solinger, Dali Yang, Yasheng Huang, Don Herzog, Meredith Woo-Cumings, Mark Frazier, Bill Hurst, Jaeyoun Won, Kevin O'Brien, Neil Diamant, Stanley Lubman, Scot Tanner, Isabelle Thireau, Ruth Rogaski, Andy Mertha, Jerry Cohen, Noga Morag-Levine, Rob Franzese, Zheng Yongnian, Edward Gu, John Campbell, Young Jin-choi, Jacob Eyferth, Larry Root, Ian Robinson, Ken Kollman, Ashutosh Varshney, and Jennifer Widner. While at the University of Michigan, I have had the help and assistance of very able research assistants. I thank Peng Du, Min-hua Huang, Juan Chen, and Lyric Chen. At Princeton University Press, I thank Chuck Myers for taking an early interest in this project and helping it through the publication process. I also thank the anonymous reviewers for suggesting additions and changes that improved the final product. Jennifer Nippins and Cindy Crumrine supplied critical help with editing and copyediting.

In China, the most grateful thanks and appreciation go to the managers and employees of the firms that allowed me to visit more than once, always made time for me, and treated me and my numerous requests graciously. Many other people also helped this project along. In particular I would like to thank Du Jinhong, Zhang Cuiying, Zhang Jun, Pang Qiong Zhen, Tu Hua, Wang Shuxin, Hu Wenbiao, Zeng Jia, Dai Jianzhong, Feng Tongqing, Ko Matsui, Murao Tatsuo, Gao Huaxin, Jiang Junlu, Wang Jianping, Tang Jianyu, Chu Hsi-Cheng, Takeo Nishishiba, Lin Yizong, Jia Zengjun, Steve Mufson, Lei Peng, Chen Weiguo, Lu Dongxia, Liu Yingqiu, Chen Weiguo, Shi Meixia, Jin Canrong, Phil Pan, Dong Baohua, Li Lingyun, Song Jing, Erika Helm, and many others. I also thank the other foreign teachers at Foreign Affairs College for their support and friendship, especially Grace Fan. In Hong Kong, Jean Hung and the Universities Service Centre, Robin Munro, Tim Pringle, and Joyce Wan all offered their help with the research. While I am very grateful for all the helpful advice and constructive criticism received over the years, the errors and omissions that remain are entirely my own.

Some of the analysis presented here draws from previously published work. Parts of chapter 2 originally appeared as "Reform and Openness: Why Chinese Economic Reforms Have Delayed Democracy," *World Politics* 54:3 (April 2002): 338–72. Parts of chapter 4 originally appeared as "'Time Is Money, Efficiency Is Life': The Transformation of Labor Relations in China," *Studies in Comparative International Development* 39:2 (Summer 2004): 11–42. I am grateful for the publishers' permission to quote from these works.

As always the deepest thanks and gratitude go to one's own family, who have had to bear many sacrifices and boring conversations. My parents, Munsey Alston and Steve Gallagher, are heartily thanked for letting me go to China in 1989 when everyone else was canceling. I thank my brothers and sister, Tim, Mike, Joe, and Kate Gallagher, for listening to me and asking the obvious questions. (What is FDI?) To my daughters, Magda and Elinor, who think that all I do is sit in front of a computer, I thank them for being patient most of the time. Finally, I thank my husband, Ken, for all his help and support. He used to help me proofread and edit but now his time is better spent on trips to the playground and the museum. This is of course just as it should be.

Shanghai
January 2004

List of Abbreviations

ACFTU	All China Federation of Trade Unions
AFC	Asian Financial Crisis
CCP	Chinese Communist Party
CDS	Coastal Development Strategy
CEMA	Chinese Enterprise Managers Association
CJV	Contractual Joint Venture
EJV	Equity Joint Venture
FDI	Foreign Direct Investment
FIE	Foreign-Invested Enterprise
GJV	Grafted Joint Venture
JV	Joint Venture
KMT	Kuomintang (Nationalist Party)
LAC	Labor Arbitration Committee
LCS	Labor Contract System
LSC	Labor Service Company
M&A	Mergers and Acquisitions
MNC	Multinational Cooperation
MOFCOM	Ministry of Commerce (formerly MOFTEC)
NICs	Newly Industrialized Countries
PRC	People's Republic of China
SEZ	Special Economic Zone
SHE	Shareholding Enterprise
SOE	State-Owned Enterprise
TEDA	Tianjin Economic and Technological Development Area
UC	Urban Collective
TVE	Township-Village Enterprise
WFOEs	Wholly Foreign-Owned Enterprise
WTO	World Trade Organization

CHAPTER ONE

Introduction

> In opening up to the outside world, we must actively make
> use of things from developed Western countries . . . but we
> must be careful not to take the decadent things for miracles,
> or ulcers for treasures.
>
> —Jiang Zemin, President of the PRC, 1997

HOW DOES AN AUTHORITARIAN STATE renegotiate its duties and obligations to society without sacrificing political control? One of the key explanations for the disintegration of socialism in the Soviet Union and Eastern Europe is that these states failed to keep up their end of the "social contract."[1] Whether through the effects of continual market reform (Hungary, Yugoslavia) or the effects of stagnation (Romania, Bulgaria), these societies were no longer willing to sacrifice autonomy and a liberalized political sphere for a dwindling supply of welfare benefits and job security. As scholars of the region point out, the fusion of economics and politics under socialism made the failure of the economy a moment of political opportunity.[2]

In the Chinese context, however, the state has extricated itself out of the "social contract" with the urban working class without losing its grip on political power. The sequencing of foreign direct investment (FDI) liberalization before significant reform of the state-owned enterprise (SOE) sector and development of domestic private industry has enhanced the staying power of the Chinese Communist Party (CCP) and delayed societal demands for political change. Early opening to FDI was an integral factor in China's success in breaking the "iron rice bowl"[3] and in spreading capitalist labor practices and new legal institutions out from the nonstate sector to the large state-owned sector of China's urban economy. In addition, the large influx of FDI and the new competitive pressures emanating from this sector helped to reformulate the ideological debate central to socialist reform: the debate over the importance of state-owned industry. This debate has been redirected from the public/private dichotomy toward a debate over the need for Chinese national industry amid ever-increasing foreign competition.

For the last ten years, the People's Republic of China has attracted more FDI than any other developing country in the world. In 2002 China surpassed the United States as the most favored destination for FDI. The policy of "reform and openness" of which FDI liberalization is a central part is widely seen as a great success—so successful, in fact, that by 2001, the Chinese leadership successfully negotiated membership in the World Trade Organization. Accession to the WTO marks China's full-fledged acceptance into the global economy and shows the leadership's determination to continue to pursue increased openness, increased foreign investment, and dramatically increased competition within the domestic economy.

There is great debate among economists and policy analysts on the economic effects of FDI.[4] An equally vigorous and perhaps more polarizing debate surrounds the political and social effects of China's FDI policy, in particular, and China's rapid integration into the global economy, in general. Advocates and supporters of "reform and openness" portray FDI as the bearer of all that is good, legal, and advanced.[5] Critics of the social consequences of FDI liberalization portray it as the Trojan horse of exploitative global capitalism.[6] This debate is unsatisfying because it often fails to acknowledge that both of these characteristics co-exist in time and space. One major reason for the polarization of this normative debate surrounding the benefits of FDI and economic integration is that these broad Manichaean conclusions are often drawn from research that is focused on particular regions or industrial sectors.[7]

FDI's political and social effects are highly complex and differ widely across different regions, firms, and individual workers. The behavior of foreign investors is also shaped by their respective home country practices and business cultures so that regions with a heavy concentration of overseas Chinese "foreign" capital look different from areas with more diverse sources of overseas funding. Normative conclusions are dependent on the region, industrial sector, and, if at the firm level, where the firm is placed within international production networks. A researcher studying foreign-invested enterprises in the footwear industry will usually come to different conclusions from a researcher examining labor practices in a multinational producing goods with its own brand name attached. Alternatively, research at greenfield development sites (where foreign and private factories are built from scratch and are often separate from local industry) will yield different insights from research at former state-owned enterprises that have been recently transformed into joint ventures. Finally, interviews with migrant workers employed at one of the many labor-intensive foreign-invested enterprises in China's coastal and southern regions will differ dramatically from interviews with the domestic managerial elite of foreign-invested enterprises in Shanghai and the north. These characteristics and China's large size make it difficult to make broad generalizations about the effects of FDI on the shape of China's developing capitalist economy and its effects on Chinese workers in particular.

Due to these constraints, the broad political consequences of FDI liberalization have either been simplified down to the good/bad dichotomy or have been overlooked. This does not mean, however, that broad, systemic effects of FDI liberalization do not exist but rather that these broad systemic effects impact regions, firms, and workers differently. These differences matter greatly. In China, the liberalization of FDI creates winners in some circles and losers in others. It has spawned competition and fragmentation, but slowly and only at the margins at first. The liberalization of FDI was dynamic and led to a contagion of capitalism across the economic and ideological boundary of public ownership. The power of FDI liberalization as a catalyst for social change is exactly here: It is its ability to create competition, to encourage the development of new institutions, both at the firm level and through the legal system, and to alter fundamentally the debate over socialist ownership by placing ownership in a more global and competitive context.

During my field research, these ideas of competition, fragmentation, and globalization came up repeatedly and among many different kinds of people. At the Beijing headquarters of the Chinese Enterprise Managers Association (CEMA), the official organization representing state enterprise managers, the representative complained bitterly that the unfair advantages granted to foreign firms made it impossible for state firms to compete. State firms needed the autonomy to hire workers, fire workers, raise salaries to retain skilled workers, and cut benefits to reduce the social welfare burden. How would Chinese industry survive without a level playing field against the foreign investors?[8]

At an SOE in Tangshan, Hebei Province, a manager made this general concern very specific. "After the Sino-Japanese joint venture opened in Qinhuangdao, we lost a large number of managers who were attracted by the higher salaries of foreign firms. . . . After that we began to pay attention to the problem of retaining talent."[9] This firm's solution was to open up the wage differentials, paying top managers wages that exceeded ten times the monthly wage of a production worker and guaranteeing housing even as it cut welfare benefits to the vast majority. Another manager in the same firm explained their staff reduction policies this way: "we want to look more and more like foreign firms."[10]

A manager at a small rural collective producing DVDs in Hebei complained that his firm had no foreign investment and little likelihood of attracting any. But the absence of foreign investment can sometimes be just as influential as large infusions. "We need to compete with joint ventures and wholly foreign-owned companies; competition is very fierce in this sector and so our management is very strict."[11] He continued as we toured the production line, showing how wages and bonuses were scrupulously tied to small errors in the workers' performance. He proudly explained how each worker was encouraged to report the mistakes of others in exchange for bonus points. A sign hung over the shop floor with the admonition "time is money, efficiency is life." This famous slogan had first appeared in the 1980s amid the foreign manufacturing plants of Shenzhen, across the border from Hong Kong, and was lauded by Deng Xiaoping as one of the positive slogans of the Special Economic Zones.[12] Now more than fifteen years later, it reappeared in a small rural factory in central China.

A harried manager in an urban collective in Tianjin, a city with a long legacy of state ownership and a growing unemployment problem, talked about the collective's attempt to get rid of its many small enterprises. "We contract the enterprises out to managers or when possible try to find an overseas Chinese investor to turn these companies around."[13] When asked how management and labor practices are affected by these changes, he shrugged and said, "If the manager takes over, we still make sure that they abide by certain regulations regarding wages and benefits. We let them reduce the staff but we take the laid-off workers back. Then they wait for more work. With foreigners, we give over complete management autonomy. We figure that they must know how to do things right to turn the company around. And we take the workers that they don't want."[14]

A low-level clerk in a Tianjin SOE that was recently leased to a Korean investor gave her impression of these changes. "After the Korean boss came in, all the older workers were fired, they were just sent home. They kept me because I'm young. The old SOE managers and the Communist Party Chief still hang around. They kept their office so that they could collect the rent. They're just like a bunch of landlords."[15]

My original research plan in 1996–97 was to study how the Chinese state managed different modes of labor practices. I planned to investigate firms varied by ownership to study how two modes of labor relations, capitalist and socialist, could coexist within China's political economy. Starting from where Margaret Pearson's study of joint ventures left off, I planned to study how different nationalities of investors, in different types of ownership structures, including wholly foreign-owned enterprises, managed labor in comparison to the labor practices in China's socialist firms, SOEs, and collectives. Like many well-intentioned research plans, my study was quickly redirected into examining why labor practices across different types of ownership were becoming more and more similar in the absence of political change and large-scale privatization.[16] The differences across the public-private divide that I expected to find were not as apparent as I expected, and moreover, they seemed to be diminishing rapidly over time as all firms adjusted to what they perceived to be an onslaught of competition and economic globalization. This discovery led me to examine more carefully China's opening up and how this process affected behavior on the ground. In particular, I examine how the liberalization process has affected labor relations in China, including labor-management relations at the firm level and state-labor relations more broadly.

In order to highlight the importance of early liberalization of FDI to China's continued path of economic reform without political liberalization, I analyze China's trajectory in comparative perspective, examining other cases of reform and liberalization across time and space. China's use of FDI liberalization is in stark contrast both to other reforming socialist states, which relied first on internal reform, and to other East Asian developmentalist states, which relied on export-driven growth without much direct foreign participation in their domestic economies. This comparative method allows us to see more clearly how one variable in the economic reform process can have diverse effects given its sequencing relative to other important reforms, especially privatization and state sector reform. This focus on this one variable is also warranted given the tendency in the literature on democratization to consider increased openness and greater exposure to global trade and investment as forces for political change. While I cannot show here whether or not this association is incorrect more generally, the Chinese case shows that economic openness can under some circumstances strengthen political authoritarianism.

The two primary alternative explanations for China's economic success amid political stability privilege other aspects of China's reform path. One explanation argues that the gradual nature of the reforms determined success, particularly in contrast to the shock therapy tactics in the 1990s in postsocialist countries.[17] Another explanation argues that the ability to implement "reforms without losers" created the social consensus to continue reform and reduced the threat of political instability.[18] The argument presented here takes the first explanation to be incomplete and the second to be wrong. The gradual nature of Chinese reform was a characteristic shared by the reforms of many other socialist states. Russia, Hungary, and Yugoslavia all have reform histories nearly as long or in some cases longer than China does. The experiments with shock therapy came only after the political revolutions of 1989 when gradual, piecemeal reform was rejected in favor of systemic reform, both political and economic. While Chinese reforms can correctly be described as gradual, other aspects of the reforms, the sequencing of reforms in particular, are more important in China's achievement of economic reform without significant political liberalization.[19]

China's reforms also have created losers, in terms of both relative economic status and political power. FDI liberalization made important contributions to the widening economic and social opportunities among Chinese regions, firms, and workers. Uneven liberalization of FDI led to increased competitive pressure between regions and firms for FDI inflows. Foreign-invested enterprises (FIEs) also increasingly competed with domestic state firms for skilled labor. These competitive pressures have led to increasing fragmentation and have reduced urban labor's resistance to reforms. Reduced resistance to reforms has delayed demands for political change. Openness and integration with the global economy have not brought a weakened Chinese state or a democratizing one. In fact, utilization of FDI as a change agent in the reform process has delayed political liberalization in China and enhanced the staying power of the CCP.

FDI played three roles in this process. First, FDI liberalization placed *competitive pressure* on regions and firms to pay attention to labor practices and regulations. In order to attract ever greater amounts of FDI, regions granted enterprises increasing managerial control and autonomy over labor practices. Domestic firms, interested in attracting infusions of foreign capital, also became increasingly willing to grant foreign investors more managerial control and more flexible labor policies. SOEs as they struggled to compete with FIEs also lobbied for a level playing field and for the extension of more flexible labor policies into the state sector. These competitive pressures, combined with learning and demonstration effects, hastened the adoption of capitalist labor practices in state firms. Second, the foreign sector served as a *laboratory* for difficult and politically sensitive reforms, in particular changes in the traditional social contract between the state and urban workers. This laboratory effect was critical in allowing the competitive pressures mentioned above to manifest themselves gradually. Third, the existence of a foreign-invested sector led to an ideological reformulation that reduced the importance of *public* ownership in China, while increasing the importance of *national* ownership. China's leaders have justified the "letting go" of state ownership in order to build up national industry that is globally competitive.

While the transition described here is from the planned economy to the market as the mechanism for supplying rapid growth, the ideological transition made by China's leaders has not been from socialism to liberalism, but rather from socialism to "state-led capitalist developmentalism."[20] Developmentalism has been used in different contexts to describe a developing state's commitment to an ideology of rapid economic development. The specific policies of developmentalism vary across time and space. Latin American developmentalism of the 1950s and 1960s included a heavy emphasis on import-substitution. East Asian capitalist developmentalism of the 1960s, 1970s and 1980s looked to export-oriented production with simultaneous protection of domestic markets and firms by a strong activist state. The underlying common theme of developmentalism persists despite changing policy, that is: state-led development in the name of rapid economic growth and the nation's entry to the realms of industrialization and modernization. As Gordon White and Robert Wade have argued, successful late development is most often a "process in which states have played a strategic role in taming domestic and international market forces and harnessing them to a national economic interest."[21] Capitalist developmentalism in the Chinese context is an ideology of rapid economic growth through state-led development and state control over society. The heavy state role is justified by the growth itself, with political pluralism or democracy rejected in favor of "social stability," which the regime takes as the foundation of rapid growth. This view of state-led development borrows heavily from the experiences of other East Asian capitalist states, in particular South Korea, Taiwan, and Singapore.[22] Unlike most of its East Asian neighbors, however, Chinese developmentalism is built upon active and large foreign participation in the domestic economy.

The study thus raises a related question, but it is a question that can be answered only as the future unfolds. That is, is heavy dependence on FDI compatible with developmentalism itself (as opposed to its mitigating effects during the transition from socialism)? Does the nationalist element inherent in developmentalism create a contradiction between state-led development and a liberal FDI policy? The study gives some reason to question the long-term compatibility of developmentalism and FDI. As Chinese society struggles to met the challenges of WTO membership, the contradictions between openness and developmentalism will become more pronounced. State enterprise reform, banking and financial reforms, and rising unemployment are all now intimately connected to increasing FDI and foreign competition. Reliance on FDI as a change agent also invites the temptation to use FDI and globalization more generally as a scapegoat for the difficulties of China's transition to capitalism.

OVERVIEW

The study proceeds as follows: In chapter 2, I present the main argument about the effects of contagious capitalism on China's domestic development. The Chinese case is discussed in comparative perspective against other reforming socialist states and East Asian developmental states. This argument is based analytically on three separate functions of FDI: as competitive pressure, as a laboratory of capitalism, and finally as ideological justification. These functions are examined in detail in four empirical chapters. Chapter 3, on competitive pressure, is an account of the evolution of foreign ownership in China from 1978 to 1999. In this chapter I show how foreign ownership has expanded over time and become increasingly integrated into China's domestic economy. I also show how ownership itself has blurred with the rise of hybrid firms that can no longer be neatly classified as "state-owned" or "foreign-owned."

Chapters 4 and 5 examine institutional changes related to the existence of these laboratories of capitalism within the Chinese domestic economy. Chapter 4 focuses on the firm level. I argue that the public-private divide is no longer important in determining labor practices. Firm-level responses to the trends detailed in chapter 3 are increasingly similar. In particular I examine two institutions that were intended to protect labor from the vagaries of the market: the labor contract system and the official trade union organization. As I show, these institutions in implementation have instead enhanced managerial autonomy and control over labor. Chapter 5 focuses on the broader institutional environment, especially the development of legal institutions to structure and mediate labor relations and labor conflict. I show how this drive for legal institutions was directly related to the problems and challenges of managing FDI. I also show that despite the increasing use of state-sanctioned labor dispute resolution processes, labor conflict is rising quickly in China with the highest rate of labor disputes in firms with foreign investment. This chapter also conveys the growing resistance of workers to their increasing marginalization at the workplace.

Chapter 6, the final empirical chapter, goes beyond the previous chapters' examination of change in economic structure, practices, and institutions to examine the underlying changes in ideology. This change in ideology is important because it demonstrates that despite a liberal FDI policy, China's ideological change has not been directed toward liberalism, but rather toward a developmentalist ideology that is inherently nationalistic. In the conclusion I relate this contradiction between ideology and practice to the potential contradictions inherent in China's FDI policy.

CHAPTER TWO

Contagious Capitalism

> Stationary capitalism is a contradiction in terms.
> —Joseph A. Schumpeter[1]

CHINA'S GRADUAL REFORM PROCESS is widely acclaimed for achieving "reform without losers."[2] For those who study labor, this does not ring quite
true.[3] There are losers, and they include many of the same Chinese citizens
who were earlier lauded as the "masters" of the country and the ruling
class: the urban employees of state industry. Why did their declining status not mortally threaten the political rule of the Chinese Communist
Party? Most analyses of this question give two answers: rapid growth and
gradualism. And indeed, these answers are partially correct. The People's
Republic of China's (PRC) average growth rate from 1979 to 1993 was
9.2 percent and the economy grew at 6–8 percent in the late 1990s despite
the ill effects of the Asian Financial Crisis of 1997.[4] Reform, from 1978
on, has been gradually and cautiously implemented, avoiding areas of the
economy that were most resistant to market reforms while allowing areas
like agriculture and rural industry to reform quickly. The argument presented here does not dispute these explanations; rather it shows that we
must also pay attention to the foundations of *gradualism with growth*.
These foundations include the successful liberalization of China's foreign
direct investment policy and its sequencing prior to other key reforms.

The sequencing of the Chinese reform process (FDI liberalization first,
private-sector development second, and significant SOE reform last)[5] has
meant a gradual and correspondingly less painful reform process for
China's urban workforce. China's reform process chipped away at the social contract between urban state-owned enterprise workers and the state,
while reducing the importance of this sector in both absolute and relative
terms. At the same time China's nonstate economy was radically expanded despite the lack of widespread privatization. A major factor in this
gradual yet radical process has been China's dramatic utilization of foreign capital, in particular FDI.[6] The foreign-invested sector functioned as
a source of new competition for the state sector, as a laboratory for sensitive labor reforms, and as an ideological justification for deeper reform.

The findings of this study challenge the accepted dogma on the relationship between globalization (defined as global economic integration)

and state capacity. It takes issue with the widely held assumption of the "international arena's negative effect on stateness" as the "presumed invariant" in our study of states.[7] In doing so, it also questions the link between economic openness and democracy.

The literature on the relationship between economic development and democracy is varied and complex, much of it jumping off from the "Lipset hypothesis" first proposed in 1959, which posited a causal relationship between economic development and democracy.[8] The literature includes theories of modernization, dependency, and most recently, globalization.[9] Modernization theories posit a causal link between economic growth (and its corollaries of increased education, communication, and mobilization) and democracy. Indeed, the belief that economic growth, development, and greater integration with the outside world will lead to a more liberal and democratic China has been the foundation of U.S. foreign policy toward China for the last twenty-five years. More recently, theories of globalization have posited that due to increased transnational flows of goods, money, ideas, and people, national economic and political systems would increasingly converge toward the "ideal" system of a market economy and a liberal democratic political system.[10] Other theories of globalization predict a decline in the sovereignty of nation-states and their capacity to govern because of the pressures and demands of an increasingly global economy.[11] The argument presented here challenges these ideas by showing how economic development amid increasing openness can contribute to the stability of authoritarian rule in China. In opening its borders to large flows of foreign capital, China's Communist leaders have made growth and globalization work for them.

FDI liberalization has helped delay political liberalization in China because it preceded the other key reforms of a socialist transition: reform and/or privatization of the state sector and the development of an indigenous capitalist class, reforms that would have created more pressure for political change. FDI's role can be summarized as follows: The formation of a foreign-invested sector of the economy creates new *competitive pressure* across regions and different types of ownership for deeper reform, provides a *laboratory* for sensitive and difficult reforms, and leads to the *ideological reformulation* of the public-versus-private industry debate. This reform process increases dynamically the chances that further reform will be carried out, thus avoiding the traps of "partial reform," which tends to create winners who then block further reform in order to preserve their special position.[12] Foreign investors are less likely to be satisfied with partial reforms and continue to push for deeper reform and liberalization. At the same time, however, this reform process reduces societal opposition to reform. As a newly created system of ownership, outside the primary state and collective sectors, the foreign-invested sector has only marginal impact on the core socialist workforce. Its expansion, however, leads gradually to the fragmentation and expansion of the industrial working class. This fragmentation and diversification brings increased competition, which reduces the political power of groups that benefited from and were protected under socialism.

In the latter half of this chapter, China's process of liberalization is compared to the experiences both of other reforming socialist economies and other East Asian developmental states. Two main differences in China's process of liberalization are important to understand why it has occurred in the absence of political change. First, China's *pattern of ownership diversification* avoided a frontal assault on socialism by opening up new types of ownership rather than reforming the core sectors first. Second, China's *mode of integration into the global economy* has occurred without the creation of a powerful private business class, relying instead on foreign capital to achieve integration with the global economy.

FDI as Competitive Pressure

The competitive pressures unleashed by FDI can be attributed to two separate types of liberalization: "competitive liberalization"[13] across China's regions and liberalization of ownership, which includes both the introduction of new types of industrial firms and "ownership recombination."[14] These liberalizing trends across both regions and ownership regimes led not only to regional competition for investment inflows but also competition between individual firms for foreign investment, and competition between foreign-invested firms and state firms for skilled labor.[15] These different modes of competition increased the importance of FDI in China's domestic economy by encouraging both regions and firms to liberalize competitively so as to become more attractive to potential investors. This liberalization enhanced the bargaining power of foreign capital leading to, if not a race to the bottom, then a race to implement more flexible labor policies, to create a more mobile labor force, and to pass laws and regulations granting more enterprise autonomy. Competition between firms for skilled labor (and profits) also created internal support within the SOE sector for a "level playing" field. This level playing field included the extension of preferential policies and laws applicable to foreign-invested enterprises to the state sector.

Regional Competition

The decentralization of the economy and the devolution of authority and decision making power to local governments are key characteristics of the Chinese reforms. Decentralization, at times described as an informal version of federalism, was key in granting local governments the ability to grow the economy and the necessity of doing so, as the central government cut spending and support, hardening local government's budget constraints.[16] Economic liberalization was, however, not a national policy that was extended equally to all regions. Preferential policies for trade and investment liberalization were granted in a piecemeal fashion that fulfilled the proclamation of China's first reformist leader, Deng Xiaoping, to "allow some people to get rich first." "Segmented deregulation"[17] of the economy led to a political dynamic of increasing competition and liberalization in which some regions that were allowed to open up first enjoyed benefits, rents, and opportunities of the international economy. This unequal treatment led to demands from closed regions for the extension of preferential policies. As these policies were extended, regions increasingly competed for inflows of both foreign and domestic investment.[18]

Local governments pushed for greater liberalization because of the benefits that accrued to areas with large inflows of foreign capital and more linkages to the international economy. These benefits were often but not exclusively monetary in nature. Localities and firms often also preferred the flexibility and autonomy that came with the establishment of industrial zones outside of the traditional urban public sector core. In fact Zweig's research on urban internationalization shows that one main consequence of the zones was to attract Chinese domestic capital from other areas, firms that were simply looking for more flexibility, autonomy, and external contacts.[19] Desire for flexibility and autonomy extended to the labor realm. Firms in these new industrial areas, particularly when they found a foreign partner, were subject to different laws and regulations from those of the core public sectors in China's cities.

Liberalization of the foreign investment and trade regime in China was not a uniform policy of national liberalization and integration with the outside world. It was at first a policy of insulated laboratories that allowed limited contact with the external capitalist economy in rural or suburban areas isolated and separate from the urban core of public ownership. Benefits that came from the extension of the policies led regions that were excluded to push for further liberalization. The liberalization of the foreign investment and trade regime sparked regional competition for inflows of both foreign and domestic capital, which further enhanced the bargaining power of capital. This dynamic of gradual liberalization across regions would have important consequences for the regulation and restructuring of labor relations.

Ownership Liberalization

"Segmented deregulation" of foreign investment and the spread of these policies through a dynamic of competitive liberalization are one crucial part of the story of the transformation of labor practices. A second equally important dimension is the changes that took place in ownership, including both the expansion of new types of enterprise ownership and the "recombination" of public and private (often foreign) ownership in the form of hybrid firms.[20] China's avoidance of shock therapy–style privatization masks the very radical changes that occurred in lieu of privatization and that were realized only by the tapping of the huge labor supply in rural areas. Migrant labor, which is estimated to range between 80 and 120 million, has fueled China's industrial transformation as the nonstate sector, especially but not only township village enterprises, absorbed large amounts of rural labor. While many migrants are employed in the growing informal economy, migrant labor is also predominant in the export zones and coastal factories funded by foreign and private capital.[21]

Evolution of foreign ownership in China took place on two dimensions: first, there was increased choice in the type of foreign investment vehicle and the range of domestic partners. Second, through this expansion of choice, there was a steady increase in the degree of managerial autonomy and the degree to which foreign investors could control decision making within the enterprise. As with the liberalization of policies across different regions, policies that dictated the permissible types of foreign investment vehicles and the allowable domestic Chinese partners were gradually yet radically liberalized over time. The 1978 containment of foreign capital through the joint venture framework had become in 1997 permission to sell off SOEs to foreign and private investors.[22] As investor autonomy and control increased, changes in labor relations that had earlier been in effect only at the margins were now taking place in the core public sectors. In some regions where the 1997 reforms had surfaced as the spontaneous innovations of local elites, this transformation happened much earlier in the early 1990s.[23]

Thus, at the firm level, competitive liberalization had similar consequences to those felt across China's regions. Competition and cooperation (through formal joint ventures or subcontracting) with foreign-invested firms required radical changes in the labor practices of Chinese firms and in the state's administration of labor. Convergence to more capitalistic labor practices at the firm level and the simultaneous blurring of ownership divisions administratively and legally made many of the institutions of state socialist labor control not only obsolete but also inimical to the continued development of the economy. This led to institutional friction between the new market-based regulations in the foreign-invested sector and the "iron rice bowl" system of employment and benefits in the state and collective sectors. As the institutions of socialism proved incapable of keeping up with the challenge, institutional decay and breakdown became widespread.[24]

Such competition, on the regional level and between firms, is a powerful force for convergence with capitalist practices of foreign firms.[25] It reduces resistance from those in state enterprise because to stand by and hold fast to "socialist enterprise" would mean losing out on the chance to gain not only capital and technology but also prestige from association with the international economy. Economic reform is pushed ahead dynamically by such competition, while resistance is reduced.

Competition between Firms for Skilled Labor

Competition between firms for skilled labor is also important as an impetus for further reform amid reduced societal resistance. As foreign-invested enterprises began to become more integrated into the domestic economy, competition increased not only for market share and profits but also for skilled labor and managerial talent. Such competition was particularly difficult for SOEs. Long accustomed to monopoly positions in the domestic market, they were often not legally able to compete in an increasingly flexible labor market, for example, by offering competitive wages to top managers and technicians or easily firing unwanted or redundant employees. Competition between SOEs and FIEs in the domestic economy led to calls from within the SOE sector for a level playing field. That is, the state sector began to perceive the preferential policies accorded to joint ventures and wholly foreign-owned enterprises as a barrier to their own development and a hindrance to fair competition.[26] This competition led by the mid-to-late 1990s to much greater support within the state sector for fundamental change, up to and including privatization of most state firms.

FDI and Laboratories for Change

The early stage of dual-track reform and "disarticulation"[27] between the foreign-invested sector and the rest of the economy was important for expanding the political space for experimentation and radical reform. The foreign-invested special economic zones (SEZs) and development zones that sprang up all over China's coast by the early 1990s became laboratories of capitalism, introducing new and destabilizing reforms of employment, social welfare, and enterprise management. Many of these new practices were encoded in laws and regulations expressly designed for the foreign sector, allowing short-term labor contracts, wage and bonus-setting autonomy for enterprise managers, and a sharp reduction in the social welfare burdens of the enterprise. Implementation of these new laws and practices avoided, however, overt conflict with the norms of socialism and the "iron rice bowl"—China's system of lifetime employment and extensive social benefits for urban workers. Workers drawn into the foreign-invested sectors and the development zones of coastal China were overwhelming young, inexperienced, and unfamiliar with the labor practices of socialist firms. Often migrant female workers from China's poorer inland regions made up the bulk of the foreign invested enterprise's production workforce.[28]

At the same time, of course, these development zones attracted older and more skilled workers, managers, and technicians away from the state and collective sectors. These workers, while socialized into the socialist enterprise system, were drawn into these capitalist laboratories because they benefited from a much less egalitarian system. The widening of wage and bonus differentials, special perquisites like manager housing and training abroad, and the perception of more opportunity for advancement all drew in China's special "human talent" (*rencai*) into the foreign-invested sectors.[29] Thus this laboratory of capitalism includes workers who are least invested in or who benefit least from the socialist system of employment. It is only as competitive pressure builds on other sectors of the economy that the effects of this laboratory are felt more broadly as other firms adopt labor practices of foreign-invested firms and the managers of these firms increasingly press for greater flexibility and autonomy.

The laboratory effect also functioned at the macrolevel of legal regulation and development. FIEs were the first to introduce and strictly implement employment contracts. In tandem with the rising labor mobility associated with short-term employment came a revolution in firm-level employment relations. Many of these firm-level changes were encoded into Chinese labor law, the development of which had been nearly moribund since the 1950s. At first, these laws were written expressly for the foreign-invested sector and were considered outside of the realm of normal socialist production. Legal analysts argued that workers in FIEs were at greater risk of exploitation and therefore labor laws should be tailored to this particular sector. A related but opposing reason for the development of specific foreign-invested laws was the need to satisfy foreign investor demands for a more flexible labor force and increased managerial autonomy over human resource issues. Labor laws for FIEs reflect both these concerns, although in implementation they tend to favor the side of management.[30]

One important characteristic of these laws is that they came to be considered part of a system of "preferential treatment" accorded to foreign firms alone. These laws and regulations increased enterprise and managerial autonomy and flexibility in almost all areas of personnel management. Regulations on hiring, firing, term of employment, nonwage benefits, and the designated role of worker representative institutions granted

FIEs significantly more flexibility and reduced burdens related to the employment of Chinese workers. The leadership justified these changes by pointing to the mandated higher wages in the foreign-invested sector. However, as mentioned above, these differences in treatment led to the demands for a level playing field among state managers and their supporters in the leadership.

Accordingly, over time, labor laws began to be developed that were not "ownership-specific"—that did not dictate enterprise behavior based on ownership type. Yet laws that were adopted for the whole economy were largely based on the laws already written for foreign-invested firms. The market logic of FIE employment law, with its notions of contract and autonomy, triumphed over socialist notions of guaranteed employment and the "working class as the master class." SOE managers were granted the rights to act like capitalist firms in order to be able to compete against them. These rights included greater managerial autonomy, the use of larger wage differentials between workers and managers in order to stop the drain of top level managers to the FIE sector, a lighter social welfare burden, and the right to lay off redundant staff. More generally, SOE managers won the right to pursue profits and efficiency over socialist goals like full employment and egalitarianism. A schematic explanation of this process is produced.[31] (See following page.)

As laboratories for change, FIEs established space outside the traditional socialist sectors, state and collective firms, in which to adopt new norms of behavior and new methods of labor management. Over time, however, due to the pressures of competitive liberalization and market competition mentioned above, a contagion of capitalist practices has occurred across once distinct ownership boundaries. At the macrolevel, the establishment of this new foreign-invested sector led to laws and regulations specifically created for this new ownership system. However, over time laws have become increasingly non–ownership specific, with the laws of the foreign sector serving as the templates for a new comprehensive body of labor and employment law.

The development of legal institutions to structure labor relations has led to a rapid increase not only in the number of laws and regulations but also in the number of labor disputes between workers and their employers. Chinese workers have not sat passively by as their entire world has been restructured and reformed to fit the new requirements of competition and efficiency. This is particularly the case with workers in foreign-invested enterprises. Labor conflict in foreign-invested enterprises far surpasses rates in other types of enterprises. In 1999 there were 456 disputes per 100,000 workers in the foreign sector, compared to 132 disputes in the private sector and 31.2 disputes in the state sector. Labor dispute trends since the passage of the National Labor Law in 1995, however,

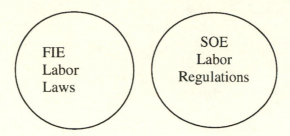

1980-1982
Labor Laws Governing Enterprises in the PRC

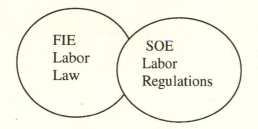

1983-1994
Labor Laws Governing Enterprises in the PRC

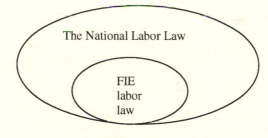

1995-
Labor Laws Governing Enterprises in the PRC

Figure 2.1. The Evolution of Labor Laws in the PRC, 1980–1995. *Source:* "Restructuring FIEs in China and Procedures to Cut Staff" (*chugoku niokeru gaisho taishi kigyo no resutora oyobi*) Kokusai Shoji Ho 27:5 (1999).

show signs of convergence between different types of firms and, perhaps more importantly, more disputes involving "recombinant" firms that no longer fit neatly into discrete ownership categories.

FDI AND IDEOLOGICAL CHANGE

Increasing convergence across different types of ownership in the realm of labor relations contributed to the ongoing debate on the function of state ownership, particularly because SOEs had already been shown to be economically inferior.[32] FDI and the competition it created at the firm and local levels affected the way state leaders thought about state ownership, leading to a radical reformulation of one of the key debates of socialist transition: the proper role of public ownership in a marketizing economy.

Socialist transitions generally began with a struggle to allow a limited role for the private economy in the hope that it will contribute to a general improvement in economic conditions and lessen some of the negative attributes of the plan—shortages, lack of consumer goods, and low-quality goods. In the 1980s, however, in most reforming socialist economies, the plan continued to falter, while the private (or mixed) economy spawned greater subversion, increased corruption, and led to declining legitimacy of the regime. Thus in the debate over public versus private, public ownership's standing continuously fell and further contributed to the dissolution of socialism in the USSR and Eastern Europe.

What we see in China is, substantively speaking, not entirely different. The SOE sector of the economy has lost out repeatedly under reform. Most SOEs have shown themselves to be immune to reform and still operating under incentives from the socialist era: the soft-budget constraint, continuing state support for failing firms, irrational investment, and politically determined personnel appointments.[33] The nonstate economy, including the foreign-invested sector, has time and time again shown itself to be more efficient, more dynamic, and more capable of bringing widespread benefits like increased employment, better goods and services, and higher levels of technological accomplishment. In the earlier stages of reform, a debate between public and private ownership was largely postponed because the dual-track system allowed both to continue side by side, the nonstate sector in success and the state sector in (often hidden) failure.[34] By the Fifteenth Party Congress in 1997, however, as the regime finally signaled its willingness to privatize large swaths of Chinese state industry, this debate was reformulated into one between Chinese national industry and foreign industry. The Chinese regime has retained its legitimacy by refashioning the debate over privatization into one of Chinese industrial survival amid ever-increasing foreign competition. Privatization (euphemistically referred to as "letting go" at the Fifteenth Party Congress) is necessary so that Chinese "national industry" can be enlivened and strengthened to meet its global competition. A nationalist perspective has replaced a socialist perspective; goals of competition have replaced the goals of socialism. State ownership, when it is retained, is justified for strategic reasons, while past justifications that relied on the moral superiority of public ownership have been jettisoned.

"Opening Up" in Comparative Perspective

Comparative analysis of China's reform policies yields insights both across types of socialist transition, comparing China to Eastern Europe and Russia, and across time, comparing China to other high-growth East Asian economies. A key factor in China's ability to reform the economy without sacrificing political control is the timing and sequencing of its foreign direct investment (FDI) liberalization. There are two key variables that are important to this comparative analysis. First, China's pattern of ownership diversification stands out in contrast to other reforming socialist economies. FDI liberalization preceded both the privatization of state industry and the development of a domestic private sector. Second, China's mode of integration into the global economy varies dramatically from the experiences of other East Asian high-growth economies, Korea and Taiwan in particular. FDI has been the dominant source of external capital for the PRC, far outweighing the more indirect, managed ties to foreign capital established by other East Asian states. I relate these two variables to the success of economic change without political liberalization, in particular how FDI liberalization has affected relations between workers and the ruling Chinese Communist Party.

FDI and Ownership Diversification: China against Eastern Europe and Russia

Janos Kornai argues that the deepest kind of reform for a socialist system is one that alters property relations.[35] Public ownership of the means of production is the defining characteristic of the political economy of classic socialist systems. Unchallenged rule of the Communist Party is its political counterpart. As the economies of socialist countries worldwide began to falter by the late 1970s, new attempts were made to modify the classic pattern. Reforms generally included both attempts to recalibrate the incentives and constraints within public ownership as well as increased toleration for diverse forms of ownership.

In the transition from socialism, FDI liberalization is only one method of diversifying industrial ownership away from the state monopoly. The two most obvious alternatives are internal reform and/or privatization of the state sector and the development of an indigenous private business class (most often accomplished in part by the legalization of the already existing second economy). Here we examine why FDI liberalization may be less politically destabilizing to a communist regime than these other reforms, which not only tend to threaten directly powerful interest groups but also strengthen and legitimate the subversive forces of the heretofore underground economy. Comparisons to the economic reforms of Russia under Gorbachev and Hungary's early legalization of private industry are made here.

Reform of State Industry

China's reforms in agriculture and foreign investment and trade went far beyond those of the Soviet Union by the end of the 1980s. In the urban and industrial reforms, however, Chinese and Soviet reforms up to the same point were not very different. Both countries attempted to improve the external and internal environments of state industry, to reduce the number of planning indicators, to put greater emphasis on profits, and to introduce management contracts to improve managerial performance. From the 1984 "Large-Scale Economic Experiment in Industry" to the 1987 Law on State Enterprises, Soviet reformers tinkered with the public ownership system in a way almost identical to the Chinese experiments that began in 1984.[36]

Chinese and Soviet reformers also met with similar problems and difficulties. Reforms in enterprises in both countries led to indiscriminate wage increases, large-scale corruption related to the ability of state managers and bureaucrats to profit from the gap between plan and market prices, and conservative and bureaucratic resistance to reforms that reduced the power of ministerial bureaucrats. Many of these issues surfaced in the popular uprising associated with the student demonstrations in Tiananmen Square in 1989. In Russia as well, failure to reform the socialist system and the concomitant problems of corruption and bureaucratic interference, "led to increasing liberal radicalization of state bureaucrats and economists because the reforms demonstrated the inability of tinkering reforms to get the USSR out its economic crisis."[37]

Why, despite these similarities in both the nature and the problems of state enterprise reform, did Soviet and Chinese reforms go in nearly opposite directions by 1989? Soviet leaders were increasingly radicalized in favor of totalistic system reform, including political liberalization, while Chinese leaders gravitated even more to gradual, piecemeal reform of the economy alone. One major difference in the nature of Chinese and Soviet industrial reforms is that the Chinese reforms in state industry were only a part of the much wider scope of industrial change. At the same time that China's SOE reforms were failing, Chinese reforms in foreign investment were starting to yield fruit; and unexpected experiments in rural collective industry were taking off.[38] By 1992, with Deng Xiaoping's Southern Tour, FDI liberalization quickened and picked up the slack of a failing, inefficient state sector. In 1992 China attracted $58 billion in contracted FDI, an increase of 384 percent from the year previous. In 1993 contracted FDI jumped another 92 percent to $111.4 billion.

The Soviet Union's exclusive reliance on SOE reform as the linchpin of its industrial reforms doomed it to failure. Such failure led directly to the subsequent radicalization and the increasing attraction of "shock therapy." Such reform leads to failure because it directly experiments with some of the most entrenched, recalcitrant, and powerful groups under socialism: bureaucrats, state managers, and state enterprise workers. SOE reform attacks the dying patient directly and with the hard-to-swallow medicine of market competition. The creation of a foreign-invested sector as a laboratory, however, gives the medicine in small doses and corrodes resistance over time. For a comparison of FDI inflows among the transitional economies, see figure 2.2 below.

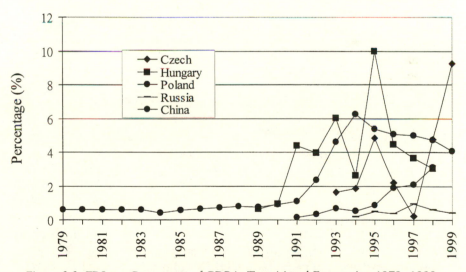

Figure 2.2. FDI as a Percentage of GDP in Transitional Economies, 1979–1999. *Source:* Data complied from the *European Bank of Reconstruction and Development Annual Yearbook* (various years); and the *China Statistical Yearbook* (various years).

SOE reform in isolation, as adopted in the USSR, also does little to spark competition between regions or firms. The soft budget constraint is still in effect because under partial reform no firm is expected to take ultimate responsibility for its losses. There are so many other parts of the economy that do not work well that enterprise failure can be anyone or no one's responsibility. Unfortunately, with the continuation of soft budgets, the atmosphere of experimentation leads to trends like irrational investment, speculation, indiscriminate wage hikes, and managerial corruption. Experimentation without fear of failure or bankruptcy makes for bad reform. The competition for FDI inflows between regions and firms that prevailed in China was absent in the Soviet Union. Funds for investment or experimentation were handed down from the state, but under the soft budget constraint, did not lead to marked increases in efficiency.

There is also little chance for SOE reform to lead to fragmentation and increased competition between workers. Amid tight labor markets and a history of labor hoarding, changes in enterprise behavior tend to strengthen worker resistance to reforms that threaten their privileged position.[39]

Finally, exclusive and primary reform of the state sector leads not to an ideological reformulation of the reform's significance, but rather to a heightened focus on the proper role of public ownership. The departure from socialism is the center of the debate and the leadership becomes extremely sensitive to charges that it is deserting its own historical platform. Unlike the Chinese case, which saw a reformulation of the debate away from public versus private to foreign versus Chinese, the Soviet debate in the late 1980s was inwardly focused. Every step away from socialism was one step closer to capitalism. Every step toward capitalism further reduced the legitimacy of the Soviet leadership and the rule of the Communist Party.

The Subversive Private Economy

Other socialist countries had long diverged from the classic socialist system, introducing reforms that encouraged the development of small-scale private economy and increased ties with the West, and generally tried to find a way to modify the rigidities of the socialist planned economy. The case of Hungary is an interesting one and has been frequently examined in comparative perspective with China. Hungary's market reforms began early and in sequencing are the most radical of any reforming socialist economy: In 1980, Hungary legalized the second economy and began to create a burgeoning private sector. In 1987, the private economy was liberalized further in response to a faltering economy. Many of these private firms worked through partnerships with state firms. The close association between private firms and state firms led to the by now familiar problems of worker outflow to private firms, moonlighting, use of public assets for private gain, and corruption.

The growth and development of the private economy in Hungary led to the erosion of state authority over time. As one academic observed, "The role of the second economy in Hungary was clearly a subversive one. It accomplished very few of the objectives the leadership had set for it, it destroyed the leadership's control over labor, and it upset its ability to plan the macro-balance of income flows. Moreover, it deprived the party leadership of its social base."[40] The tight relationship between the private economy and the state sector led to a situation where the Party's core at the enterprise level benefited and supported continual liberalization. Despite the fact that the private economy was doing little to improve the overall scope of reform (and in fact probably delaying it because private owners and state managers alike benefited from the partialness of the reforms), "[d]iscontinuing the reforms would have meant that the leadership would have had to turn against the party's own ranks."[41]

The Hungarian legalization of the second economy and Chinese introduction of a foreign-invested sector created laboratories of capitalism within a socialist economy. The private economy in Hungary gradually infiltrated the state sector and led to the reduction of societal and bureaucratic resistance to reforms. In fact, as Rona-Tas argues, the success of the private economy led to greatly increased support among managers and party activists for greater reform and reduced the state's ability to control the reform process. The laboratories in both countries had a subversive effect on state socialism by placing great economic pressure on the state sector. This economic pressure led to broad demands for deeper reform. It is on the political front that their effects have been quite different.

The development of a private economy and a private entrepreneurial class creates an obvious alternative to socialist rule. As in the Soviet Union, the ideological debate is centered around the issue of public ownership versus private enterprise. As public enterprise falters and slows during the 1980s, the second economy hums along and satisfies the domestic population in a way unfamiliar under socialist planning. The wisdom of state ownership is cast increasingly in doubt and the supporters of the second economy (who are now both in the second economy and in the state economy) expand while resistance declines.[42] Unlike China, where the ideological debate was reformulated along foreign and nationalist lines, the Hungarian debate became more sharply focused on the private/public dichotomy. It is the subversive success of the second economy that seals the fate of socialism. It is the rise of an alternative ruling elite (private entrepreneurs and their collaborators within the state) and the development

of the "new interest politics" that bring demands for political liberalization and the end of the monopoly on political power.[43]

FDI and Integration in the Global Economy: China against Korea and Taiwan

The second variable of FDI liberalization, as the mode of integration into
the global economy, yields insights across time rather than space. Comparisons are often made between China and its East Asian neighbors,
economies known for rapid economic growth through a heavy reliance
on export-oriented industrialization promoted by an activist state.[44]
China's early and continued opening to FDI, however, stands in stark contrast to the experiences of other East Asian states, Japan, Korea, and Taiwan in particular. Although their industrial structures and development
trajectories differ in important ways from each other, these East Asian
economies were built on strong domestic business classes often closely al-
lied with interventionist states. Foreign participation in the domestic
economy was extremely small despite the export-orientation of their development paths. Due to the limited space, we focus on the experiences
of Korea and Taiwan. See figure 2.3 below.

China's path toward greater integration with the global economy began
with foreign direct investment, and FDI remains today the most significant form of foreign capital. Korea and Taiwan, however, chose quite different paths, limiting severely the amount and nature of FDI while pursuing export-led industrialization through the promotion of domestic

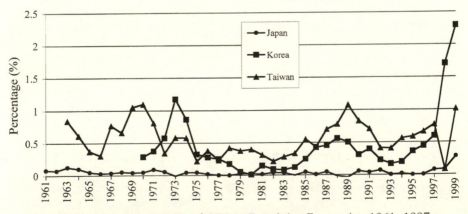

Figure 2.3. FDI as a Percentage of GDP in East Asian Economies, 1961–1997.
Source: Data complied from *International Financial Statistical Yearbook* (Washington, D.C.: International Monetary Fund, various years); *The Statistical Yearbook of the Republic of China* (Taipei: Executive Yuan, various years.)

firms.[45] The Korean and Taiwanese governments chose domestic economies that were quite closed and protected but with an outward orientation that spurred efficiency and technological development up the production ladder over time. China's leadership has chosen much greater integration with the global economy, with foreign capital flowing in as exports flow out.

How is this difference between China and other East Asian states important to our understanding of the democratization process? The development and strengthening of the domestic business classes in Korea and Taiwan was due in large part to the close relationship between the state and business during the period of high growth. Over time the growing autonomy and independence of the private business class (the large chaebols in Korea and the ethnic Taiwanese small and medium enterprises in Taiwan) led to pressure for political change. The business elites were not liberal democrats. However, their growing independence made the united front of authoritarian government and domestic capitalism increasingly untenable. This fissure between state and business in the late 1970s and early 1980s led to increased support and political space for the democratization movements in both countries.[46]

In the PRC, however, there is little chance for the leaders of the private economy to play a central role in China's political change in the near future. The delayed development of private industry has resulted in a sector that, while growing rapidly in terms of employment and output, remains small in scale, often dependent on local governments for support, and still facing discrimination in credit opportunities.[47] In fundamental ways, FDI has become the substitute for large-scale private industry in China. This substitution has important effects on the possibilities for democratization in China. While foreign investment may indirectly improve the environment for future democratization, through the promotion of the rule of law, transparency, and the freer flow of information, in the short term its presence has afforded the regime more time and more political space to pursue economic reform without political liberalization.

Domestic Business and the Developmental State

Korea and Taiwan experienced rapid economic growth in the postwar period despite near economic collapse after the end of their civil wars in the early 1950s. Growth was achieved through policies of state-led industrial development that continuously pursued export markets abroad while leaving their domestic economies quite closed. In the 1960s both countries relied on labor-intensive manufacturing and the open markets of the United States. By the 1970s, experiencing a slowdown in rapid growth and new competition from other developing countries in low-level manufacturing, both countries looked to move up the production ladder. Following the Japanese model, these states began to shape policies that would shift their industries toward heavy industry in Korea and high-tech, petrochemicals, and plastics in Taiwan.[48]

Although the state and business were acting in concert and business was obviously benefiting from the policies, these actions would change the balance of power between the developmental state and the domestic private business class, strengthening the business class against the state in both cases. Of course there are important and very large differences between the industrial structures of Taiwan and Korea. Taiwan's economy is largely populated with small and medium-size enterprises that are privately owned, often by ethnic Taiwanese. The Korean business elite was embodied in the "chaebol," the large diversified industrial groups that were modeled after the Japanese system of *keiretsu,* a system of vertically linked companies with interlocking ownership and relationships.

Links between the government and business groups in South Korea were direct. These vertical pressures could not be easily countered, because intermediate or independent local institutions were weak, repressed, or absent. A homogeneous and nationalistic big business class thus was available in South Korea to carry out the government's objectives in terms of domestic and overseas investments and external trade.[49]

The heavy industrialization drive in the 1970s in Korea further increased the importance of the Korean chaebols. In the early 1980s, during a time of economic crisis and political instability, the Chun regime encouraged policies of financial and economic liberalization that were intended to curb somewhat the importance of big business and end the practice of guaranteed policy loans to Korea's biggest firms. But the general trend of increasing power and influence for the chaebols at the expense of the Korean state did not end and, in fact, intensified. The chaebols' share of the economy continued to grow, with the top ten chaebols' contribution to total manufacturing sales reaching 67 percent in 1984.[50] Moreover, the opening of the Korean economy in the early 1980s granted big business alternative paths for capital financing on the international capital markets and less reliance on the state for credit.[51]

Taiwan's movement in the 1970s and 1980s to strengthen and diversify their economy targeted many small to medium-sized Taiwanese firms that were owned by ethnic Taiwanese. The growth of Taiwan's private industry over time intensified the ethnic cleavage between the mainlander-dominated political elite and the ethnically Taiwanese economic elite. In combination with changes with the leadership (the liberalizing rule of Chiang Ching-kuo and the increasing Taiwanization of the ruling party, the Kuomintang (KMT), Taiwan's private business class grew increasingly powerful.[52]

Neither the Korean nor the Taiwanese business class became frontrunners in the push for democratization. However, the changing balance of power between the state and business did have ramifications on politics and did increase pressure from other social forces for democratization. Karl Fields writes on Korea: "In Korea, the symbiotic collaboration between powerful bureaucrats and giant chaebol achieved the mutually beneficial objective of rapid, Fordist, economic growth. But the social and political consequences of this developmental strategy and the increasing strength and financial autonomy of the big business sector have significantly altered the nature of state–big business relations and the mutuality of benefits."[53]

In China, however, the development of private industry has lagged behind the liberalization of FDI. The development of private industry has been subjected to informal bureaucratic discrimination, barriers to capital and financing, and barriers to expansion both across different regions and into the global economy.[54] Even with China's accession to the WTO, the relationship between the ruling Party-State and the private business elite remains contested. CCP support for domestic private enterprise, in the form of allowing entrepreneurs to join the CCP, has led to a divisive debate between conservatives and reformers on the proper nature of the CCP and its relationship to capitalists.[55]

China's developmental trajectory, while modeled in some ways after its East Asian neighbors, diverges in its widespread use of FDI in place of a strong domestic private enterprise. This may change in the future as China's leadership grows increasingly concerned with the ability of the remaining state sector firms to compete internationally and the growing dominance of foreign firms in China's domestic marketplace. At this point, however, this difference in development paths is likely to affect the direction of political change in China.

It is unlikely that China's domestic private business elite will play a significant role in politics in the near future. The private sector was given constitutional protection in 1999, and the constitution was revised again in early 2004 to provide protection of private property. These changes indicate that the CCP leadership is paying more attention to the interests of China's new wealthy elite. The CCP also adopted a new policy of "three represents" in which the CCP now purports to represent the interests of China's advanced productive forces and therefore, in return, allows private entrepreneurs to join the Communist Party.[56] This welcoming of "red capitalists" by the party might be seen as a sign of the CCP hedging its bets when it comes to the long-term performance of the SOE sector.[57] If it is the private sector supplying the domestic economy with the most new opportunities, why not fuse the ancien régime with the potential seeds of its own destruction?

CONCLUSION

The sequencing of reforms in China, in particular the early and competitive liberalization of FDI vis-à-vis other reforms, has led to a delay in political change by enhancing the capacity of the CCP to implement difficult reforms while maintaining a political monopoly. This path of reform at first protected, then fragmented, and finally marginalized the urban working class: the social class most privileged under socialism and, historically, the class in whose name the Communist Party rules. This process had led to the gradual but radical transformation of labor relations, a transformation that is no longer limited to the newly created nonstate sector but which has been extended into the socialist core.

The competitive pressures inherent in the liberalization of FDI, across regions and firms, has led to increased convergence with capitalism and reduced urban labor's resistance to reforms. The foreign-invested sector of the economy acted like a laboratory for the difficult and sensitive reforms of a marketizing socialist economy, but competition pushed these reforms across ownership boundaries. Finally, the presence of foreign competition and the looming specter of the WTO has reformulated the transition debate over public and private industry into a debate over foreign versus Chinese competition. The Chinese Communist Party has survived intact despite their declining commitment to their core principles (state ownership, elevated role of the working class, notions of economic justice). These core principles have been rejected in favor of principles of nationalism, Chinese industry, and the ability of China to compete in the international economy.

In light of problems of transition in some Eastern European countries and Russia, there may be benefits to delayed political change in China. Integration into the global economy, the increased use of legal institutions to mediate conflict, and the influence of a small but growing middle class may together slowly build up a more stable societal foundation for democratization, something that was absent during the 1989 student-led Tiananmen Pro democracy Movement. This is not an argument to say that the "Chinese are not ready for democracy"—many countries can go through democratization and be unprepared; in fact, historically this has probably been the case for most countries. This argument merely points out that there may be benefits to continued authoritarianism, in particular the broader social foundations for democratization, including a growing middle class and the development of institutions to mediate societal conflict.[58] For example, legal institutions are developing to mediate mostly, but not only, economic conflicts. Many different social groups are increasing using the law to protect their rights or protest perceived injustice, as chapter 5 demonstrates. The state itself promotes these institutions as a way to stave off demands for further political liberalization and to channel societal demands into channels under its control. Social groups do not enjoy complete autonomy and these legal institutions still do not work well, but like an iterated game, people become more adept at using them to their favor. As incomes grow, particularly, citizens have expanded access to lawyers, and there is growing consciousness about civil and political rights. This increasing contentiousness extends beyond China's middle class to aggrieved farmers in China's countryside and workers in both the sweatshops of the south and the rustbelt of the north.[59]

China's integration with the world economy has surely contributed to these trends as China's legal system has incorporated bodies of law necessary for increased contact with the outside world.[60] China also regularly uses international codes of conduct and covenants as models for their own domestic legal development.[61] Economic integration has helped this progress and given greater justification for convergence with other countries. Legal institutionalization and convergence in labor practices are not sufficient for political change. However, as shall be shown in chapter 5, the turn toward the law has dramatically increased the expectations of workers who believe that these new institutions should offer them protection and due process. In the longer term, the creation of these new institutions will increase pressure on the state to respond more effectively to those who have lost out in economic reform, in terms of both economic security and political position.

An important qualification of the general argument presented here is the conclusion that political change has been *delayed,* not stopped. The transition debate has been reformulated, not forgotten altogether. The influence of FDI liberalization and integration with the global economy has differential effects over time. In the short term, "reform with openness" can produce economic change without political liberalization. Reform with openness reduces societal resistance to reform, buying the existing regime time to implement politically difficult reforms and to reformulate the ideological foundation of their legitimacy to rule. In comparison to East European and Soviet Union reforms, the Chinese reforms avoided a full-frontal attack on the existing institutions of state socialism, including the work-unit system of urban employment.[62] Instead, these institutions eroded slowly over time in a losing competition with the market.

CHAPTER THREE

Blurring Boundaries:
Foreign Direct Investment and the Evolution
of Enterprise Ownership in China

"Taking the Motherland Public"[1]

SINCE 1978 A KEY ELEMENT OF CHINA'S ECONOMIC REFORM has been the opening to foreign investment and trade. This policy has turned out to be one of the most successful reform policies. From 1979 to 2002, China drew in over $446 billion in utilized foreign FDI, second only to the United States worldwide. (See table 3.1) Compared to other socialist or postsocialist economies, China's ability to attract FDI is unprecedented. Russia, a reforming economy that has also looked to foreign investment as an engine of growth and restructuring, attracted a mere $14.3 billion in FDI in the 1990s. Compared to other large developing countries, China is again in a league of its own, attracting over $430 billion in net FDI since 1990 against Brazil's $138.3 billion and Mexico's $113.5 billion.[2]

China's ability to attract large inflows of FDI seems at odds with the traditional assumptions about the nature of foreign investor preferences and contrary also to the normally assumed preferences of the CCP. Foreign investors care about reduced risk, clear property rights, a stable institutional setting, and a clear chance for profits. Ruling communist parties, one might assume, cherish stability, control, the preservation of economic sovereignty, and the protection of state-owned industry and state-sector workers. Yet since 1979 FDI has become an increasingly significant part of the Chinese economy. In 2002, foreign-invested enterprises contributed 24.5 percent to China's industrial growth, while exports manufactured by FIEs accounted for over 50 percent of China's total exports.[3] From 1993 to 1997, FDI as a proportion of gross fixed capital formation was 14.56 percent, much higher than the more closed economies of Korea and Taiwan (1.06 percent and 2.78 percent respectively) and even higher than Malaysia (14.12 percent) and Thailand (3.76 percent), countries that are considered relatively open to FDI.[4]

The initial decision to liberalize the economy and allow FDI was made in the late 1970s in the aftermath of the Cultural Revolution. It was a calculated decision to allow limited FDI in order to overcome a dire capital

TABLE 3.1
Foreign Direct Investment in China, 1990–2002

Year	Contracted FDI (U.S. $billion)	Change on previous year (%)	Utilized FDI (U.S. $billion)	Change on Previous Year (%)
1990	6.6	+18	3.5	+3
1991	12.0	+82	4.4	+26
1992	58.1	+384	11.0	+150
1993	111.4	+92	27.5	+150
1994	82.7	−26	33.8	+23
1995	91.3	+10	37.5	+11
1996	73.3	−20	41.4	+9
1997	51.7	−29	45.2	+8
1998	52.1	+2	45.5	+1
1999	41.54	−20.2	40.39	−11.2
2000	62.66	+50.8	40.77	+.94
2001	69.19	+10.4	46.85	+14.9
2002	82.7	+19.5	52.7	+12.4
TOTAL	795.29		430.51	

Source: Compiled from China Ministry of Commerce, www.mofcom.gov.cn. and "Foreign Investment in Brief," U.S.-China Business Council, www.uschina.org/public/briefinvest/html.

shortage and a dearth of technology, modern industrial equipment, and managerial know-how. FDI was to be a supplement to China's primary socialist, state-owned economy. The original vision of state leaders was to see FDI as a passive tool, something that could be controlled and manipulated to fit the goals of China's leadership. Keeping FDI under control was important for political reasons, because the last time that foreign capital had thrived on Chinese soil, China ended up a humiliated, nearly colonized, wrecked empire. Nor did the large-scale presence of Western and Asian capital fit with China's economic goals of nationalistic economic development and rapid growth, such as that enjoyed earlier by Japan, Korea, and Taiwan.

It has been stated by others that China is now heavily dependent on foreign capital.[5] In this chapter, however, it is not the degree of China's dependence on FDI that is examined but rather the process of FDI liberalization and integration with China's domestic economy. This process was extremely dynamic, path dependent, and largely unintended. Earlier policies placed important restrictions on later reform.

Understanding this process is important to demonstrate the link between FDI integration into the domestic economy and the contagion of capitalist labor practices across the public/private ownership divide. There are in fact many illustrations of FDI as an agent of change, from the strictly economic to the social and the political. This examination of the evolution of foreign ownership, including the diversification of ownership types and the blurring of boundaries between established types of ownership through "ownership recombination," shows that FDI in China has not only grown in numerical terms and across geographic areas, but that its impact has spread across enterprise ownership types. With this increasing integration, FDI has gained a political significance that outweighs (and will probably outlive) its economic effects. In other words, FDI may or may not be a long-term engine of growth, but in these crucial reform years, it has been an important engine of reform and continued economic liberalization.

Three forces have advanced the integration of FDI into the domestic economy. First, the process and sequencing of economic reform, in particular the early opening to FDI, the delayed development of a domestic private economy, and the delayed reform of the SOE sector, has increased the importance of foreign capital's contribution to China's overall economy. Second, FDI was given political significance early on by the central leadership. The "Open Policy" was used as a tool to gain provincial support for reform. The central government allowed several coastal regions to prosper early through preferential FDI policies and thus gained key provincial support for controversial reforms. After FDI was extended more widely, performance and effectiveness of local government officials was measured based on their ability to attract and retain FDI. Thus local officials found their interests to be strikingly similar to those of foreign investors or, at least, local officials were increasingly pressured to please foreign investors as a way to promote their regions and their own careers. Finally, external trends in globalization and the changing preferences of foreign investors also led such investors to push for deeper, more integrated economic relationships on the mainland. Foreign investors increasingly emphasized greater opportunities in the Chinese domestic market as well as more effective management control at the firm level.

In brief, this chapter establishes the links between FDI and the transformation of labor relations not only within the limited "foreign-invested" sector but also across ownership types, most importantly into the core of socialism: the state-owned enterprise. It is a nuts-and-bolts account of the path of FDI liberalization from the early days of isolated development zones to the current practice of allowing foreign investors to buy state companies lock, stock, and barrel. Through the diversification and blurring of ownership, firm-level labor relations and the state's regulation of labor relations have been much changed, as the chapters that follow will demonstrate. As ownership types have diversified, foreign investors have gained greater autonomy and control at the enterprise level, and their opportunities to invest in many different types of enterprises have increased. State enterprise managers have found a method to overcome the strictures of state sector employment and authority relations. Finally, local officials have found foreign investors to be a new source of employment and tax revenue and as potential buyers of burdensome state firms. Thus the mechanism for change in labor relations is found here, in the diversification of ownership types open to foreign investment and the increasingly murky boundaries among ownership sectors.

CHAPTER OVERVIEW

Part one of this chapter is a brief overview of the relevant literature on FDI in China. Heretofore the literature has done well in explaining the initial reasons for a liberal FDI policy and in explaining why foreign investors have responded so enthusiastically to China's investment opportunities. This literature has not, however, examined closely enough the political incentives of a liberal FDI policy. The continuous liberalization of FDI is due to a dynamic reform process that increased the supporters of reform. Through the continual expansion of the benefits of FDI to both local officials and SOE managers, they too became ardent supporters of increased liberalization. Some of these incentives, although not all, lie in the realm of labor relations, including transforming firm-level management and authority relations, relieving local employment pressures, and, more broadly, aiding the development of labor markets.

Part two gives a detailed account of the changes in FDI that have taken place since 1978. This section focuses both on changes in government policy and investor reactions as well as on more spontaneous phenomena at the local and firm levels that also led to changes in ownership structure. This section demonstrates the "blurring" of ownership boundaries in China through the expansion of new types of ownership as well as through ownership recombination, which is the fusing of the public and nonstate sectors through novel forms of organization.[6]

Part three shows how this trend of increased autonomy and managerial control of foreign capital and blurring lines between ownership types have been able to proceed. The competitive pressure unleashed by FDI liberalization, across regions and firms for FDI inflows and between foreign and state firms for skilled labor, explains the trends detailed empirically in the second section.

FDI IN CHINA

China's ability to attract FDI is well known. To the envy of many other developing countries, China has consistently attracted the lion's share of FDI from the developed world. In 1994, 49 percent of all FDI inflows to the developing world went to China.[7] In 1999, China continued to lead the developing countries in FDI inflows, and in 2002 China surpassed even the United States as the most favored destination for foreign direct investment.[8] China has also succeeded in attracting multinational companies interested in China as a production base for export and for its large domestic market. Many of the characteristics of China's political economy make an explanation of China's success seem facile. It has a very large, relatively well educated, low-cost workforce; it is politically stable; and it has a large and growing consumer market. Prior to its accession to the WTO in 2001, China also had relatively high tariff barriers, another reason for foreign companies to locate production within its borders rather than choosing to import from without.[9]

Explaining FDI in China, however, involves two components: explaining why there is a high supply of investment from foreigners and explaining why there is high demand for FDI from within.[10] Much of the analysis focuses on the former component, leaving the latter to be assumed as natural and logical. Indeed, there are important logical reasons for the Chinese leadership to have looked to FDI as a source of investment in 1979. China faced a capital shortage, lacked advanced technology, and the Chinese domestic managerial class was small and inexperienced. But there are also important reasons for China to be wary of foreign capital: a history of foreign invasion and imperialism during the nineteenth and twentieth centuries; a ruling Communist Party that jealously guards its monopoly on economic and political decision making; and, finally, a strong nationalistic component to economic growth that places high importance on China's relative power vis-à-vis other nation-states. Indeed these fears of foreign capital led to the policies of autarky and self-reliance under Mao Zedong; these were policies that eschewed dependence on the economic wealth of other countries, capitalist and socialist alike.

The domestic debate regarding foreign capital has waxed and waned in China throughout the reform period. Using foreign capital to aid China's development was a crucial part of the reform process, but it was not an uncontested one. It was and continues to be highly controversial and sensitive because it touches on issues close to the hearts of the CCP and many ordinary Chinese. The presence of FDI on Chinese soil reminds some Chinese of an earlier, bitter period when China was too weak to control foreign capital, when the presence of foreign capital was a precursor to foreign militaries on China's soil.

In this context, China's relatively liberal FDI regime becomes somewhat more difficult to explain. Why did China's leaders consistently liberalize FDI throughout the 1980s and 1990s? Did the fears of foreign capital exploitation diminish over time? Did the government find that it was effective at establishing controls over FDI such that greater flows could be tolerated? Did the FDI policy have such success in attracting capital and technology to justify further liberalization?

These questions cannot be answered definitively in favor of increased FDI. For example, by 1993 it was apparent that foreign capital exploitation, in the form of labor abuses and substandard working conditions, did occur quite regularly.[11] It was also clear that due to the increasing economic decentralization, controlling FDI and the behavior of foreign investors was difficult.[12] Finally, most leaders were openly disappointed with the amount and quality of technology brought in by foreign firms.[13] Yet China's FDI policy evolved gradually toward greater liberalization in spite of these difficulties.

In short, the supply of FDI to China is more easily understood than the increasing demand for FDI from within China. To understand how the demand grew and intensified over time we need to look at less overt changes and to look beyond the concrete legislation and regulation of FDI. In particular we need to understand the interaction between FDI regulations and behavior at the micro level, including local officials, state-owned enterprise managers, and foreign investors. It is this dynamic process that is most often overlooked in discussions on FDI, in which each step in policy liberalization is taken to be part of a natural progression of the Open Policy.[14] This perspective, however, mistakes gradual policy liberalization as planned or premeditated policy liberalization.

It is somewhat strange that FDI policy would be understood as a deliberate, planned out strategy of increased liberalization and openness. Almost all other aspects of China's reforms, from agriculture to rural industrial growth, have been interpreted as dynamic and unintended, with central policy following local policy innovations.[15] The crucial difference between FDI policy and other aspects of reform is the emphasis placed on the role of laws and regulations as necessary precursors to investor interest. Foreign investors' demands are greater than those of local entrepreneurs. Foreign investors are choosing to invest in China while local entrepreneurs have little choice but to keep their capital in China. This ability to choose makes foreign investors more discerning and careful to protect their investments from unforeseen problems. Foreign investors also tend to place much greater emphasis on the development of a strong legal infrastructure. China, however, was able to attract foreign investment despite a wobbly and incomplete legal system by first attracting many overseas Chinese investors who were able to use their cultural ties and social networks to overcome the uncertainty of the investment environment.[16]

Despite the initial importance of government-initiated liberalizing policies, FDI liberalization has been the result of two interacting mechanisms: the liberalization of state policies and regulations regarding foreign investment (especially the lifting of regional and sectoral restrictions on FDI) and the spontaneous policy innovations of local officials, state-owned enterprise managers, and foreign investors. This dynamic perspective on reform is seen in many important works on China's political economy, yet most of these works are either written too early to incorporate the boom in FDI in the mid-to-late 1990s or are focused on domestic examples of dynamism.[17]

Yasheng Huang's examination of the role of FDI does incorporate the later period from 1992, which saw dramatic increases in the flow of FDI. This approach is more comprehensive than the typical economistic approaches, which seem largely to explain the supply of FDI but not the domestic demand.[18] Like other analyses of FDI, however, Huang portrays FDI liberalization as deliberate state policy. He asks, " Why should policy makers in China liberalize the FDI control regime and choose a heavy FDI-dependent financing scheme?"[19] After demonstrating that China's dependence on FDI is in stark contrast to the earlier policies of Japan and Korea, he states that "[t]his heavy reliance on FDI is an indication of Chinese willingness to cede a considerable degree of operational autonomy to foreign investors."[20] Huang also notes that this reliance has had many deleterious effects on the health of the Chinese economy. For example, the credit supply to domestic private firms was tightly restricted so that Chinese banks could continue to loan to failing SOEs. Moreover, foreign-invested firms received preferential treatment in personnel autonomy (hiring, firing, and welfare benefits) that were denied domestic firms. This significantly enhanced the competitive position of foreign firms vis-à-vis state firms that continued to support generous and comprehensive welfare benefits and continued to find it difficult politically to fire or lay off workers. Huang explains the state's willingness to "choose" a development strategy that has yielded such perverse effects with a political explanation, arguing that this development strategy was pursued in order to preserve state ownership and state control over the economy. Treating China's FDI liberalization as a deliberate and well-thought-out strategy of development ignores the true nature of FDI liberalization, which was dynamic and gradual with state policy often changing to reflect practices on the ground. Rather than viewing FDI liberalization merely as a misguided policy choice, the argument here emphasizes how FDI liberalization was pushed forward by momentum from below, especially by the converging interests of foreign investors, local officials, and later even state enterprise managers.

This interaction effect between state policy and bottom-up innovation was compounded by external changes that also increased the importance of FDI worldwide and within East Asia. These factors include rising wages in Japan, Korea, and Taiwan, the lifting of direct investment restrictions by Taiwan, and the increased use of FDI by multinationals throughout the late 1980s and 1990s. Moreover, the sequencing of China's reforms (fast liberalization of FDI, slow reform of the SOE sector, and delayed liberalization of the urban private sector) also enhanced the importance of FDI as a source of capital and employment opportunity.

THE EVOLUTION OF FOREIGN OWNERSHIP

In 1978 with the inauguration of the Open Policy, Chinese leaders hoped to emulate the successes of its East Asian neighbors by throwing off the decades of Maoist autarky and self-reliance and establishing ties with the global capitalist economy. There were significant economic and political barriers. In 1978 China lacked foreign exchange to purchase technology, it lacked the management skills needed to reform industry, and it lacked the strong political-security ties to the U.S. that facilitated Taiwan and Korea's export-led drive. Moreover, whereas Korea and Taiwan were able to build alliances between state leaders and private business, the PRC had eradicated its domestic capitalist class. The PRC had reformist leaders at the center but a decrepit industrial sector in a state of post–Cultural Revolution disarray.[21]

These practical barriers to internally driven reform (along the lines of Taiwan and Korea) were significant. Coming off the radicalism of the Cultural Revolution, the ideological barriers to allowing the return of foreign capitalists to Chinese soil were perhaps even greater. Western and Japanese firms had been booted out with great fanfare in the early years of the communist republic. Vilified as exploiters of Chinese labor and profiting off the misfortunes of a poor, war-torn country, foreign capitalists played a starring role in the Chinese communist story of the near death and rebirth of the Chinese nation. These obstacles to reform and historically based ideas about foreign capital shaped the early policy choices of the Chinese leadership, which in turn set reform and China's FDI policy on a specific course.

The obstacles, both practical and ideological, that lay in front of China's modernization drive were reduced by a political anomaly: the existence of potential "patriotic FDI" from the ethnic Chinese living in the surrounding capitalist economies. Due to China's weak international position in the last 150 years, Chinese capitalism continued to flourish just beyond China's borders, in Hong Kong, Macao, Taiwan, as well as in Southeast Asia. Within these dynamic communities lay a vast wealth of capital, entrepreneurship, and technical and management skills. These communities retained strong cultural, linguistic, and familial ties to the mainland. Political obstacles, particularly between Taiwan and the mainland, had at-

tenuated those ties, but as relations became less bellicose and the Cold War
waned worldwide, investment from overseas Chinese looked increasingly
attractive. On the other side, rising labor costs and a desire to move up the
production ladder to higher value-added, high-tech goods and services provided Taiwanese and Hong Kong investors ample reasons to move production of labor-intensive, low-end goods offshore to the PRC.[22]

This overseas Chinese connection was a critical factor alleviating the
ideological barriers to FDI. Early reform propaganda promoted the idea
of patriotic Chinese coming back to the motherland for the most unselfish
of reasons: to build a richer and stronger China.[23] The fact that these
savvy entrepreneurs would make a killing in labor-intensive, low-level
manufacturing was the unspoken flip side of the story. For example, Wei
Yuming, former vice-minister of Foreign Economic Relations and Trade
stated: "Our government grants preferential treatment to overseas Chinese, compatriots from Hong Kong and Macao, and Taiwan compatriots
who invest in the mainland. They long for the prosperity of the motherland in the possible shortest [sic] time. Some think fondly of their hometowns, in hoping that they can do a bit towards the construction of their
hometowns."[24]

Reliance on overseas Chinese investment alleviated but did not erase
the PRC leadership's fear of foreign capital domination. Overseas investment was to be limited geographically and in their contact with the mainstream domestic economy. In the early years of reform, FDI was allowed
only in strictly controlled development zones situated near China's borders. The state would carefully monitor the "pollution" that flowed outward from these laboratories of capitalism.[25] In reality, however, this decision to allow liberalization in some areas but not others began a
dynamic of competition that weakened attempts at state control.

Special Economic Zones, 1979–1984

The decision to allow FDI was made in 1979 when the first Sino-foreign
joint venture law was promulgated.[26] In 1980, four SEZs were established
in China's southeast. Zhuhai, Shenzhen, Shantou, all in Guangdong
Province, and Xiamen in Fujian Province were situated close to the capitalist economies of Macao, Hong Kong, and Taiwan, but in areas that
were still largely rural and agricultural. For our purposes the most important characteristic of this early FDI policy was the way in which FIEs
were separate from the domestic economy. Barry Naughton argues that
the SEZ policy was one of many policies of "disarticulation, in which suc-
cessive sections of the economy are separated from the planned core,
which persists."[27] The SEZs, in particular, "initially had almost no links
to the remainder of the economy."[28]

Within the SEZs, foreign investors were allowed to set up joint ventures with state-owned firms. Initially the share of foreign ownership was controlled and the chairman of the board of directors was restricted to being a Chinese national. Because the domestic partner was always a state-sector firm, certain institutions and practices carried over into the newly formed companies. The Chinese managers were also supplied by the domestic parent company; there were very few opportunities to hire managerial or technical staff independently. Internal migration into the SEZs was strictly limited in the early reform period, further limiting the employee pool. SEZ firms at the outset were allowed some degree of labor flexibility and autonomy, but due to the strong influence of the Chinese parent firm, the institutions, practices, and problems characteristic of state firms tended to carry over.[29]

By 1984 the central leadership came to the conclusion that the SEZ policy was a mixed success at best. As the core of China's attempt to build up export-led industrial capacity, the SEZs had failed to perform as hoped. High-tech industry was not thriving, and the SEZs still required large infusions of state money for infrastructure development. Coupled with several high-profile cases of corruption, crime, and "unsocialist" behavior, like prostitution, in the SEZs, the conservatives in the central leadership were ready to declare the Open Policy a failure.[30] Reformers, Zhao Ziyang in particular, were forced to find a new direction for the Open Policy.

Foreign investors, particularly the capital-rich, high-tech firms of the West and Japan were also not satisfied with the conditions for investment in China. Overall FDI inflows remained low. A key complaint of foreign investors was the rigidity and lack of autonomy in personnel management.[31]

The Coastal Development Strategy, 1984–1992

The Coastal Development Strategy (CDS) was a radically expanded version of the Open Policy and was effective as the glue to hold together several reform coalitions: groups who benefited from increased openness and who would lobby the central government for such policies. In fact, it probably can be said that the CDS created too many active and latent reform coalitions for the central government to control and manage effectively. But beleaguered reformists in the central government needed to find new supporters of reform to battle the growing conservative opposition in the central government and in the military. "The CDS could potentially purchase political support from representatives of the coastal provinces, while also delivering a considerable economic benefit to the country as a whole."[32]

While the CDS policy of opening up China's entire coastal area was announced in early 1988, facets of this policy began to be implemented as early as 1984. They include the decision in 1984 to open up fourteen coastal cities to FDI with preferential policies similar to although not quite as liberal as those awarded to the SEZs. These new open areas were encouraged to set up economic and development zones in an increased attempt to capture FDI inflows. In May 1985 three development triangles, in the Guangdong Pearl River Delta, in the Minnan River region, and in the Yangtze Delta, were granted status as "coastal open areas" and awarded policies similar to the fourteen coastal cities. Finally, the 1988 Coastal Development Strategy as laid out by Zhao Ziyang not only expanded these liberalizing policies to the entire coast, but also introduced a new development strategy: China would begin to use its comparative advantage to attract labor-intensive manufacturing.[33] In this way China would begin to compete in the global marketplace as a new location for the inexpensive manufacturing of exports.

The CDS was successful in generating the support that then premier and reformist leader Zhao Ziyang anticipated. Coastal provincial and local leaders leapt at the chance to exploit opportunities using FDI and new liberalized regulations guiding foreign trade. The increases in growth, industrial capacity, and the transfer of high-tech equipment and management skills benefited the entire economy. Moreover, Zhao was successful in creating an external reform coalition: a multinational group of foreign investors, from overseas Chinese investors to Western multinationals, who began to have entrenched and long-term interests in the liberalization of the Chinese economy.[34]

The CDS decentralized decision making over foreign investment and liberalized FDI policy in several ways. It granted local officials much greater autonomy in authorizing projects with foreign investment. Local governments could now approve projects up to $30 million. Foreign investors could also form partnerships with township-village enterprises (TVEs), enterprises that while still considered public are run more like private firms, with harder budget constraints and more attention to profitability. TVEs also have much lower welfare and wage burdens and hire from a more flexible labor pool of unemployed workers, surplus agricultural workers, and rural migrants. The central leadership also drew back somewhat from its focus on high-tech, capital-intensive projects and began to allow low-tech, labor-intensive industries to enter. These industries had less prestige and did not match the developmentalist aspirations of some central leaders, but they were a much better fit with China's comparative advantage.

The CDS also clarified and liberalized preferential policies for foreign investors. In addition to devolving decision-making authority to local governments (considerably enhancing the bargaining power of individual investors), the central government dropped the prohibition on wholly foreign-owned enterprises (WFOEs) in the PRC.[35] Foreign investors no longer had to search for a local partner, hire their workers, and risk an uncooperative or inexperienced partner. Preferential tax and land-use policies were expanded as different coastal regions began to compete for FDI inflows. As Naughton writes of the CDS: "These measures implied the end of the government's attempt to micromanage foreign investment. Furthermore, by greatly expanding the number of potential partners and hosts for foreign investors, the measures substantially reduced the bargaining power of any individual unit on the mainland side. Foreign investors could now shop among any number of potential partners to find the best conditions."[36]

Preferential policies were also enacted to attract Taiwanese and Hong Kong investors exclusively.[37] Because the majority of FDI inflows into China have come from overseas Chinese investors, these policies were especially significant in granting much greater autonomy and control to foreign investors. These policies were an important signal to local officials on how far liberalization could go. "[T]ogether these actions by the central government clearly signaled local governments that they were being actively encouraged to court Taiwanese investors and that they could not get in trouble for cutting a too favorable deal with a Taiwanese counterpart."[38] Overseas Chinese investors were permitted to lease out or rent factories and take over all management and short-term financial responsibility. Without changing the designated ownership of a firm (and thereby preserving the ideological restriction on privatization), this policy effectively transformed the inner workings of many firms.

The CDS was extremely successful in opening up the Chinese economy to foreign trade and foreign investment, spurring growth on the coast, and gaining new supporters of the reform program. It also spiked the interest and envy of inland leaders. The CDS exacerbated economic inequality between the inland and coastal regions. Regions not authorized to set up development zones with preferential policies for foreign investors found it extremely difficult to compete with the coast. The inland provinces also lacked the human capital and infrastructure advantages of the coast, so that the CDS added insult to injury by widening the historical gap between the advanced coast and the backward inland areas. Thus the pro-reform coalition added a new albeit disgruntled group: inland leaders excluded from the boom who wanted to see the coastal policies extended nationwide.[39]

As the income gap widened, pressure on the central government to extend the CDS grew. Inland provinces watched with envy as the coast boomed and FDI poured in. The central government, eager to make these poor areas more self-sufficient (and to build a larger revenue base), finally relented in 1994 when the preferential polices of the CDS were extended to all provinces. Coupled with a more general pro-reform atmosphere associated with Deng Xiaoping's "Southern Tour" in 1992 to the booming provinces bordering Hong Kong, this decision heralded a new period of rapid growth and foreign investment. It also extended nationwide the competitive drive for FDI that had already been occurring in the coastal provinces. Thousands of local governments set up development zones in a mad dash to court foreign investors, announced tax and land-use fee breaks, and offered foreign investors access to low-cost labor.[40] This "competitive liberalization" between regions accelerated the trends of expanded foreign investment autonomy and control.

Yang describes the logic of competitive liberalization and "bandwagoning" by inland provinces and reform laggards: "While initially the open policy was confined to a few special economic zones, by the early 1990's, China's opening had become multi-dimensional both geographically and economically. Yet the political momentum for reform in 1992 was far more than the opening up of border regions. Fundamentally it empowered localities to pursue local interests through the offering of various preferential policies and the designation of special zones."[41]

The competitive liberalization that began once the CDS policies were more widely extended once again expanded the bargaining power of foreign investors. Local officials were now competing with other localities across China for foreign capital. Greater inflows of FDI translated into greater local autonomy and financial independence as well as into political prestige for local government and party officials. The increase in the importance of FDI, combined with expanded opportunities to attract it, improved the investment environment, translating into more managerial control and less bureaucratic interference.

The CDS resulted in two trends in foreign ownership of enterprises in China: an increase in foreign investor autonomy and an expansion of foreign investor control at the firm level. These trends stem from the increase in the bargaining power of foreign investors vis-à-vis local officials and potential domestic joint venture partners. Evidence of these trends is threefold: the increasing popularity of WFOEs (as opposed to equity joint ventures or contractual joint ventures); the diversification of joint venture (JV) domestic partners and types of JV cooperation; and the tendency for increased foreign equity stakes in existing joint ventures. These are described in greater detail below. While these trends were magnified and had even greater significance in the late 1990s, their genesis was during the CDS period.

Wholly Foreign Owned Enterprises

The most marked change in how foreign investors set up firms in China is their growing preference for "going it alone" by setting up WFOEs. WFOEs were first permitted in 1986 but expanded slowly until the 1990s. By 1995 the proportion of WFOEs had grown to 27 percent and, by the end of 2002 over 64 percent of all new foreign firms in China were wholly foreign owned.[42] A consultant to Western companies recommended in 1997 that in order to exercise greater control, more foreign investors should go it alone in China:

> Why are WFOEs taking hold in the current environment? The answer is not because of a change in China's legal or regulatory codes. Instead, pioneering companies, frustrated by the limitations and underperformance of EJVs [equity joint ventures], have begun experimenting with WFOEs. Many of these companies have met only minimal resistance from the authorities. Chinese officials are proving far more concerned about what outside investors bring to the country—in terms of jobs, technology, and foreign exchange—than how their deals are structured. At the same time, foreign investors are finding that WFOEs, *because of the flexibility and managerial control* they deliver, make an excellent fit with China's competitive situation today. The bottom line: WFOEs may well be the win-win China strategy that businesspeople around the world have been waiting for.[43] (emphasis added)

From 1996 to 1999 WFOEs grew in relative number to the more traditional equity and contractual joint ventures, showing a clear trend toward foreign investor autonomy and control. In fact, even as FDI in aggregate has declined since the 1997 Asian Financial Crisis, WFOEs have been the only type of enterprise to grow steadily. See table 3.2 below.

Foreign managers of WFOEs contend that not having a Chinese partner is beneficial in several ways.[44] First, there are no demands to hire redundant workers from the Chinese firm. Since redundancy in Chinese state enterprises is estimated to be at least 20 percent, this demand can be particularly important to the Chinese side and a major focus of negotiations. Without a Chinese partner, a WFOE can hire openly through advertisements, job fairs, or interviews at schools and colleges. Foreign firms can also contact the local labor bureau to enlist the government's help in finding eligible workers, but again since the foreign company alone sets eligibility requirements and screens the candidates themselves, they can freely reject workers they find unsuitable.[45] Second, the managerial staff will also be openly hired, unlike traditional joint ventures in which employees are transferred from the Chinese side. Taiwanese investors, in particular, seem to value this autonomy because they fear gov-

TABLE 3.2
Number of Foreign-invested Enterprises, by Type, 1996–2002

	EJVs[a]	CJVs[b]	WFOEs[c]	SHEs w/FDI[d]	WFOEs Percentage of Total
1996	12,628	2,849	9,062	No data	36.9
1997	9,046	2,371	9,604	6	45.6
1998	8,146	2,010	9,674	9	48.7
1999	7,050	1,656	8,201	3	48.4
2000	8,560	1,755	12,199	9	54.1
2001	8,895	1,589	15,640	11	59.8
2002	10,380	1,595	22,173	19	64.8

Source: Compiled from statistics of the Ministry of Foreign Trade and Economic Cooperation, www.moftec.gov.cn/moftec/official/html/statistics_data, and U.S.-China Business Council, http://www.uschina.org/statistics/03-01.html. These statistics are now available at the Ministry of Commerce Web site, www.mofcom.cn, which absorbed the former MOFTEC in 2003.

Notes:
[a]EJVs: equity joint ventures
[b]CJVs: contractual joint ventures
[c]WFOEs: wholly foreign-owned enterprises
[d]SHEs: shareholding enterprises with foreign-investment

ernment interference or "spying" by former SOE managers. Other investors as well who have concerns about industrial secrets or the illegal transfer of technology also value a managerial staff without divided loyalties.[46]

Finally, Chinese law requires that all firms with more than twenty-five employees, foreign or domestic, establish a labor union under the auspices of the official trade union, the All-China Federation of Trade Unions (ACFTU). Enterprise management must then set aside 2 percent of the wage bill for union activities and, depending on the size of the enterprise, have a certain number of full-time union staff. There is significant difference in the rate of unionization of JVs and WFOEs. JVs, especially JVs with state-owned companies, tend to establish a trade union as a matter of course, copying the institutional structure of the parent firm. Union cadres are usually imported from the parent firm and are well schooled in the bureaucratic, "transmission-belt" role of Chinese-style trade unions. WFOEs, on the other hand, are much less likely to have a union. It is estimated that as few as 10 percent of WFOEs have established trade unions.[47] Moreover, even if WFOEs establish a union, these unions tend to be weaker and co-opted by management. As one Chinese human resources manager commented on the union's role in her JV, "our union can do the work of the government, so it's a good thing to have it in a foreign company."[48] This governmental role of the union is, on the other hand, not held in high esteem by many foreign managers.

A second trend is the diversification in the types of joint ventures and the expansion of potential partners for cooperation. This is most apparent in the increase in "grafted joint ventures," where rather than forming an independent JV with a state-owned partner, the foreign investor effectively absorbs a state-owned plant (usually one that is losing money) at a low price. The foreign investors then try to turn the firm around by introducing new management practices, cutting excess workers, and importing better equipment.

The third trend is an expansion of the foreign share in Sino-foreign joint ventures, with the foreign investors partly buying out the Chinese side, enlarging their ownership stake and gaining more seats on the board of directors.[49] In many sectors, the foreign partner is also now permitted to buy out the total Chinese share, effectively transforming itself into a WFOE. In a study by the U.S.-China Business Council of twenty-two FIES in China, it found that once regulations on foreign equity stake were liberalized, two-thirds of the foreign companies upped their stake, emphasizing their desire for autonomy and control. Half of the firms interviewed increased their stake by 50–75 percent of the total investment, while 20 percent acquired complete control (turning a JV into a WFOE). After this consolidation of ownership, only 10 percent of the firms had less than a majority stake in their firms, and 40 percent had between 81 and 100 percent of ownership.[50]

This section has established the origin of these trends in the liberalizing policies associated with the CDS. However, these strategies for foreign investors to gain more enterprise control spread quickly in the mid-late 1990s when the need for foreign capital as a means to revive the languishing state sector intensified. These trends intensified once local officials (and reformist central leaders) sanctioned the use of FDI as a means to solve the state sector problem.

"LETTING GO THE SMALL:" FDI AND THE SALE OF SOEs, 1992–

Foreign investor autonomy and control expanded once again when the Chinese leadership decided to push the languishing SOE reforms forward by allowing FDI participation. This period is treated separately from the dynamics of competitive liberalization, which was a phenomenon across regions. This second phenomenon does not cross spatial borders as much as it crosses ideological ones: from the nonstate foreign-invested sector to the state-owned sector, the hallowed core of socialism. When combined these dual pressures had powerful effects on further liberalization.

In the late 1980s the trends of increased autonomy and control mostly reflected the interests of foreign capital and were realized in part by foreign investors' enhanced bargaining position. The government reactively liberalized FDI policies at the behest of foreign investors unhappy with the business environment.[51] In the 1990s, however, these trends accelerated due to a domestic crisis: over half of all SOEs were losing money and most were deeply in debt. Reformist leaders now saw FDI as a means to salvage the state-owned sector from bankruptcy, financial crisis, and rampant unemployment.

The changes in the leadership's SOE reform policy were announced during the Fifteenth Congress of the CCP in late 1997 but had been in the works for months.[52] The new policy was touted with the slogan "Hold the Big, Release the Small" (*zhuada, fangxiao*), signaling the government's willingness to allow many small and medium-sized SOEs to change ownership hands, effectively allowing large-scale privatization although the government resisted using those words (*siying hua*).[53] Gu writes: "What is striking in China's case is that, through acquisition of Chinese SOEs by foreign investors, a de facto privatization is—to some extent—taking place in a country where the central government has inhibited privatization on the basis of political and ideological considerations."[54]

The Fifteenth Congress did not signal anything new or novel from the center; rather it bequeathed official approval of phenomena that had been occurring in many localities since 1992. "The 15th Congress merely set the ideological tone by officially acknowledging the need to clear out the redundant workforce and to allow the state to abandon its medium and small enterprises step by step."[55] The 1997 policy changes marked a decision to allow large-scale ownership recombination, allowing the merging of the public sector with private capital, both domestic and foreign.[56]

Foreign investment has figured significantly in the state's "letting go" of its small and medium enterprises through a rapid increase in the number of "grafted" joint ventures, the foreign acquisition of state firms, and the renting of factories to foreigners on long-term leases. Accurate information on such activity is mostly anecdotal or region-specific. Official statistics regularly underreport such activity because local officials fear punishment for selling off state-owned assets too cheaply.[57] Chinese journalists and academics have, however, exposed these phenomena through a vigorous debate on the future of Chinese "national industry."[58]

Representatives of foreign business greeted the policies of the Fifteenth Party Congress with the hope that investors' interest in China would deepen despite the economic turndown in Asia following the financial crisis. The U.S.-China Business Council told its members: "[T]he wholesale restructuring of State-owned enterprises promised during the 15th Communist Party Congress presents a range of new opportunities for foreign investment. Foreign investors are now allowed to merge, lease, or buy out medium-sized and small SOEs with the hope that foreign capital, technology, and management experience will put the ailing firms back into the black."[59]

New investors looked to this opportunity as a way to bypass the long waiting period for profits by tapping directly into an established company. In 1998 Eastman Kodak bought three state-owned photographic film enterprises. This deal, wrote the *Financial Times,* "heralded the possibility of a new style of foreign investment. Rather than pouring large sums of money, many years, and considerable corporate energy into a greenfield operation, western companies are looking at the merits of waiting until they can buy into established ventures."[60]

Local Chinese governments were, perhaps, even more enthusiastic than foreign investors. A reporter in Hebei Province captured the new atmosphere:

After two decades of mostly fruitless efforts to turn state-owned companies into market-oriented profit machines, Chinese leaders decided to wash their hands of all but the biggest ones. City and provincial authorities, responding with more gusto than usual to signals from Beijing, plunged into a frenzy of public auctions and cozy backroom deals; some even traveled to Hong Kong to stage trade fairs with entire factories for sale. Nor were they picky about who they sold to: Workers, managers, private businessmen and even foreigners snapped up the once-proud assets "of the whole people"—symbols of China's status as a socialist nation—and turned them into private property.[61]

The central government estimated that as of November 1998, Liaoning Province in China's northeast, a bulwark of state industry, had sold off 60 percent of its small and medium-sized enterprises, while the coastal and southern provinces had sold off over 80 percent.[62] In Fuzhou, the capital of coastal Fujian Province, the number of SOEs was slashed from 592 to below 300 by the end of April 1999. Over 65 percent of Fuzhou's SOEs turned to foreign investment for restructuring, prompting the city's mayor to say, "[n]ot only has capital from the foreign countries injected new vitality into industry, it has also brought advanced technical equipment and modern management mechanisms."[63]

Foreign participation in the restructuring process is realized in a number of different ways. Two of the most common methods are examined below. The first is the acceleration in "grafted joint venture" (GJV) formation between foreign and Chinese firms. The second is the increase of foreign participation in the Chinese stock markets and the increasing "blurring" between the B-share market (purchase restricted to foreigners) and other shares that are restricted to domestic individual and institutional investors. By 2001, with China's accession to the WTO, policies designed to gradually unify the B-share and A-share markets began to be implemented.

Grafted Joint Ventures

"Grafted joint venture" (*jiajie waizi* or *jiajie gaizao*) is a colloquial expression that encompasses several different kinds of merger and acquisition activity between foreign investors and state-owned enterprises. The Chinese term is from horticulture—the grafting of a new branch to the trunk of a sickly tree in order to revive it.[64] The increase in grafted joint ventures is directly related to the declining fortunes of the SOE sector, a veritable forest of sickly trees.[65] In reality, GJVs are a type of merger and acquisition (M&A: the wholesale acquisition of one company by another or the merging of two separate companies to form a new entity), but because the Chinese leadership mostly excluded foreign investors from the formal merger and acquisition process until 2002, they were not counted in the official statistics.[66] As one researcher writes, this new form of joint venture is fundamentally different from previous types and more akin to outright privatization:

> Having been legalized since 1979, establishment of joint ventures is politically and ideologically much less controversial than M&A. Many foreign investors have thus chosen to conduct M&A in China under the banner of joint ventures. Hence, in the Chinese context, M&A can be regarded as a specific form of joint venture. However, there is a difference that, whereas joint venture usually refers to formation of new enterprises and "creation of new economic composition" M&A involves injection of foreign capital into existing SOEs. Since only M&A but not joint venture would *result in transfer of state ownership to foreign hands,* we regard M&A in particular but not joint venture in general as a form of foreign participation in China's privatization.[67] (emphasis added)

There is no clear legal distinction between GJVs and regular JVs. The term "grafted joint venture" can actually describe a wide range of behavior, from a foreign investor buying a controlling stake in a state firm to a foreign investor buying up 100 percent of a firm's equity. The most important distinction between GJVs and regular JVs is the effect on the internal running of the Chinese parent firm. In a GJV the foreign investor becomes involved in the internal management and structure of the existing SOE, whereas normal JVs entail the formation of a new enterprise and have fewer points of contact between the running of the parent SOE and the newly formed JV. In many cases the number of employees transferred to the new JV is low, involving mostly managerial or technical staff. Production workers are often recent entrants into the labor force, fresh from schools or from the countryside. Although both kinds of enterprises introduce capitalist labor practices and greater labor discipline, the "subjects" of these changes tend to be different. In GJVs the foreign investor must work with the existing plant and workforce. More reforms are necessary and the reforms are more difficult due to the entrenched practices of the parent firm.

As mentioned above, statistics on GJVs are incomplete because they still fall under the broader category of joint ventures. However, in a study of GJVs in 1997, Edward Gu was able to compile some regional statistical data that demonstrate the rapidly growing popularity of GJVs as a means to restructure SOEs and attract FDI. For example, in Yantai, Shandong Province, by 1994, 44 percent of all FDI was funneled into the restructuring of SOEs or county-level collectives. In 1993 alone, 22 percent of all JVs in Qingdao, Shandong were GJVs. In Dalian, Liaoning Province, by the end of 1993 $1.3 billion of foreign capital was used to restructure over nine hundred SOEs.[68] New data in a recent OECD report on FDI offer the most persuasive information that GJVs and similar kinds of foreign acquisition of state firms are quite common phenomena. This report found that in 1999 60 percent of China's FDI inflows took the form of mergers and acquisitions.[69] The U.S.–China Business Council found that through November 2002, foreign investors spent $13.9 billion purchasing Chinese firms. This was an increase of 180 percent from the year before.[70]

GJVs are springing up in both the dynamic coastal regions, where the private and foreign sectors are well developed, as well as in the rust-belt regions of northeastern China, an area long dominated by state firms and now facing rampant unemployment. Were they a strictly region-specific phenomenon, occurring only in Fujian or Guangdong, it could be argued that they are simply the result of the close ties between these regional economies and overseas Chinese investors in Taiwan and Hong Kong. The appearance of GJVs in Dalian, Taiyuan, and Tianjin indicates that they are indeed a national phenomenon of privatization through the use of foreign capital. They are extremely controversial because they often result in the loss of state assets, either by selling the SOE too cheaply or, even worse, selling off the best parts of the SOE too cheaply. Conservatives charge that when a foreign investor acquires only part of the SOE, the most profitable workshops, the youngest and best-educated workers, and the most up-to-date equipment are absorbed into the new entity. The original factory is left as a hollow shell, full only of elderly workers and retirees and some outdated equipment. They can then choose bankruptcy or continue to rely on meager and sporadic government handouts to survive.[71]

The highest profile case of foreign investors buying up SOEs was that of China Strategy Co., Ltd. (CS), a firm led by an overseas Chinese businessman from Singapore, Oei Hong Leong. CS shareholders include Morgan Stanley, an American investment bank, and Li Ka-shing, a famous Hong Kong tycoon.[72] Known as the "China Strategy Phenomenon" in the Chinese press, China Strategy attracted attention because it was the first large-scale, cross-regional transfer of state-owned firms to a foreign owner. Chinese analysts also regarded it as an example of a new stage of FDI in which foreign investors bought up even failing state firms in a bid to capture established market share in important industries.[73]

CS expanded its presence on the Chinese mainland first by buying up all the SOEs in one geographic area. In 1992, CS bought all thirty-seven SOEs in the city of Quanzhou, not coincidentally Oei's ancestral home, establishing several GJVs with CS holding a controlling stake of 60 percent. It then also began to expand sectorally across China by buying up SOEs in a single industry. CS acquired SOEs in the rubber industry, the beer industry, and attempted a buyout of a top pharmaceutical company that was canceled at the last moment by the central government.

The case of CS and others like it—for example, Zhuhai City in Guangdong Province, which sold off all SOEs to foreign investors—raised the discomfort of central leaders who feared that state assets were being sold off too quickly and at too low a price. From 1995 to the 2002, there was considerable disagreement at the top whether the problem was the price of SOEs or the fact that so many were being sold to foreigners.[74] By 2003, however there was a renewed commitment to push forward SOE sales to foreign and private investors.[75] Due to the urgency of the SOE problem, the government, instead of halting the sale of state assets, has eased some of the rules placed on mergers. Under the regulations governing bankruptcies and mergers, the acquiring company in a merger must absorb the workforce of the acquired company, but because both sides believe that the surplus workforce is a major cause of the firm's problems, there are negotiations on how to "settle" the excess workforce. In "mergers" that involve foreign investors, legal responsibility for the welfare and employment of the acquired firm's workers was until a new regulation in 2003 even more unclear, because such a merger still qualified as a kind of "joint venture."[76]

In M&As, Settlement of the redundant workers is simply part of the negotiation process. In a special series on mergers, the *China Business Times* explains that the seller can ask for a higher price and use the proceeds to settle redundant workers or the buyer can get a lower price and agree to accept all workers. Downsizing is now a matter of course in most mergers and acquisitions.[77] A Western investment banker involved in these deals stated, "hundreds of things . . . can go wrong—debt, excess labor, management. But what few realize is all of this is negotiable. . . . Given the growing urgency of economic restructuring, the government is increasingly willing to negotiate these problem areas out of the picture."[78] An acquisition of a Wuhan firm by a Hong Kong company resulted in the firing of 1,300 workers out of a total 2000. When Proctor and Gamble formed a GJV with a Nanchang City (Jiangxi Province) factory, it hired only 242 technical staff and laid off 1,600 others.[79] A Western consultant to the Shenyang City government, a heavily industrialized city in the northeast with severe unemployment, demonstrates this willingness to negotiate. "In Shenyang, for example, the government has approved a plan whereby excess workers can be bought out for 15,000 yuan ($1,800) a piece, including pensions and all future commitments."[80]

Local governments are often the most ardent supporters of grafting SOEs with foreign investors, not least because it helps relieve them of their own social welfare burdens. Each GJV resolves the problem of redundant workers differently and behavior can range. In a GJV between a food processing SOE in Zhuhai (Guangdong Province) and China Strategy, the foreign investor absorbed all the workers of the original factory and continued to provide their social welfare benefits. In many other cases, however, the foreign investors bargain hard to absorb a very limited number of SOE workers (preferring the younger and better educated), who are then hired on a contract basis with limited welfare benefits. Older workers are asked to retire early and responsibility for their retirement and the pensions of those already retired falls to the local government. In some negotiations workers are offered a one-time severance package (*maiduan gongling*) and are encouraged to go out and fend for themselves as individual entrepreneurs.[81]

Analysts, both foreign and Chinese, have long pointed out that the most difficult negotiations deal with the problem of redundant employees (in the SOE) and the consistent demand from the foreign side to have full autonomy over personnel choices. Foreign-Chinese M&As have led to large-scale protests and strikes by workers who feel that their interests have been completely ignored during the negotiation process.[82] More frequently than overt protests, however, is the successful division of the workforce into a young or skilled desirable section and an unskilled, usually older, undesirable section.[83] The foreign investor absorbs some of the workers, the local government takes over responsibility for retirees, and most workers in between are shoved toward the market. One reason that negotiations tend to be successful is that conditions inside the existing SOE are already so dire, workers take what they can get, and with foreign capital around they are likely to get a little more than they would otherwise. For example, when China Strategy bought up *all* the SOEs in the city of Quanzhou in Fujian Province, out of a total 15,356 workers, 6,000 had already been sent home, designated as "waiting for work" and were receiving a meager subsidy only sporadically. As many as 3,472 retirees were also no longer receiving adequate support.[84]

Shareholding Companies and Foreign Equity Ownership

Foreign investment may also be expanded through foreign acquisition of shares of stockholding companies. In 1990 and 1991 the Shanghai and Shenzhen stock exchanges were opened. At the time only "A-shares" were issued, shares that could be purchased only by Chinese citizens. In February 1992, "B-shares" were issued on both exchanges; these shares could be purchased only by foreign investors and were denominated in U.S. dollars in Shanghai and in Hong Kong dollars in Shenzhen. B-shares were seen as a necessary means to attract external funds and to acclimate Chinese firms to international accounting practices and other financial practices that ensured fairness and transparency.[85]

Shareholding enterprises (SHEs) have existed in the PRC since 1984, but the process of converting wholly owned state enterprises into shareholding enterprises was adversely affected by the political crisis in June 1989. As with other types of state sector reform, however, SHEs began to grow rapidly in the early to mid-1990s, so that by the first half of 1999, SHEs numbered over 230,000, an increase of 9.2 percent over the end of 1998.[86] In his study of foreign participation in Chinese stock markets, Shu-yun Ma demonstrates that there is significant "blurring" between types of shares and increasing participation by foreign capital across all types of shares. These trends have proceeded in four ways: (1) companies are allowed to issue increasing amounts of equity in B-shares; (2) companies that can list B-shares no longer have geographical restrictions; (3) restrictions on foreign ownership of A-shares and Chinese ownership of B-shares have been relaxed and (4) some "spontaneous conversion" of shares held by domestic institutional investors to B-shares has been allowed, although still not yet officially sanctioned.

Increasing Equity in B-Shares

The central government now allows a larger percentage of a company's total capital stock to be issued in B-shares. In 1995 the government allowed Shenzhen-listed Jiangling Auto Company to sell 80 percent of its B-shares to the Ford Motor Company, giving it a 20 percent stake in the company and making it the second largest shareholder. Also the government is increasing the amount of B-shares, especially in strategic industries like high-tech, energy, transport, and telecommunications. Issues of

B-shares will be given priority and companies issuing both A- and B-shares must first issue B-shares. These changes give foreign investors more opportunities to invest and allow current investors to expand their share of ownership.

Geographical Restrictions Lifted

Because the Shanghai and Shenzhen exchanges are locally run and managed, for several years there were no nationwide laws or regulations guiding these stock exchanges. Firms from other regions found it difficult to list B-shares since the local government granted firms B-share quotas (and often favored local firms). This ended in 1995 when the State Council announced the first nationwide law on B-shares. This law did not place any geographical restrictions on issuers of B-shares.[87] This change opens many more stock-listed firms to foreign ownership.

"Spontaneous Conversion"

Spontaneous conversion of A-shares to B-shares occurs when a company attempts to enlarge the proportion of B-shares relative to the firm's total capital or even, for firms listed on only the A-index, to introduce some degree of foreign ownership. This effectively allows a state-owned shareholding enterprise to transform itself into a "foreign-invested" enterprise. Because this allows foreign investors to buy state assets outright, leaders worried about the loss of state assets to foreigners have criticized this phenomenon.

In 1995 a wholly state-owned shareholding company, Beijing Light Bus, sold 40 million state-held shares to Isuzu Motor and Itochu of Japan. This gave the Japanese companies a 25 percent stake. The first case of this kind, it set a precedent for foreign acquisition of Chinese stockholding companies. Central leaders became even more worried when a Japanese general manager was appointed, thus reducing Chinese control of the company even though it was still 75 percent Chinese owned.[88] This case demonstrates how increased foreign ownership of a Chinese company can have direct effects on management.

After the Beijing Light Bus acquisition and a few others, the central government banned conversion of state and corporate shares to foreign shares until the drafting of relevant legislation, some of which was finally issued in 2002.[89] Ma argues that uncertainty and disagreement at the top level of the CCP delayed the establishment of an official policy. Ma states, "when senior-level criticism and irregular activities emerged, the government banned the practice, but did not actually enforce the rule."[90]

As with general M&A activity, by 2002 the government was once more pursuing a more liberal policy. The government has made some movement toward an official policy setting how much equity can be sold and who, if anyone, is restricted from buying state property.[91] But the trend is unmistakable: greater liberalization of the SOE reform policy and expanded participation of foreign capital.

As in other instances where central policy lags behind innovative localities, in response to a general decline in FDI inflows in 1998, the Shanghai government announced an aggressive drive to market state-owned companies to foreign investors. The Shanghai Assets and Equity Exchange, which handles transactions of limited companies and unlisted stock companies, has shifted its focus from handling nonstate companies to SOEs. In 1997, transactions involving state assets accounted for 43.5 percent of the total.[92]

The A and B Markets: Toward Gradual Unification

After a year-long decline of A-share prices in 1994, the government announced the decision to allow Sino-foreign joint venture investment companies to enter the A-share market. After the successful implementation of this policy, the government pledged to further open the A-share gradually to "credible" foreign investors.[93] In November 2002 a provisional rule was issued allowing large foreign institutional investors to make limited investments in the A-share market.

The B-share market has been increasingly open to Chinese citizens who reside abroad and to domestic Chinese citizens who hold foreign exchange. In February 2001, the Chinese government eased restrictions on the purchase of B-shares by mainland investors.[94] Since Chinese citizens have been illegally active in the B-share market for some time (either by having Hong Kong friends and relatives buy shares or by the local flouting of the regulations), these new regulations are seen to be sanctioning practices already well in place.[95] These changes were also heralded "as a prelude to a merger of the B market with the much larger, domestic market in A shares, and the eventual opening of that market to foreigners."[96] Such an intention was announced later that year as China's entry to the WTO became imminent. Foreign participation in the stock market in the wake of WTO-spawned competition was seen as necessary to ensure stock price stability and to expose Chinese domestic firms to new sources of capital investment.[97]

Treatment of State and Nonstate Firms

Along with the concrete changes in policies and practices that are listed above, other more symbolic changes have occurred that allow for greater legitimate participation by foreign and, increasingly, domestic private firms. In 1997, 1999, and 2004 the Chinese leadership improved the constitutional standing of China's private economy. This change followed the announcement at the Fifteenth Party Congress that the "leading role" of the state sector was in strategic terms, but not in a quantitative sense.[98] That is, the state will now concentrate ownership in a few strategic areas of the economy, allowing large parts of the economy to be of private, foreign, and mixed ownership. The constitutional upgrading of the private economy from a "complementary" role to the state-owned economy to "an important element" in the national economy was more than an ideological change of heart. In 1999 the prohibition on foreign-private economic cooperation in China was lifted, making it easier for smaller foreign firms to establish a foothold in China.[99] Several large multinational corporations (MNCs), including Microsoft, also heralded the change since it would allow them to form strategic partnerships with many of China's high-tech private businesses.[100] Following the constitutional change, the Shanghai City government quickly adopted a policy encouraging foreign investment in its private enterprises.[101] While not directly affecting the SOE sector, this change does increase foreign investor choice and bargaining power in decisions on how and with whom to invest. Foreign firms are no longer restricted to alliances with state or collective firms.

As further evidence of the sea change in official attitudes toward ownership that has taken place, many coastal regions now discriminate against state firms, through the buyouts and acquisitions mentioned above (by selling off all the SOEs, like Quanzhou for example) or through administrative regulations. For example, the Shenzhen SEZ government announced in July 1999 that solely state-owned firms are *no longer allowed to set up in the SEZ*. The policy is effective immediately for small firms and will apply to medium and large firms gradually over the next eight years. A Guangdong-based paper stated, "[t]he Shenzhen SEZ government's plan to phase out state-owned enterprise as the main force in the area's economy will not be difficult because the zone already has several firms with foreign investment and private firms."[102]

The previous section has traced the evolution of foreign participation in the Chinese economy from the early days of isolation in the SEZs to the most recent period of expanded foreign ownership in nearly all types of Chinese firms. Expanded foreign ownership has come about in myriad forms, from the "grafting" of foreign and Chinese ventures, to greater foreign participation in the Chinese stock market, to the formation of foreign-private companies. "Process-tracing" of FDI liberalization highlights how foreign investor autonomy and control have grown with the expansion of investment opportunities, the liberalization of investment regulations, and the rise of hybrid ownership types. Increasing foreign participation and ownership despite significant suspicion among senior leaders toward foreign capital and a historically antagonistic relationship between the CCP and foreign capital is due to an FDI liberalization policy that was region-specific and highly decentralized.

COMPETITIVE LIBERALIZATION AND ITS EFFECTS

The gradual expansion and integration of foreign capital in the Chinese economy are results of the competitive pressures unleashed by FDI. The logic of a "region-specific" FDI policy created "competitive liberalization" between regions and firms for FDI inflows. This Open Policy expanded the economic and political significance of FDI for local officials, and granted foreign investors greater bargaining power vis-à-vis local governments and firms. Second, the partial or unfinished reform of the state sector and the concomitant regional liberalization of FDI policy created opportunities for cooperation between SOE managers, local officials, and foreign investors. SOE managers and local officials, recognizing the competitive threat of foreign-invested firms, led a push for greater foreign participation in SOE reform, which widened the investment opportunities for foreign investors and expanded their bargaining power even further.

There is a final, exogenous reason for continued liberalization and integration of FDI. The investment goals of foreign investors changed from a search for low-cost, export-oriented production to long-term exploitation of the Chinese domestic market. This strategic goal for greater access to the Chinese domestic market led to a greater emphasis on management control and autonomy. Foreign investors looked to strengthen relations with Chinese domestic firms to take advantage of market reputation, distribution networks, and government connections in order to increase their domestic market competitiveness (through grafted joint ventures, for example). However, they also sought greater control and larger equity shares within these joint ventures than they had in the past. Unhappy with the bureaucratic nature of joint venture alliances and more confident of going it alone, foreign investors established WFOEs with increasing frequency or raised their ownership stake in existing JVs.

Local Initiative and Central Incentives

Beijing first used FDI as an incentive policy to gain provincial support for reform. The central leadership granted special preferential policies to coastal regions to attract FDI and thus hoped to balance conservative opposition toward reform at the center and in the military.[103] With the success of the CDS and an economic boom in the coastal provinces, inland provinces grew increasingly envious and "bandwagoned" with other pro-reform coalitions to press for further liberalization.[104] As FDI policy was liberalized, localities began an intense, competitive drive for FDI inflows.

Local governments wanted to attract FDI because it brought in capital, technology, management skills, and employment opportunities. At the same time, the central government was reducing financial support to the regions, leaving them more self-sufficient. Revenue from domestic companies were unreliable; the SOE sector was increasingly bankrupt and the small private sector was difficult to tax. FDI was an enviable source of increased revenue. Finally, foreign investment was a mark of political prestige; it was used increasingly as a measurement of local government performance and effectiveness. Leaders of regions that attracted large inflows of FDI, especially Western or Japanese investment, were lauded in the national media.

FDI's growing political significance is also related to its increasing integration into local economies. When FDI was limited to the SEZs and a few coastal localities, its influence on the state sector was minimal. These regions historically had small industrial sectors, remaining largely rural and agricultural. Moreover, "greenfield" development further cut off FDI from contact with the developed economies of these regions. Economic development zones were havens of wide, paved highways and clean, tiled factories amid rice fields and small villages. As FDI expanded into other areas, areas with a large SOE presence, development could not imitate the experiences of the early successes in Fujian and Guangdong Provinces, which had relied on a large rural labor surplus and low levels of industrialization. These areas faced different problems: a large number of unemployed or underemployed state-sector workers and debt-ridden factories with outdated equipment and managers ill equipped to function in a market economy. Local officials in these regions looked for ways to increase foreign capital's participation and integration in the local economy (through GJVs, auctions, or the leasing of SOEs, for example). On the other hand, early foreign investment on the coast seemed to be mostly excluded and separate from the local economy.

The local initiatives in attracting FDI followed the incentives set by the central government. The competitive drive for FDI was a natural result of the region-specific Open Policy and the political and economic importance given to FDI by the central government. China's success in attracting FDI was achieved in spite of the central government's own worries about how to control and manage it. Even today when the Chinese government still restricts FDI from key sectors, it has moved further and further away from its original conception of foreign capital as a minor player in China's national development.[105]

Partial Reform of the State Sector

SOE reform, either through privatization or internal restructuring, is a critical reform for all reforming socialist or postcommunist states. The Chinese SOE sector has been reformed early and often by the Chinese state, but always within the parameters of continued state ownership of "important" sectors of the economy and retention of the state sector as the "mainstay" of the national economy. However, in order to achieve rapid growth rates, the Chinese government could not wait for the SOE sector to produce efficiently and yield profits. Instead the government relied on the nonstate sector as the engine for economic growth. To use Barry Naughton's phrase, the Chinese state allowed the economy to "grow out of the plan," which meant expanding the nonstate sectors while allowing the planned sector to decline in both absolute and relative terms.[106] The relative decline of the SOE sector and the rapid growth of foreign-invested firms left the state with little choice but to tap foreign capital in the process of privatization. Gu captures the state's predicament well: "The central government is facing a dilemma: on the one hand, the introduction of foreign investment has proved to be a powerful stimulant for the development of China's economy, which is a major factor in the reform government's legitimacy; but, on the other hand, the corporatization of SOEs as a result of the formation of GJVs would erode and eventually destroy the system of state ownership. However the central government is not a monolithic bloc."[107]

The institutional innovation of GJVs was not the work of the central government; rather it was a reaction to the pressures that partial reform placed on local officials and SOE managers. The central state made SOE reform a priority, cut subsidies, and then pressured local governments to find ways to turn these companies around. "Local governments are more enthusiastic than the central government in developing the private sector because it is they who face striking workers and have to find jobs for them."[108] GJVs and the more general sale of small and medium-sized SOEs to private and foreign capital were the work of these "institutional entrepreneurs" at the local level: SOE managers, local officials, and foreign investors.[109] Caught in the bind of partial or unfinished reform, foreign investment meant two important things: capital infusions into debt-ridden firms and the chance to reorganize firms more efficiently and flexibly. In return, foreign investors gained considerable control and autonomy in the restructuring of state firms.

Central officials were also influenced and constrained by their earlier policy choice to allow the nonstate economy to expand around the state sector. The relative decline of the state sector posed an increasingly difficult dilemma to central leaders: continue to try to save the entire state system (through piecemeal reform) or cut their losses and save a greatly reduced number of state firms. As a "developmentalist" regime, strongly influenced by the development trajectories of its neighbors, Japan, Korea, and Taiwan, the Chinese reformers are dedicated to the creation of global Chinese firms: a Chinese Mitsubishi, a Chinese Hyundai, or a Chinese General Motors.[110] The attraction of saving a few firms and then building them up as opposed to saving many firms (with much less chance of success) is apparent. Moreover, as multinational after multinational entered the Chinese market, the leadership grew worried that the window of opportunity for the development of strong, national firms was closing. The increased competition that the foreign-invested sector introduced to the Chinese economy made partial reform increasingly unpalatable and possibly lethal to the long-term success of China's "national" economy. This gave the state even more reason to winnow the state sector down to a manageable number. As the minister of the State and Economic Trade Commission explained the "Hold the Big, Release the Small" policy: "Key support will be given to large-scale enterprise groups that combine industrial, technical, and trading enterprises; and that are also cross-regional, conglomerate in nature, and incorporate different systems of ownership. This will allow them to become central participants in domestic and international market competition."[111]

Ironically, of course, by the time this decision to "release" small and medium sized firms was made in the late 1990s, foreign investors were the natural targets for local officials and SOE managers eager to divest. The competition was also the potential buyer of China's state firms.

The Changing Goals of Foreign Investors

Since the introduction of FDI in 1979, foreign investors have consistently pushed for greater access to the Chinese domestic market and for greater management control over their operations in China. That these were the preferences of foreign investors does not alone explain why they were fulfilled. The two dynamics above, of competitive liberalization and of partial reform, explain how foreign investor bargaining power increased over time, helping to realize the goals of increased access and increased control. In order to explain the origins of foreign investors' preferences, we need to look both at the investment environment in China and more generally at changes in production cycles and global capital flows.

Foreign firms in China emphasized control and autonomy partially because all JVs are defined by a struggle between the partners for control over the company's future. In China, where culture and business practices clashed quite frequently, even in ventures with overseas Chinese, this struggle for control was all the more pronounced. Many foreign investors also argue that control is critical to the survival of their company. Many companies have been severely disappointed with their performance in China and blamed the investment environment, the bureaucratic interference in firms, and corrupt or inept government officials. Some firms see the move toward increased control and ownership stake as a last-ditch effort to make profits in the Chinese market.[112]

Foreign firms were also responding to a more positive trend: the rapid growth of the Chinese economy and the development of a consumer-oriented market economy. Firms of all types, but especially Western and Japanese firms, sought greater access to a growing and huge consumer market. Even firms from Hong Kong and Taiwan, which had first invested in China to produce goods at low cost for the export markets of the West, began to deepen their commitment to China's domestic market and make long-term investment plans.[113] This longer-term outlook made investors more attentive to the issues of integration in the local economy and stronger managerial control over the firm's performance in China.

Finally the rapid growth of FDI in the 1990s was a global trend not restricted to the PRC, although it was one of the major recipients of global FDI flows. In the last few years, FDI has grown more quickly than foreign trade, reflecting the changing strategies of "global firms." This trend has been especially important for developing countries. In its 1999 Global Development Finance report the World Bank found that, "FDI flows to developing countries increased more than six fold from 1990 to 1998, and their share of global FDI has risen from 25% in 1991 to an estimated 42% in 1998."[114] Due to the declining costs of communication and transportation, many firms now set up production facilities around the world. For firms eyeing the long-term development of the Chinese economy, investing early has often been thought to be a crucial strategy to develop market reputation, government connections, and knowledge about the local economy.

Rising wages and appreciating currencies in the East Asian newly industrialized countries (NICs) also explain the steady rise of FDI from China's neighbors, especially Hong Kong, Taiwan, Korea, and Japan. These economies began to move production offshore to the PRC in the late 1980s and 1990s as East Asian firms faced increasingly severe competitive pressures. Reducing production costs through FDI was one solution to their declining competitive advantage in world markets.

CONCLUSION

Competitive liberalization describes a contagion of "development zone fever" across regions, moving inland from the booming coast and sweeping reform skeptics and political conservatives aside. As the state sector languished in a state of partial reform and decay, state managers and officials became interested in using FDI to deepen reform of the state sector. In order to beat this new competition, the state sector would have to join them first. FDI liberalization continued apace across regions and firms, transforming the role of foreign capital from its early incarnation as an isolated supplement to the mainstay of China's economy, the state-owned sector, to the main source of capital to rescue this supposed "mainstay." As more regions opened to FDI, a contagion also spread, in a slower and less dramatic fashion, from the laboratory-like foreign-invested sector to the state sector. This contagion included the transmission of new modes of labor management and managerial control of the workplace.

CHAPTER FOUR

The Unmitigated Market:

CONTRACT LABOR AND THE PROBLEM OF
REPRESENTATION IN CHINESE FIRMS

> "Time is Money, Efficiency is Life"
> —Slogan posted in a rural collective factory, Hebei

IN THE ABSENCE OF LARGE-SCALE PRIVATIZATION and with the continued existence of large public and collective sectors, China's transition, although still incomplete in many ways, has resulted in the transformation of labor relations and the widespread adoption of capitalist labor practices by firms of all ownership types.[1] The distinction between public and private firms in labor practices has blurred in tandem with continuous economic deregulation, increased competition within the domestic economy, and China's continued economic integration with the global economy. Public ownership as a core characteristic of socialism is increasingly irrelevant for the determination of labor relations. To paraphrase Richard Nixon, "We are all capitalists now." China's slow and piecemeal movement toward privatization has not impeded the transformation of labor relations. In many ways changes in labor practices have preceded more radical changes in property rights and in the absence of political change.

Earlier research did find significant variation between firms based on ownership. For example, Jonathan Unger and Anita Chan wrote in 1996: "The economic reforms have led to a bifurcation of Chinese industry: (i) a non-state sector of private Chinese firms, foreign-managed enterprises, and the so-called collective firms that come under very local control; and (ii) the state-owned and large collective enterprises. Depending on the sector they participate in, Chinese industrial workers enter into very different kinds of relationships with their respective management, work under quite different conditions, and enjoy different benefits and levels of job security."[2] Dorothy Solinger found a similar bifurcation in the workforce between migrants and the regular employees of the state and collective sectors. However, her analysis of the sustainability of this bifurcation is quite prescient as it concludes with a prediction that the then current conditions of migrants in China's nonstate sectors signaled the future for workers in the public sectors.[3] It is highly possible, following the argument laid out here, that the divergence noted in earlier research was simply capturing the lag between reform's effects in the nonstate sector and the then more protected public sectors.

The question of possible divergence from capitalist labor practices in China is important not only to our understanding of China's reform process, which unlike other postsocialist countries has maintained communist rule, but also to the general literature on contemporary global capitalism. The literature on national divergence and "varieties of capitalism" has overwhelmingly focused on the advanced industrialized world, in particular the continuing differences between Anglo-American liberal capitalism and the more regulated and state-dominated patterns seen in much of Western Europe and Japan.[4] Variation in labor and social welfare policies has been central to this ongoing debate. Globalization theorists argue that increased economic globalization, especially the globalization of production with increasing capital mobility, has weakened the bargaining power of labor. Not only is labor constrained by its relative lack of mobility; different countries are in competition for the jobs that investment brings, and the impulse to protect labor rights and job security has declined accordingly.[5] Thus national divergences will wane over time as labor policies are adjusted in favor of mobile capital. This literature with its focus on comparisons between advanced industrialized states, however, should also be extended to examining trends in the countries to which capital is increasingly flowing. Production in many industries is not shifting between Germany and the U.S. or the United States and Japan but rather from these countries to the developing world, including China, Southeast Asia, Latin American, and Central Europe. How these countries respond to the pressures of globalization, in particular competition for the flows of foreign investment, also informs us about the ability of particular places to diverge from common free-market practices or even to choose from the varieties of capitalism practiced in the advanced industrialized world.

I argue here that Chinese labor practices have shifted overwhelmingly toward favoring firm autonomy, flexibility, and managerial control of worker organizations. Attempts by the state to retain some aspects of socialism, including greater employment stability, longer-term employment relations, and active worker organizations, have not met with much success.[6] As detailed in chapter 3, the effects of globalization have been magnified by the way in which liberalization and openness occurred, as a gradual process of uneven application and selective regional benefits.[7] This process spawned competition and change in labor practices, including marked increases in managerial autonomy and labor flexibility. The "segmented" nature of this process, however, reduced its political threat to the ruling Communist Party leadership.[8] Competition for investment in

China was regional as well as a part of a larger global phenomenon. China and India compete for FDI but so do Shanghai and Tianjin.[9] The transformation to capitalist labor practices at the firm level has been achieved with the help of globalization and "opening up" as local firms and local governments have struggled to meet the demands of foreign investors and global markets. The much-needed antidotes to this shift to capitalism, however, a state regulatory and legal regime that is capable of mitigating its excesses and effective organizations to represent labor, are not yet well established.

This chapter examines the firm-level consequences of this lopsided achievement of China's move to the market; capitalist labor practices have spread but two modes of labor's protection—a legal regime of labor rights and an effective mode of collective organization—have failed in implementation. Rather, the basic characteristics of contemporary labor relations include substantial managerial control and autonomy, the atomization and fragmentation of the workforce through the individual contract system, and management domination or suppression of worker organizations.

The wide range of practices that are employed in Chinese firms, from the infamous sweatshops of the south to the highly evolved human resource regimes of multinationals in Shanghai, are themselves indications of one crucial characteristic of labor relations in China today: the overwhelming power of management to determine a firm's internal labor practices. Due to a lack of capacity on the part of the official trade union and a significant lack of will on the part of developmentalist local governments, firm management or owners overwhelmingly determine labor practices, which is why a researcher can find glaring differences between firms even in the same development zone.[10] Second, there is substantial employer flexibility due to the uneven implementation of new labor laws and regulations. Labor relations between workers and employers are increasingly based on the notion of contract, which entails a mutual agreement between individual workers and managers. These agreements can be legally binding official documents or simple oral agreements; the labor contract's crucial characteristic is its individual nature and its impermanency. Labor contracts in China are short-term and are also amenable to early termination. The notion of contract as the foundation of labor relations fundamentally shapes interactions between workers and managers. By its individualized nature, reliance on contract places workers at a great disadvantage and in a very weak bargaining position. Initiatives by the central government and central trade union to improve labor relations and equalize the labor relationship by implementing mitigating laws and regulations, including those that require unionization and collective bargaining, have mostly failed. Finally, management domination of worker organizations, especially the trade union, further accentuates these characteristics of managerial control and autonomy and worker fragmentation and atomization through individualized labor relations. Despite the organizational presence of the All-China Federation of Trade Unions (ACFTU) in many firms and recent efforts to unionize workers in the new nonstate sectors, managerial domination or outright suppression of worker organizations is the overwhelming norm.

Given the many varieties of capitalism and the great regional diversity of China, is it possible to generalize about the emerging picture of labor relations there? The focus here on the decline in importance of ownership and the rise of capitalist practices in both public and private firms does not conclude that there is one single version of capitalism that is emerging in China. Differences of industrial sector, region, and nationality still matter in determining the particular characteristics of firms. Moreover, the research on which this book is based was conducted in China's urban industrial coastal cities, mainly Tianjin, Tangshan in Hebei Province, and Shanghai and its surrounding areas. The processes detailed here, especially as the result of large inflows of foreign investment and a rapid development of a domestic private sector, may have different consequences in areas where state sector employment still dominates and alternative sources of investment and connections to global markets are sorely lacking. As much research on the northeast and central China have shown, these regions have experienced reform largely as a process of being left behind rather than the process described here of greater integration and convergence with global labor practices.

Policy Liberalization and Labor Flexibility

How did the regional liberalization of investment policy, the expansion of ownership types, and the increasing occurrence of ownership "recombination" detailed in chapter 3 transform labor practices? For newly created firms, including township-village enterprises (TVEs), WFOEs, and domestic private firms, labor practices were from the beginning less affected by the legacies of socialism than by the pressure of global production. Foreign investment came mostly from other East Asian economies that were looking for cheaper manufacturing of labor-intensive products. Many of these firms felt the pressures of rising wages and democratization in other Asian economies, making manufacturing in China more attractive. Similarly, TVEs, although rising out of the ashes of the commune system, operated with harder budget constraints and the pressures of subcontracting for SOEs and foreign manufacturers.[11] Suppressing the cost of labor is critical to these types of firms as is labor flexibility. It is the combination of these economic pressures of firms with the developmentalist orientation of local governments under regional decentralization that produces an environment conducive to labor exploitation with a concomitant lack of emphasis on labor conditions and workers' rights. The incentives, both political and economic, of attracting investment and export markets on the part of local governments has led to an overwhelming emphasis on firm autonomy and flexibility at the expense of workers' safety, health, and rights.

Changes in the core public sectors, especially SOEs, came more slowly as reform on the margins did not immediately threaten socialist labor practices, including the "iron rice bowl" and secure employment. Even changes in SOE wage policies to improve productivity and material incentives were often implemented in traditional egalitarian fashion and were not linked directly to improvements in productivity.[12] Legal and regulatory reforms, including the labor contract system, were implemented slowly and in a piecemeal fashion from 1986 to 1997.[13] The use of labor contracts was often just a formality and not a real threat to employment until SOE reform was accelerated in the mid-to-late 1990s. One SOE manager reported that although his firm signed contracts in 1993 with all employees, management held off the invocation of contracts (for termination) because of the fear that it would make workers' thinking "unstable."[14] Ten years later, however, this SOE was laying people off through the expiration and early termination of their labor contracts.[15]

Fundamental changes in SOE labor practices came gradually as competition and influence from the growing nonstate sector discussed above expanded and began to seriously threaten the existence of a viable public sector. It was the relative performance of SOEs vis-à-vis the new nonstate sector that led to a more widespread adoption of capitalist labor practices and calls from state managers for a level playing field with other firms. In practice, these calls meant an expansion of managerial autonomy, especially the right to fire, as well as reductions in the welfare burden. The rate of change was also dynamic as ownership recombination (the merging of state firms to nonstate firms, both foreign and private) was a major facet of the privatization measures following the fifteenth Party Congress in 1997.

Chinese Firms under Socialism, Pre-1978

How did Chinese firms behave under the socialist system? And how did the reforms affect their behavior and performance? Despite much learning from and adaptation to the Soviet system of enterprise management, Chinese firms differed in significant ways from firms in other socialist countries.[16]

First, the Chinese system of work-unit (*danwei*) socialism was a complex form of social organization that went beyond typical employee-employer ties, even compared to the relatively stable bond of employment in pre-1989 Eastern Europe and Russia. The *danwei* evolved out of the chaos and poverty of the Sino-Japanese War and the Chinese Civil War.[17] It was a system of control and organization of China's urban citizenry that bound workers to their enterprise, often for life. Under heavy state guidance, workers were assigned to a work-unit upon leaving school. In this work-unit he would receive employment at a low wage but with extensive welfare benefits furnished directly by the enterprise, including housing, medical care, and a pension. Benefits and wages did vary across different types of firms; high-level state firms offered the most extensive benefits, while lower-level firms offered less; and state-owned firms supplied better benefits than locally owned, collective firms.[18] Generally speaking, however, wages were low across the board, creating an urban society that valued egalitarianism. Society was "atomized" in the sense that the work-unit's overwhelming influence on an individual's life tended to isolate each unit, making them worlds unto themselves. Ironically, this had a homogenizing effect on urban society, creating similar life experiences and social expectations across the urban landscape.[19]

The flip side of the work-unit's role as a supplier of welfare benefits was its role as the basic unit of state control and surveillance over urban residents. The work-unit system ensured that labor mobility remained virtually nonexistent, in contrast to many other communist societies in Europe. The work-unit not only was the sole source of crucial life necessities, making it impossible for a worker to survive without his work-unit, but it also recorded and monitored for the state an individual's political attitude and behavior, both on and off the job. The work-unit controlled the life chances of each worker through control of the dossier (*dang'an*). Moreover, job transfers were impossible until the former work-unit released the dossier to the hiring work-unit. These cell-like structures of state penetration and domination over society narrowed the distance between the ordinary citizens and high officialdom by creating a grass-roots level organization in which the state provided welfare in exchange for power over people's lives.

The notion of neotraditionalism depicts this system well, and analysis using the framework of neotraditionalism penetrates deeply into the day-to-day machinations within the firm.[20] Research into the inner workings of firms revealed that political control was realized individually through party cadres' ties with activist workers. This led to the bifurcation and division between politically active workers and nonactivists with vertical ties of clientelism running up and down the factory. The firm was a political institution as much as an economic institution, and it was a very intimate institution at that, with power wielded as a personal tool.

Under socialism then, Chinese firms were highly stable and workers were almost completely dependent on the firm and its management not only for their wages but also for their benefits, subsidies, and housing. Yet this "organized dependence" of workers on the firm was matched by the management's own dependence on workers due to the fact that workers enjoyed permanent job security. The importance of this mutuality of dependence was recognized in the critiques of neotraditionalism and in Walder's own amendments in his later work.[21] The Chinese labor force was rigid not only because workers found it hard to leave their welfare benefits supplied by the firm but also because it was politically unacceptable (and not economically rational under the soft budget constraint) for managers to trim their workforce.

Active but Not Efficient

The importance placed on political attitude and behavior (and by extension the quality of personal ties to management and the party) made the factory very good at fomenting political campaigns and workers' mobilization at times when the external environment demanded them. But it made the factory less adept at normal productive work. Managers and technicians in charge of overseeing production were relegated to secondary positions, while CCP officials called the shots. In fact, the entire history of the period from postliberation to the end of the Cultural Revolution in the 1970s shows an almost continuous decline of managerial power (the experts) and a continued rise in the power of the Party (the reds). The dominance of the party at the enterprise level politicized the Chinese workplace, divided the workforce, and relegated economic considerations like productivity, efficiency, and material incentives to the eerie netherworld of political incorrectness. Workers could be activated to participate in political campaigns or mad dashes to meet state plan requirements, but there was little ability in and less attention to normal, stable production and regular increases in efficiency and quality. Managers did not have the power to insist on such improvements. Workers had little or no incentive to do so. Material perquisites were realized through one's political connections and activist credentials, not through emphasis on bonuses and wage increases, which were criticized as economistic and unsocialist.

The Party Rules

As noted above, the organizational structure of Chinese firms was bifurcated between management and CCP officials. This structure was the result of attempts in the 1950s to revive factory production after the Chinese Civil War (1946–49). Communist leaders decided to allow managers from the Republican Era to continue into the transition period but under the direction of the newly established CCP branches. This "Party Command System" later was seen as a rebuke to the Stalinist system of one-man management, which many leaders believed violated the principles of democratic centralism. The CCP was further strengthened in the political struggles with the trade union in the later 1950s. This debate swirled around the issue of the union's dual responsibilities to workers and the CCP, under whose aegis the union existed. Mao Zedong finally decided this issue in favor of CCP dominance as he also condemned union activities that supported narrow worker interests at the purported expense of the CCP and national unity. Unwilling to devolve authority to either management or the trade union, the CCP continually strengthened its position within the enterprise.[22]

CCP dominance of the enterprise had important consequences for the other organizational structures within the enterprise and for the general configuration of authority relations. Management was weak and ineffectual unless it worked in tandem with CCP directives and mandates. This was generally meant to place political objectives above economic ones. Managerial autonomy was suspect, and as long as the CCP controlled career opportunities for managers, managers were tied to the system of party command. CCP dominance had even greater deleterious effects for the trade union organization. The trade union's mandate was unclear and contradictory from the beginning of the CCP's rule in China. It was to protect the rights of workers, but from whom? The Party? But the CCP ruled in the name of the Chinese proletariat, how could it also exploit or injure workers? From management? But here the union was trumped by CCP power. If the workers had a conflict with management, they went to the CCP, not the union, because the CCP's position was much stronger and more dominant. In general this weakening of the union left it as a mere transmission belt of CCP propaganda and as an administrative appendage of the CCP until the central union's dissolution and breakdown during the Cultural Revolution.[23]

In brief, the Chinese firm's most marked characteristics were its striking lack of *labor mobility*, even in comparison to firms in other socialist systems; a related work-unit-based distribution of welfare and benefits that bound workers closely to their firm, usually for life; and finally, a politicized atmosphere with the party in command and management in a secondary and weaker position. As might be expected, the reform period brought great changes to this rarified institution, but it was change that came in fits and starts, accompanied by many unanticipated consequences. Labor relations under the partial reform period can be summed up by three characteristics: the breakdown of mutual dependence, a changing and unstable relationship between the CCP and management within firms, and a rapidly changing external environment.

THE ERA OF PARTIAL REFORM, 1978–1992

Management and the Party: The Center Absorbs the Core

Throughout the 1980s and early 1990s, management gained greater power and autonomy within firms at the direct expense of CCP leadership in firms.[24] This statement however requires two qualifications. First, it is more precise to say that management positions gained greater decision-making power and autonomy, while party positions (as party positions) suffered a decline in their authority and influence.[25] Yet rather than reflecting a clear decline in CCP power, this change reflects the *melding of party and management goals and the melding of party and management positions*. Second, this change is most fundamentally a reflection of internal CCP change and signals the end of a war of attrition between reformers and conservatives. Managers didn't beat out the party; the party joined with management in pursuit of common, largely economic goals. This is most often reflected in Chinese firms when the general manager serves simultaneously as the party secretary.

The party's decline in firms began with the early attempts to root out the remnants of Cultural Revolution institutions from factories and to reestablish other institutions that had been suspended during the Cultural Revolution, most notably the revival of trade union branches. These early changes diluted the concentration of power in party hands, giving some power back to both management and mass organizations. But the CCP remained the "core" of the enterprise organization, and party interference into management decisions continued with little real change. Management's hand was finally strengthened through the passage of the Enterprise Law in 1988, which stated clearly that the management superseded CCP authority in every aspect of factory life, not only production.[26] The Enterprise Law heralded the passing of the era of the "Party in command" and the rise of the "Director Responsibility System." This new emphasis on legal recognition and the "legal representative" of the enterprise granted the manager more autonomy and power as well as powerful recourse to the idea of a "legal obligation" to stable production and economic performance.[27] As You Ji notes of the Enterprise Law, "it also indicated the extent to which the party center came to grips with the changed nature of a state firm, which, it concluded, was an economic body."[28]

The enterprise's identity as an economic institution was solidified with the practice of encouraging CCP secretaries to serve concurrently in a production or management-related job. Managers who have joined the party after reaching management levels often cast the decision to join as a career decision. Promotions to lead larger or more important factories are easier if one is a CCP member.[29] Up until 1992 there were some restrictions on this policy of "one shoulder, two posts"; for example, enterprises with more than one hundred workers were not to implement this policy, ensuring that the party position was full-time. However, in the post-1992 era these restrictions rapidly fell by the wayside. At the firm level, party officials were increasingly, first and foremost, enterprise managers.[30] Party officials that did not concurrently hold management positions found themselves out in the cold, with their political ties to workers severely attenuated. As one party official reported, the attitude of workers toward the party is "wage and bonuses aren't determined by you; for housing and welfare, I don't go to you; when I have a problem and go to you, you don't resolve it, so I mock you."[31]

The trade union in particular complained bitterly about this new policy because it robbed them of a dual authority structure and severely hampered their bargaining power. Previously the party secretary would resolve disputes between management and the union, granting the union some degree of independence from management. This is no longer the case. As one trade union advocate stated, this "new leadership pattern leaves unions in a very awkward position. Traditionally, both the manager and the union president would turn to the party secretary for arbitration in case of disputes. Now the manager is also the party secretary! . . . This one-man-with-two-posts leadership pattern is indeed very unfavorable to trade unions."[32]

The victory of management is related to the political unrest of the late 1980s, a period of intellectual ferment and an overheated economy. The explosion of urban unrest in 1989, the year after the passage of the Enterprise Law, had a somewhat ironic effect on later enterprise reforms: it ensured the ascendancy of management over other factory organizations. Although the events of 1989 did lead to a period of retrenchment and renewed emphasis on politics and ideology, it was short-lived and shallow. Conservative retrenchment policies never effectively challenged the fact that enterprises were now economic bodies, pursuing investment and growth. The significance of 1989 is that it closed down attempts at political reform while economic reform continued nearly apace. Management autonomy continued to increase, because it was perceived to be a necessary part of economic reform. Organizations designed to balance management power, like the union, weakened because union reform was political and possibly threatening to the CCP's hold on power, a point that was made all the more obvious by the establishment of independent unions during the Prodemocracy Movement of spring 1989. Evolutionary economic changes continued, however, and sped up after Deng Xiao-ping's visit to southern China in 1992, where he encouraged reforms to go faster and deeper. The evolutionary nature of the reform and the reti-cence of the central government to deal explicitly with political issues, such as the role of the union, allowed management to "win" by default.[33]

During the early and middle reform period, from 1978 until 1992, re-forms in the state-sector firms occurred in relative isolation. That is, struc-tural reform of the state sector and the simultaneous development of a foreign-invested and domestic private sector proceeded on parallel tracks. Separate laws were promulgated for the foreign sector, most foreign plants were set up in "greenfield" development zones away from traditional state industry, the foreign acquisition of state firms was forbidden, and the ex-plosive growth of township-village enterprises was largely a rural phe-nomenon. Learning or informal borrowing of foreign practices certainly did occur, although it is often hard to document, but in general the state sector was treated as an isolated patient in a separate ward. The charac-teristics of the "partially reformed" Chinese firm reflect this division and relative isolation. The external environment was changing quickly but the internal one was not. Gradually the external environment began to im-pede into the state sector, and this melding of intentional, internal reforms and external encroachment on state sector firms further complicated the SOE environment.[34]

The Breakdown of Mutual Dependence

The reforms began the slow, gradual breakdown of organized depen-dence, a type of dependence that had been stable and long-term: virtually impossible for workers to break.[35] Workers are, of course, almost every-where dependent to varying degrees on their employer for compensation. But in a market economy, workers have greater autonomy and agency at the expense of stability. Organized dependence established a lifetime tie between worker and enterprise, severely limiting the courses of action possible for individual workers. This began to change under reform, but workers benefited from the increasing mobility before state managers did. This initial gap in mobility (workers were able to exploit nonstate em-ployment opportunities but managers were not permitted to fire) had im-portant effects on the decay of organized dependence.[36]

The rise of nonstate employment opportunities did not mean that work-ers left state firms in large numbers. Survey research from the early 1990s did show rapid increases in mobility, particularly to FIEs and particularly by skilled workers, but these increases were from a very low starting point.[37] Most were unable to, in fact, because losing a state-sector job also meant the loss of state-sector benefits, most importantly, housing and medical care. The breakdown of organized dependence first meant the rise of several different kinds of informal agreements between firm and worker that allowed workers to leave their job but to keep their benefits. In this way, state firms began to hemorrhage their best and most skilled workers while continuing to provide them with extensive benefits.

Moonlighting was the most common informal practice and certainly the earliest to appear. Moonlighting, working in the private sector or simply plying your trade as an individual entrepreneur, was first and foremost a way to make more money while retaining the benefits and perquisites of a state-sector job. In the early years of reform, firms tolerated moonlighting and at times even encouraged factorywide collective moonlighting.[38] Resistance to moonlighting increased over time, however, as state managers complained that they lost their best workers but had to continue to pay them.

As the pressure to shed excess workers mounted, the state began to encourage practices more akin to partial unemployment. "Stop salary, keep post" (*tingxin liuzhi*) allowed workers to keep their benefits and the labor relationship with their enterprise, but they were no longer required to go to work and could pursue second jobs or entrepreneurial activity. This change in practice reflects state goals to speed up reform but control large-scale unemployment. Allowing workers to keep their benefits but not their salary relieved some of this burden. Through this system SOE workers were gradually acclimated to the concept of a labor market and given some time to find their bearings in this new environment. A somewhat similar practice was the taking of long-term vacations or sick leave in which the worker retains benefits but not all of his salary (*changqi fangjia*).[39] Many state firms encouraged older workers to take "internal retirement" (*neibu tuixiu*), which reduced their monthly payment but guaranteed the continuation of crucial benefits like housing and medical care.[40]

Fear of social instability made it difficult for the state to match greater job mobility among workers with an equal gift to managers: the right to fire and lay off. The loosening of employment ties between worker and enterprise favored the best workers, often the youngest and the highly skilled, while "grandfathering" the workers least likely to succeed in this new environment. The status of older workers as permanent workers (*guding zhigong*) continued. In 1986 the labor contract system was introduced but applied only to new employees. Even when the labor contract system was applied more widely in the years following, workers with ten years or more of employment were permitted to sign long-term contracts with no set date of expiration. This "two-tier" system of employment in state firms not only created divisions in the workforce, it also left the management unable to fire the least productive workers and to retain the younger, more technically skilled workers. The right to permanent employment continued within the contract system, but as Warner found, this right was reserved "for those who look" while "those who work" could go elsewhere.[41] Managers could now lose their best employees, faced competition with the nonstate sector in hiring new employees, and still were unable to lay off or fire many of their own employees. With underemployment rates in SOEs estimated at 30–50 percent of the workforce, SOEs were in an increasingly disadvantageous position.[42] As seen below, new pressures to enhance employee welfare and increase wages exacerbated this one-sided decay of mutual dependence.

Enterprise reform designed to rationalize state firms and increase efficiency led to unexpected changes in the traditional "organized dependent" relationship between workers and managers. Namely, the tendency for managers to resort to legal and illegal measures to boost employee wages, bonuses, and benefits was a result of the more autonomous enterprise environment under reform. But why would managers, with newly enhanced abilities to respond to market forces, squander their resources on employee bonuses and expanded benefits? Upon closer examination it is clear that these changes are related to the permanent employment status of most state workers.

As state firms were pressured to begin to respond to market signals, managers quickly raised workers' wages. Wage and bonus increases were justified by the long period of wage stagnation under Maoist policies that emphasized moral over material incentives. However, these increases continued unchecked and with little connection to comparable gains in productivity. This tendency to appease workers' demands for higher wages is related to the lack of labor mobility and the increased need for managers to garner employee compliance: "While in the past I have tended to stress the dependence of China's workers on the enterprise and management, China's reforms have highlighted the dependence of managers upon their permanent labour force. The absence of a labour market gives the current labour force a monopoly on the supply of labour."[43]

The tendency to appease workers is also linked to the way in which managers were evaluated. It became apparent that the performance of partially reformed firms was extremely difficult to measure, so instead managers were held accountable for the basic conditions of their employees. Due to the inherent problems of a semiplanned economy (bottlenecks, supply problems, quality of inputs, among others), it was almost always possible for a manager to find an external reason for problems with his firm's performance. Employee welfare served as one of the few ways that state officials could objectively measure the performance and management of the enterprise. It was more difficult to excuse problems or concerns of the workforce, since this was one of the few areas that the manager could now control and show improvement in. There is also an ideological component. In the early reform period, blatantly capitalist goals such as maximization of profits and reduction of input costs were simply not acceptable as the be-all and end-all of SOE production. Under socialism, if profits and efficiency were to be emphasized, it was a reasonable and just expectation for workers to expect egalitarian distribution of the increased profits.

External Changes and Opportunities

The flip side of this new dependence of managers on their workforce was the expansion of nonstate employment opportunities. New entrants into the workforce were gaining greater autonomy in choosing their employment. Workers were beginning to move from the state sector to the rapidly growing collective, foreign, and private sectors. While SOE managers did have a problem of underemployment, they also faced a severe shortage of skilled, educated workers.[44] This problem of attracting and retaining desirable workers was greatly exacerbated by the growth of the nonstate sector and contributed to the emphasis that managers placed on extensive welfare benefits—perquisites that usually did not exist in the nonstate sector.

In sum, partial reform benefited the nonstate sector at the expense of the state sector as the long-term economic viability of the state sector worsened during this period. Partial reform relaxed the degree of workers' dependence on the firm while managers remained unable to fire or lay off workers. Managers' dependence on their immobile workforce also led to large wage and benefit increases with little comparable increase in productivity or profits. At the same time, organizational reforms benefited management at the expense of the CCP, with CCP and management goals and positions showing convergence over this period of reform. Thus the increased dependence of management on workers was balanced by their more long-lasting victory over party control.[45] Managers were increasingly in a position to press for more far-reaching changes, most importantly, a reduction in their welfare burden and the right to cut staff. As the external environment changed rapidly in the early-to-mid 1990s, the pressure to cut staff and relieve the welfare burden increased dramatically. Not only had SOE reform failed to turn these enterprises around; they now faced new competition from the nonstate sector.[46] As the reforms deepened in 1992, the historic divide between state and nonstate owned firms began to erode.

Contagious Capitalism, 1992–

The wide range of practices that are employed in Chinese firms, from the infamous sweatshops of the south to the highly evolved human resource regimes of multinationals in Shanghai, are themselves indications of one crucial characteristic of labor relations in China today: the overwhelming power of management to determine a firm's internal labor practices. Due to a lack of capacity on the part of the official trade union and a significant lack of will on the part of developmentalist local governments, firm management or owners overwhelmingly determine labor practices. There is substantial employer flexibility due to the uneven implementation of new labor laws and regulations. If firm autonomy and choice is now paramount for setting labor practices, how can we accurately analyze the overall condition of labor relations in China today? Most importantly, we should consider the firm-level realization of management choice and autonomy as one of the key characteristics of the general condition. Variation and diversity at the firm level is one result of a more general situation in which regional liberalization and economic decentralization have sharpened competition for investment inflows.

Contracts and Employment Insecurity

Labor relations in China have been in a state of flux and transformation since the 1980s as the nonstate sectors developed and the core public sectors gradually felt the quickening of reform. By the mid-to-late 1990s a clearer picture of the Chinese state's conception of labor relations began to emerge as key labor legislation was promulgated and the Communist Party began to move on deep restructuring of the core public sectors with the measures implemented in the wake of the Fifteeenth Party Congress. The official conception of labor relations in a "socialist market economy" includes a heavy dose of state regulation and oversight through laws and regulations with a relatively large degree of freedom of individual choice, for both employer and employee, in employment. Collective worker organization is legally mandated at all firms with twenty-five or more employees through the establishment of a grass-roots branch of the ACFTU. The trade union has the legal right to sit in on management meetings that may affect employee welfare, to be notified of any employee termination, and to negotiate collective contracts with management on behalf of the workforce. These two protective institutions—legal labor rights and collective organization—are in theory designed to mitigate the negative consequences of labor markets and to prevent full commodification. Laws and regulations mark the boundaries of the freedom of contract by providing basic minimum requirements—for example limits on hours worked, vacation time granted, and mandatory provision of social in-surance. Collective organization of workers provides a framework for collective bargaining and interest representation of workers at the workplace.

This framework for labor relations is heavily reliant on an effective rule of law and state capacity to implement and enforce the law. In practice institutions designed to protect workers are instead used against them. Freedom of choice (workers choose their jobs and employers choose their workers) has developed and been institutionalized rapidly since 1997. This freedom has benefited employers and skilled employees, freeing them from the strictures of the work-unit system of employment. For most other employees, this newfound freedom comes mainly in the guise of extreme employment insecurity. For employers freedom of choice has been achieved through the implementation of the individual labor contract system and the newfound ability that it grants not only to hire more freely but also to let workers go as needed or desired. The employment relationship is based on the individual labor contract, which is an agreement between the employer and the individual worker.

The protective institution designed to mitigate this emphasis on choice and flexibility—state oversight, supervision, and constraint on the freedom of contract through the rule of law—has largely failed to materialize. China has made important strides in its development of labor and employment law but implementation and enforcement of these codes have lagged far behind their legislation. Local enforcement of the labor law and other regulations is extremely weak and compromised by the need to attract and retain investment and grow the local economy. Supervision and oversight of the labor law is spotty; local bureaus responsible are understaffed and underfunded. Implementation of China's legal framework for labor has mainly succeeded in fulfilling the needs of enterprise managers—by shortening and attenuating the employment relationship, rather than increasing the rights of workers. Moreover, several important national laws that might clarify difficult issues and grant workers greater rights and entitlements have been held up at the drafting stage due to bureaucratic and ministerial infighting.[47]

The widespread use of rural migrant labor from other regions or provinces is a further disincentive to pursue local enterprises aggressively for infractions and violations. Many local officials do not seem to consider these workers as their responsibility and often pass local regulations that deny migrant workers basic rights.[48] Finally, cozy government–business relations and deep-seated corruption further weaken the state's capacity to supply legal institutions and a regulatory framework that can adequately protect the weaker signatory of the labor contract: individual workers.

This current atomization of workers through the individual contract system is from an already weak collective position. The ACFTU, the officially sanctioned union organization, has historically been a weak and subordinate mass organization. Since 1949 the trade union has had to balance representation of workers' interests with its subordinate role to the CCP and the party's pursuit of broader collective goals, most recently articulated as rapid economic growth and development. Trade union activists that championed workers' interests met resistance from the CCP early on and were suppressed or deposed.[49] As Walder has argued, authority relations in Chinese factories under socialism were clientelistic, with vertical relationships fragmenting and dividing the workforce. Employment security and benefits were protected through the work-unit (*danwei*) system, which guaranteed lifetime jobs and benefits, and *not* through any collective organizational power of workers. The switch to labor contracts and the weakening of the danwei system of employment has exacerbated the already weak and dependent position of Chinese workers vis-à-vis management. Despite the implementation of the labor contract as one part of a "rule of law" project led by the state, workers have been left with little protection or power to challenge or change the employment relationship.

There are, of course, important differences in how contracts have been implemented in different sectors. Many public sector firms have switched from lifetime employment to short-term contracts, while many nonstate firms have been encouraged by the government to implement short-term contracts as an improvement from at-will employment and extreme employment insecurity. Despite these different starting points, there are several trends that cut across sectors and point to an increasingly insecure employment environment for China's industrial workforce.

First, despite initial attempts by the Ministry of Labor to encourage long-term or open-ended contracts as well as to implement laws that require written contracts signed by both parties, the labor contract regime in China is increasingly short-term and informal. Among all the firms visited by this author, contracts ranged from one to two years for production level workers and were used to enhance labor flexibility and managerial power. One SOE switched to the labor contract system in 1993 and since then has slowly expanded the system to include all workers with short, one-to-two-year contracts for all workers, except for those closest to retirement.[50] Workers with a bad work attitude *(biaoxian buhao),* who are not hardworking or who cannot fulfill production goals sign one-year contracts. Workers who have received some form of administrative punishment or internal CCP warning also sign one-year contracts. Using one-year contracts as a probationary period for politically suspect workers allows the company to threaten the job security of troublesome or activist workers. Temporary workers outside of the production plan and registered workers within the plan also sign one-year contracts. One-year contracts for temporary workers extend the flexibility that the FIE sector has long enjoyed without adding to the SOE's welfare burden. Workers who are waiting for employment (*daiye*) also sign one-year contracts.[51] The use of one-year contracts for redundant workers or workers with no regular work assignment also indicates that SOEs are increasingly able to dismiss surplus workers, albeit in a gradual manner that allows the worker one year to find new employment while still drawing a salary.

Foreign-invested firms also resort almost exclusively to short-term employment contracts. Although the government had tried to pressure firms to sign longer contracts, by 1999, most labor contracts for FIE workers were one-year contracts, with renewal contingent upon the agreement of both sides. Some Japanese companies used a combination of a long apprenticeship period, a one-year contract, and then a possible extension to a two-year contract. This practice grants the company a long period of reduced labor costs (an apprentice has no insurance and receives a living stipend, not a wage) with the opportunity to evaluate the employee before offering even the security of a one-year contract. The use of apprenticeship labor is also common in Taiwanese companies. Young rural migrants enter the factory directly from technical school and receive reduced wages and no contract. These practices further reduce labor costs and also allow the company a fairly long period of time to evaluate workers before offering contract employment. There is also no requirement that apprentices receive a contract once the apprenticeship has ended, which raises the possibility that some FIEs endlessly recycle young migrant labor.[52]

"Nasty, brutish, and short" describes the conditions in many other firms that use illegal labor contracts or other illegal means to maintain control over their workforce. For example, some labor contracts may require workers to pay a security deposit to work at the firm. Firms may lock workers in the factory grounds or confiscate their identity cards, making it dangerous for workers to leave and impossible to be employed elsewhere. Even with a labor contract, dismissals are arbitrary, dependent on the production process and the firm's economic health. There is no job security. The Hebei rural collective signed one-year contracts with its employees, but the manager was confident that he could fire anyone at anytime. He served jointly as the enterprise's trade union chairman, which ruled out opposition from the trade union in the event of terminations. At the Tianjin urban collective, working under the contract management system, the general management had devolved the responsibility of signing contracts to the managers of each individual firm. These contracts are often not in compliance with Chinese labor laws and supervision from the central office is lax.[53] The urban collective's trade union had been absorbed into the general affairs office in order to reduce costs.

Despite the overwhelming influence on short-term labor contracts and flexible employment for production staff, many firms use the labor contract system to try to retain badly needed and coveted skilled labor. Some SOEs continue use of "open-ended contracts" as a means to encourage skilled staff loyalty. Open-ended contracts are more difficult to break without paying a fine and therefore are used by the company to limit the mobility of technical workers. These regulations ensure that skilled workers will have much more difficulty switching jobs once they sign an open-ended contract. Because the worker will have to break the contractual agreement to switch jobs, the company can delay or prevent this process by withholding his dossier, without which he would be unable to be employed elsewhere. The company can also demand compensation for any training received. Disputes involving breach of contract have increased dramatically, particularly cases where an SOE sues workers leaving to enter the private or foreign sector.[54] These types of contract regulations strengthen the SOE's power to retain skilled employees without competing with the higher salaries and extensive perquisites that are offered to skilled employees of some FIEs. FIEs that offer training abroad and extensive educational benefits to skilled workers also try to use longer-term contracts to encourage job stability and stem personnel losses to their competitors.[55]

In comparison to the emphasis at the firm level on individual labor contracts to maximize flexibility for the vast majority, the role of the collective contract system has remained minimal. Collective contracts have been successfully encouraged only in large, well-run firms; most often these firms seem to be profitable state firms or large joint ventures with American or European investors. Even here, however, research has found that collective contracts are often the result of the local CCP's direct intervention into the signing process so that the contract becomes in effect an agreement between the local party-state and the firm's management. In most nonstate firms, collective contracts remain inconsequential, either nonexistent or easily co-opted by a much stronger management and turned into a meaningless "form."[56] In the legal resolution of labor conflict, collective contracts have also had a negligible impact, even in regions where the implementation of collective contracts has been pushed. For example, the Shanghai local labor arbitration commissions arbitrated over thirteen thousand labor disputes in 2001, yet not one dispute was in regard to a collective contract.[57] As one trade union official remarked, "We won't re-sign collective contracts again in three years unless we are forced to, because this thing has no meaning."[58]

The weakness of collective negotiations and contracts is in stark contrast to increased tendencies of enterprise managers to share information, tactics, and even set wage-setting guidelines to improve retention and reduce competition in labor markets. Japanese firms in Shanghai and Tianjin report that enterprise managers meet regularly to set wage guidelines and to share information about troublesome workers.[59] In research on the Suzhou Industrial Park one researcher found that electronic firms in the park had formed the "Human Resources Club of Electronics Companies in Suzhou Industrial Park." The main duties of this "club" were to lobby collectively the local governments on issues related to labor legislation and regulations and to "negotiate among members of the club issues regarding recruitment, retention, turnover, salaries and benefits."[60] Investors from the United States, Japan, and Korea dominated the club's membership.

In sum the implementation of the labor contract system has created a system of employment relations that place much greater emphasis on flexibility than stability and on the individual over the collective. This is despite the original intentions of Chinese labor officials and others who believed that labor contracts would offer increased employment security and longer-term employment relations. In firms with labor contracts, employment security is usually guaranteed for a year at best. In the many firms that do not use formal labor contracts, employment in reality is simply "at will."[61]

One-year employment contracts may seem relatively secure in comparison, for example, to the United States, where much employment is simply at will; however, the trend in China is toward even less security and the further degradation of the contract system itself. Nearly ten years after the passage of the National Labor Law, many firms have already found ways to avoid even the relative rigidity of the contract system, preferring instead to hire new workers on other more flexible terms. These include the apprenticeship system mentioned above and the subcontracting of workers through labor service companies. A Japanese JV in Shanghai had expanded its workforce from three hundred to eight hundred production line workers between 1996 and 2003. Yet after the initial hiring of the three hundred local Shanghai workers, some of whom were transferred from the SOE partner, the remaining five hundred have been migrant workers hired indirectly through a local Shanghai district labor service company. These workers, mainly from Anhui and Shaanxi Provinces, are not given benefits nor do they participate in social insurance. They are hired on three-month contracts. According to one manager, the firm does not need to fire workers; it simply waits for the contracts to expire.[62] The Tangshan SOE also used similar strategies to ensure a more flexible work-force by hiring workers from its subsidiaries on short-term projects without transferring the labor contract or the terms of employment. This allowed the core workforce of the SOE to enjoy relative employment security while forcing much more uncertain terms on new workers.[63] Moreover, by 2003 the SOE was no longer using subsidiaries to absorb redundant labor but was instead resorting to layoffs, terminations, and severance buyouts.[64] Links between subsidiaries and the core company were used to make labor more flexible, but unlike the mid-1990s, they were not being used to reallocate workers who were no longer needed.

The implementation of the individual labor contract system and the renewed attention to labor flexibility has further increased the insecurity and dependency of Chinese workers on enterprise management. The regulatory framework initiated by the government has been implemented only haphazardly. The lopsided implementation of individual labor contracts with a negligible emphasis on collective contracts and collective negotiations has led to the atomization of the workforce. The large influx of rural migrants through subcontracted labor, apprenticeships, and even illegal practices such as bonded labor has revived practices seem in the pre-Communist era as the state has taken a less active role in the administration of employment.[65]

MANAGEMENT DOMINATION OVER OR SUPPRESSION OF WORKER ORGANIZATIONS

The preceding discussion regarding managerial control and autonomy in the setting of labor contracts has emphasized the degree to which individualized employment relations amid market reform have improved the relative power position of enterprises at the expense of individual workers. In addition to the state's supply of legal labor rights as a protective institution for labor, collective organization of workers is also a means to temper the unequal bargaining relationship between enterprises and individual workers. As a socialist state, China has a long history of trade unionism and a highly developed union organization, the ACFTU, which serves as the umbrella organization for all legal unions in China. Independent unions or other types of worker organizations are illegal in China, and labor activists suffer long prison terms for attempting to organize workers outside of this official framework.

The following section details how managerial domination or suppression of worker organizations has been achieved despite the presence of the ACFTU and repeated attempts by the government to extend the union's presence and influence in the new nonstate sectors. We begin with the structure and history of the ACFTU itself and then turn to changes within firms that have contributed to the marginalization of the trade union and management domination over issues involving worker organizations.

The ACFTU is the national federation of Chinese trade unions, which includes industrial unions, local-level trade union offices, and enterprise-level trade union branches. Higher levels approve appointments at lower levels. The trade union organization at every level is also subordinate to the Communist Party bureaucracy. In the tradition of Leninist democratic centralism, the union, like other mass organizations, should act as a transmission belt conveying worker concerns and suggestions to higher levels while ensuring that central policies and edicts reach down to the workplace. As in most state socialist economies, this dual function of the union weakens its ability as a body representing workers in conflicts with management or the state.[66] At the national level, the union is subordinate to the CCP and the wishes of central CCP and state leaders. As a bureaucratic organization, the union is weak without the economic resources or bureaucratic control over policy that empower the other bureaucracies that influence labor policies, in particular the Ministry of Labor and Social Security.[67]

The ACFTU has a long history of affiliation with the CCP, appearing in its earliest form in the 1920s when the CCP and the Republican Party (KMT) were locked in a bitter struggle for political control of a divided nation. This history is marked by several periods in which the trade union attempted to stake out a certain degree of independence from the CCP. After 1949 these attempts became more difficult to justify as private and foreign ownership were eliminated. The CCP's central role in enterprise management reduced the union's position to that of a handmaiden of the party, with its responsibilities within enterprises largely limited to welfare and entertainment tasks. Union leaders who advocated for greater independence from the CCP were purged, most famously the long-time labor organizer and first vice chairman of the ACFTU, Li Lisan in 1951.[68] The trade union was an early target of the leftist leaders and Red Guard brigades during the Cultural Revolution who accused trade union leaders of "economism," "welfare trade unionism," and other types of behavior that mostly entailed highlighting the particular interests of workers.[69] These attacks on the ACFTU resulted in a ten-year hiatus during which the ACFTU was largely inoperative.

When the union returned to enterprises after its dissolution during the Cultural Revolution, important changes were already taking place in the management of state firms and in the expansion of the nonstate sector. As reforms progressed through the 1980s and 1990s, the union's position did not markedly improve, despite the dramatic expansion of the nonstate sector, which theoretically justified a more active union presence to balance against the power of enterprise owners and managers. There are two reasons for the union's continued weakness. First, enterprise reform within the core public sectors increasingly favored management's economic goals over the political goals traditionally touted by the party or union officials. As a subordinate organization to the party, the union lost influence. Enterprise reform, in particular the expansion of enterprise autonomy, granted factory managers wide discretionary power over issues such as wages, capital investment, and production plans that were previously decided by higher authorities. Management became more professional. As the party identified increasingly with management goals and supported management in its decision making, the union found itself with no powerful ally in the firm.[70] As management and party goals become increasingly intertwined, it also became common for the top manager of the firm to serve simultaneously as party secretary. The merging of these two once separate positions also served to reduce the influence of the union.[71]

Second, the rapid diversification in enterprise ownership through foreign investment, stockholding conversions, mergers, bankruptcies, factory leasing, and the rise of a private sector led to a rapid increase of enterprises that never had unions in the first place or that had "restructured" their unions out of existence. Thus the entire trade union institution found itself marginalized in the most dynamic sectors of the Chinese economy.

Although Chinese trade union law requires that all firms with twenty-five workers or more must have a trade union if requested by the workers, unionization rates vary greatly across types of firms. Due to the historical legacy of socialism and the preexistence of trade unions in SOEs, SOEs continue to have the highest rate of unionization. Joint ventures between SOEs and foreign companies are also likely to have a trade union organization, with personnel transferred over from the parent SOE. Large MNCs with well-developed human resource practices also tend to allow trade union formation, although this is not universal. Foreign firms whose owners are not of ethnic Chinese origin also seem more inclined to allow unionization, viewing the presence of a union as a means to improve communication with and cross-cultural understanding of their workforce.[72] Ethnic Chinese investors from overseas seem far less inclined to establish unions. These differences notwithstanding, however, the general trend of trade union organization in China is toward greater managerial control and oversight of worker organization, if not out-and-out suppression of worker organization.

"Access without Autonomy": Management Domination of Trade Unions

Firms that have enterprise-level trade unions use unions as a tool of management and as a stabilizing institution between workers and management. The role of the trade union is to mediate disputes and to relay worker opinions to management. It is a middleman more than it is a representative of the workforce, with little or no decision-making power.[73] Management dominates union leadership, usually managers from the enterprise's personnel department. The company's management in agreement with the local union bureau usually selects union representatives. The election of union officials occurs after the field of candidates has been narrowed and approved by management.

Gordon White aptly termed reform period unions as having "access without autonomy."[74] By the late 1990s this form of representation had extended throughout the SOE sector and into the "higher end" foreign-invested firms. SOEs and some foreign firms converged toward this form of representation, but they were coming from opposite directions. Foreign firms had a very low rate of unionization, while SOEs had highly bureaucratized union offices with full-time union cadres. Market forces and rising labor tensions were pushing both types of firms to find a new mode of labor control.

Unionization of Foreign-Invested Firms

The number of FIEs increased rapidly in the late 1980s and early 1990s, but unionization failed to keep pace. Prior to 1994, unionization at foreign firms was abysmally low, less than 10 percent, despite regulations specifically calling for unionization in foreign firms. Unionization of the FIE sector was encouraged by the government, but it was not enforced, and many foreign managers resisted unionization. Pearson's study of joint-ventures in the 1980s found that trade union organizations were either extremely weak or nonexistent, compromised either through foreign managers' resistance or attempts by local government officials to guarantee enterprise autonomy. [75] In the economic boom regions of the South, Hong Kong, Macao, and Taiwanese investment led to rapid industrialization of rural and suburban areas. Workers in these firms were often former peasants unfamiliar with factory organization in general and unions in particular. With little job security, these unskilled workers had little power to push for unionization themselves.[76] Nor were local governments enthusiastically pushing for unionization, concentrating on economic growth and development, and increased foreign investment. Trade unions were not a key concern. This continued until the 1990s when a rash of strikes and walkouts in the FIE sector alerted the leadership to the tinderbox nature of labor relations in these largely unregulated firms. As international and domestic media coverage of these conflicts increased, foreign investors expressed concern about stability and the Chinese media expressed anger at the treatment of Chinese workers by foreign bosses. The vice minister of Labor stated bluntly that unless labor legislation was quickly introduced, the strikes would only increase. Labor officials also worried about new demands from workers to set up independent unions in FIEs.[77]

Unionization of foreign firms did pick up and several cities achieved relatively high rates of unionization. By 1998 three-quarters of eligible FIEs had established trade unions.[78] Many of the largest and most popular development zones boasted high rates of unionization. By 1999 a labor union had become a more regular fixture in many foreign firms—indeed many foreign firms found that a union improved communication and overall labor relations without unduly interfering in management decisions or production.[79] Like SOE unions, FIE unions have access to management but they lack autonomy to represent workers fully. The main difference between the FIE and SOE unions is the way in which this access is achieved. In FIEs, the bureaucratic ties run between the enterprise union and the local development zone bureaucracies. The union's access to foreign management is through the legitimacy and power of the local level union. SOE unions have bureaucratic ties to the firm's management. Thus SOE unions tend to have more direct access to firm management, whereas FIE unions use ties to the local bureaucracy to pressure foreign management. However, the direct nature of the SOE ties does not necessarily translate into increased power. This point will be expanded upon below.

FIE Unions as Administrative Arms of Local Government

In development zones, the local bureaucracy plays a vital role in attracting FDI and managing the zone to please investors. Here the government is part administrator and part chamber of commerce. The trade union bureaucracy is part of the total developmentalist machine. In the Tianjin and Shanghai development zones visited, unions are set up and enterprise-level representatives are appointed as a bureaucratic process led by the development zone's union office. In She-kou, a special economic zone (SEZ) in Guangdong Province, the district union chair is a voting member of Shekou's board of directors and the party committee. The union has a role in resolving labor disputes, in reemployment programs, and in worker health and safety protection. They also direct the process of unionization in new FIEs and disseminate new labor regulations and government edicts.[80] These SEZ unions are not necessarily weak. A union chairman who is concurrently on the district board of directors and party committee is likely quite powerful. This "access without autonomy" grants the union a monopoly on worker representation but it places stability and economic development over other union responsibilities.

Japanese firms, in particular, seem the most adept at using this bureaucratic structure (local union bureau, enterprise-level union, and management) to achieve relatively stable labor relations. Compared to many other foreign-invested firms, they have higher rates of unionization and use unions effectively as a mediating institution between managers and workers.[81] Japanese firms fill the top union position with high-level Chinese managers, often the human resources manager or deputy manager. Japanese managers put emphasis on achieving consensual labor relations with the union chairman serving as a mediator between the foreign management and the Chinese workers.[82]

In a Sino-Japanese joint venture in Tianjin's development zone, relations were somewhat antagonistic but the union clearly had a role in worker representation and dispute resolution. It is significant that in this firm, the workers requested the establishment of a union, rather than waiting for an administrative edict from above. Due to this difference, the union chairman was actually elected (rather than appointed) and had been reelected in succession for three years. This union chairman argued that his union was "a real union, not like the unions in SOEs," and yet at the same time he jointly served as the personnel manager. The Chinese manager cast himself as the defender of Chinese interests in the firm against a band of noncooperative, misunderstanding Japanese.[83] And, in fact, he had achieved some success. Not coincidentally, employee benefits had been increased from 28 percent of base salary to 71 percent from 1997 to 1999. This occurred at a time when the Tianjin Economic and Technological Development Area (TEDA) government cut the welfare requirement from over 60 percent to just 49 percent, in a bid to be more competitive with Shanghai and development zones in the south.[84] However, his position as union chairman was obviously compromised by his joint position as personnel manager.

Japanese firms' success with this bureaucratic system is in sharp contrast to other Asian investors including overseas Chinese and Korean investors.[85] In a survey of 837 Japanese firms in China, 47.3 percent of firms surveyed reported that they were satisfied with the "cooperative" unions. Only 1.5 percent reported that they were satisfied with the unions although they were "not cooperative." Another 1.5 percent reported that they were unsatisfied with the uncooperative unions. The survey also reported that 11.7 percent of the firms reported strikes or walkouts, mainly in disputes over wages. Most of these strikes were resolved in less than one day (48.4 percent) with 29 percent resolved after one day. These were also spontaneous outbursts of discontent with no reported union participation.[86] Although the survey shows that some Japanese executives worry about the union interfering in management decisions, both the survey and the case studies reveal a relatively cooperative relationship between Japanese management and the unions. This cooperative relationship reflects the long-term investment plans of Japanese investors in China who express the need to establish a positive public image and to retain a stable and well-skilled workforce.[87]

Japanese investors are also adept at cultivating relations with the local union bureaucracy. In the Dalian Economic Development Zone where Japanese investors dominate, the union acts in cooperation with local governments and Japanese investors to preempt large-scale strikes and coordinate labor relations. The zone-level union joined with the labor bureau in formulating regulations on "collective work stoppages."[88] Noting that media coverage of earlier strikes (which numbered over 30 from 1992 to 1994) adversely affected Dalian's reputation among foreign investors, these regulations make it extremely dangerous for workers to organize protests. Workers must notify authorities seventy-two hours in advance of any work stoppage so that authorities can "sound the warning bell" and also warn the workers that they will be severely punished. In the event of a strike the union acts in cooperation with the Public Security Bureau (PSB) and the Labor Bureau to manage the conflict and resume production as quickly as possible. The union's role is to act as intermediary between the workers and management while the Labor Bureau supervises the process. The PSB is used as a show of force to dissuade workers from violent or destructive acts. The first priority is to resume production, call a meeting of workers and start negotiations. Both sides should "recognize their mistakes" and choose representatives (it is unclear whether workers can represent themselves) with the union relaying the proceedings to the workers. The Dalian Labor Bureau also recommends that China pass a no-strike law similar to those, the article notes, in England, Switzerland and Australia.[89] The union takes an active role in the dispute resolution process in Dalian but as these proposed regulations show, its role is to control worker protest (if not preempt it), mediate negotiations, and encourage workers to return to work immediately.

American firms in China report significant problems with human resource management, but unlike many Asian investors they do not seem to experience as many extreme situations such as strikes, work stoppages, and sabotage.[90] American managers have difficulty finding skilled workers and managers and even more retaining them. Poaching of employees by other FIEs is common.[91] Because the average size of American investment is large and their higher public profile, stable labor relations are a priority for both the government and the firms. While no data are available on unionization rates by national origin of investor, unionization of American firms is probably quite high, although lower than in Japanese-invested firms.[92] Labor lawyers report that there are palpable differences in labor dispute resolution cases that involve European and American firms. These firms tend to adhere to labor regulations and grant unions more decision-making input.[93] Disputes, when they do arise, are negotiated quickly. For example, in the American WFOE in Tianjin, a regulation was passed that required all workers to be searched upon leaving the factory premises to reduce employee theft of materials. Workers promptly protested this new practice, proclaiming that the American company was "violating their human rights."[94]

Foreign firms with high international profiles and public relation concerns over their investments in China are more likely not only to have unions but to allow unions greater responsibility and input. The result can be a management-empowered union, in which management pushes for better realization of the union role as set out in China's own legislation.[95]

Restructuring and Union Downsizing in SOEs

Although SOE and FIE unions have different institutional foundations, the pace of convergence is due to the growing market pressures on SOE firms. As mentioned earlier, the bureaucratic structures of FIE unions link the union to the local governmental bureaucracy. SOE unions, on the other hand, are increasingly incorporated into the enterprise management structure. This incorporation process, often coinciding with a period of restructuring, can grant the union an official position within a reformed firm, but it remains a weak junior partner vis-à-vis management.

With the deepening of SOE reform in 1994, ownership diversification has meant a rapid expansion in firms that (while perhaps still officially state owned) have undergone significant changes in management, often followed by drastic restructuring and downsizing.[96] These include mergers, bankruptcies, leasing, renting, and outright acquisition of state-owned firms. Union offices are often the target of the restructuring, leading to the closure, merger, or downsizing of union offices.[97] In a provincewide survey of Ningxia in China's northwest it was found that 56.2 percent of unions had been merged with other offices or disbanded. In most cases of merging, the trade union was absorbed into the firm's party branch.[98] Reports from other areas seem to indicate that this is a nationwide phenomenon.[99]

The Supreme People's Court of China has ruled that basic-level unions have legal personhood, making it easier for unions to sue when manage-

ment arbitrarily disbands their offices. The Court also stated that it is illegal to appropriate, transfer, or freeze union accounts when the enterprise is in financial straits.[100] But in reality unions have little financial independence from enterprise management. Financial constraints on the
union contribute to an institutional dependency on management that
leaves unions helpless and passive during the restructuring process. Many
enterprises simply absorb union fees into their administrative budget or
fail to dispense the required 2 percent of their total wage bill to the union
office.[101] The salaries of union cadres are paid by the enterprise, leading
to a situation where management's mantra is "you receive my money, you
listen to me." One indication of this phenomenon is the widespread failure of enterprise-level mediation committees. These committees, led by
the union chairman, are responsible for the mediation of labor disputes.
The lack of job security of union officials who have signed labor contracts
with management inhibits their commitment to mediation. Many union
chairmen who by law serve as the mediation committee chair hold a joint
administrative position. Some union leaders even represent the enterprise
in arbitration proceedings against workers.[102]

Joint-Posting in FIEs and SOEs

Other practices are become more similar across SOEs and FIEs, in particular the joint posting of union officials. Most union officials in FIEs and
SOEs now jointly serve in management positions, most often in human
resources and personnel.[103] Joint posting is a practice used by one of the
model union organizations, the Shekou SEZ union in Guangdong
Province. Shekou has an extremely high rate of unionization, reaching 98
percent in the last few years.[104] In an internal report in 1993 of the 250
enterprise-level unions, only two had full-time union posts. Thirty-three
of the union chairmen were also general managers, 110 served jointly as
deputy managers, and 115 union chairmen were middle managers, workshop directors, or workers.[105] The joint-posting policy is consistent with
the union's goals, which are first and foremost to encourage production
and strengthen "unity" between foreign capital and workers. The Shekou
system has expanded to other regions with FIEs in Tianjin and Shanghai
using the joint-posting system. Sino-Japanese joint ventures also seem to
prefer this system, with union chairmen regularly serving concurrently as
personnel managers or deputy managers.[106]

The practice of joint posting dilutes the power of the union. The conflict of interest it presents is most severe in joint ventures where joint posting as personnel manager and union chairman is common. Top union officials oppose this policy, realizing that it weakens the union's capacity to

bargain collectively and effectively and severely affects workers' confidence in the union.[107] One researcher notes that a union chairman who is concurrently party secretary, assistant manager, or a relative of the employer is not able to act as an advocate for workers. The union generally advocates that "the problem of joint positions" be quickly settled with the office of the union chairman as a special, full-time position without managerial responsibilities.[108]

Joint posting is not limited to the foreign sector. As seen above, union restructuring often means the amalgamation of the union offices into a larger administrative office. The union chairman might be a party official or a mid-to-high-level production manager. In the Tangshan SOE, which had converted to a state-controlled stockholding company in 1994, the union chairman was a *voting* member of the board of directors and a *stockholder*. Like FIE union chairmen who hold joint positions in human resource management, this practice clearly compromises the union's role as the representative of workers' rights and interests. It is unclear whether the practice of the union chair as company stockholder and voting board member is widespread among stockholding SOEs, but statistics from other regions indicate that it may be an unusual practice. In a survey of sixteen hundred firms in Hubei Province, only 2.5 percent of the stockholding firms had a labor representative on the board of directors.[109] In a report of sixteen firms in Shenyang City, none had a union member on the board of directors.[110]

Even if the practice of assigning a board of director seat to the union chairman becomes more widespread (as the union hopes), it is questionable whether or not it would improve worker representation or exacerbate the existing conflict of interest.[111] Does the union have more power because the chairman can vote against motions that are unduly harmful to workers? Or does the chairman's own stake in the economic performance of the company compromise his union role? The Tangshan SOE union chairman adamantly stated that the union's power had increased under enterprise reform, particularly through his presence on the board of directors. He cited a recent decision by the factory general manager to increase the enterprise's contribution to an employee housing fund. After the workers complained that the company contribution was too low, the union chairman negotiated with management to increase its contribution.[112] It is difficult to assess how this practice affects the union. Clearly the loyalty of the union chairman is divided. It may be that in comparison to stockholding companies without union representatives on the board of directors, his influence is greater. But the role of the union is dependent, then, on the chairman's personal choices as this structure allows him to act as manager, as union chairman, or as a stockholder.

Serve the Foreign Investor! The Communist Party in FIEs

Despite some reluctance to allow unions on the part of some FIEs, many large multinationals seem to welcome the role played not only by the firms' branch of the ACFTU but also the role played by the Communist Party, which seems to increasingly have branch committees within foreign enterprises. These organizations employ traditional Chinese socialist methods (thought work, propaganda, tight organization) to train the workforce to accept their role in the factory as loyal employees of a foreign company that often has extremely high demands and an exhausting work schedule. It is an ironic marriage of neoliberal capitalism with socialist tools of control.

In some cases, firms with global "no unions" policy allow CCP party branches as an apparent compromise with the local authorities. For example, a large MNC in Tianjin has continued for over fifteen years without a trade union despite various national campaigns to encourage unionization of foreign firms. This company, however, has a well developed CCP branch system and an "Employee Standing Committee" that fulfills many typical union responsibilities, including entertainment, welfare policy coordination, and the handling of special issues related to women workers (women make up 80 percent of their production workforce). The separate propaganda boards of the two organizations complement each other in a kind of numbing repetition of human resource management slogans and patriotic propaganda. While the Employee Standing Committee emphasized employee excellence, the party emphasized its role as a bridge between China and foreign investors. "Encourage understanding of foreign investment!" one slogan read while others lauded the recent feats of China's new leaders. When asked what the party branch did exactly in the firm, one employee replied "patriotism, propaganda, and stability. Foreigners are surprised that we have the Party, but what do you expect in China?" Clearly discomfited by the fact that I could read the slogans and announcements as we toured the plant, she asked that I speak to her boss about it. "We aren't really supposed to talk about this with you."[113]

Leadership of party and union organizations are often combined in one person who serves jointly as party secretary and union chairman. In the Tianjin American WFOE the party secretary was also the head of the Employee Standing Committee, although workers were allowed to elect their workshop representatives for the committee. In a large Sino-American JV in Shanghai, the party secretary and the union chairman shared an office and were clearly the main middlemen between foreign management and the production workforce. In another large Sino-American JV in Shanghai, the party secretary was also the union chair.

These leaders are compensated at the level of upper management; they are mainly there to mediate between the company's economic goals and the desires and demands of the employees. This is not interest representation of the workforce, but rather the more traditional transmission belt style trade unionism of Leninism—with the difference that the union and the party serve the interests of the foreign company. These leaders do "thought work" to convince the workers to accept new modes of production, long work shifts, cuts or changes in benefits, and other adjustments to global capitalism. The propaganda boards of these organizations are not very different from what one sees in Chinese SOEs with their mixture of corporate HR (human resources) and patriotic exhortation. "It's so nice to have a trade union that works with us rather than against us," is how one American manager put it when asked about their relationship with the trade union.[114] Tired of working with oppositional trade unions in the United States and Britain, this manager expressed relief that things in China were different. In a Sino-Japanese JV in Shanghai, the structure was similar. The general manager was also the party secretary while the union chairman position was filled by the assistant manager of the general affairs department. The party's role was "to encourage workers, to promote workers' activism and set high production goals for workers."[115]

Neither Access Nor Autonomy: Management Suppression of Trade Unions

Many other firms eschew the union system altogether and rely on a personalistic management style that does not tolerate organized worker representation. In firms visited by the author, small domestic firms, even publicly owned firms, did not have functioning unions. The urban collective union structure, once a regular institution in collective firms, has been emasculated by the contract management (*chengbao*) system. Among FIEs, Taiwanese firms seem most opposed to the establishment of enterprise level union organization. These firms rely on highly autocratic managers, often purposefully using local managers to control "their" workers. For example, firms in Guangdong were reported to hire Sichuanese managers to control Sichuanese migrant workers.[116] Taiwanese managers cite localization as the main way to reduce labor tension. "Chinese," one manager said, "don't like to be managed by *huaqiao* (overseas Chinese)."[117] Formal institutions that mediate between labor and management are absent. Some researchers have found evidence of informal organizations that workers form to achieve some sense of collective power. These organizations are often based on native-place affiliation. If the workers are migrant, their "*baogongtou*" (the person who contracts out the labor of workers) may serve as their representative in negotiations with management or the local government. These informal institutions are vulnerable to managerial opposition and have no legitimate, legal standing within the enterprise.

A rural collective in Hebei, a "national joint venture"[118] between an older collective firm and a university in Beijing was a typical example of the new firms in China's rural and suburban areas. The formation of this joint venture involved the near liquidation of the older collective and the transfer of management and land to the new firm. The original workers of the rural collective were left behind at the old company (which had stopped production) as this new venture hired sixteen- and seventeen-year-old youths from nearby villages to manufacture DVDs using equipment acquired with the capital infusion from Beijing. The enterprise had what the general manager called a "temporary union" that he said did nothing but give out free tea and sugar to the otherwise benefitless young peasant workforce. This general manager was also the union chairman. In leaving the old workers and the old enterprise structure behind, the new company was able to restructure labor relations with a younger, less demanding workforce. By ridding the new enterprise of older, more demanding, and experienced workers, the enterprise is unlikely to hear any new demands for unionization.[119]

The emasculation of the union also has occurred in the urban collective sector, mainly through implementation of the contract management system and more recently through the actual privatization of many small-to-medium firms. In a Tianjin urban collective, each individual enterprise is contracted out to individual managers who are under no obligation to establish a grass-roots-level trade union. The collective's central administration had also restructured its management system, with the central trade union dissolved into the General Affairs Office.[120] Thus at the enterprise level there was no union representation and at the administrative level, the union had been absorbed into a larger administrative office.

FIEs that ignore the regulation to unionize are one of the biggest problems for the Chinese state because these firms tend to have abusive management, the worst working conditions, and the most explosive disputes. Indeed the Taiwanese WFOEs visited were the only firms that reported openly in interviews significant labor problems, including strikes, sabotage, and tense relations with workers.[121] Unlike a joint venture that has several former SOE managers join the new company, these independent enterprises have much greater independence to structure labor relations as they see fit. Often this can lead to extremely harsh and militaristic labor systems.[122]

The mutual contempt and ill will between workers and managers was most obvious in Taiwanese WFOEs. Despite a common language and culture, labor relations in these firms were overtly tense and antagonistic.

Managers made no attempts to disguise their loathing of the workforce and the strict measures necessary to produce efficiency and quality. "These workers are all peasants, they don't know how to behave, they spit, they jaywalk, they have no discipline," is how one manager described the problems he has encountered since relocating to a mainland factory, while justifying the need for "militaristic" labor discipline.[123] A manager in another department of the same factory bitterly complained about the attempts his largely young female workforce made to get time off for child rearing. "One hour of breast-feeding for them is one-hour of loss for me. Anyway, I know that they don't really need that time. Their kids are back in villages. They just want to rest."[124]

Both managers and workers, when interviewed separately, characterized their relations exactly the same way while blaming the other side. Managers complained that because workers only cared about money and not about the future of the company, they could be made to work hard only through material rewards and punishments. Workers complained that because their Taiwanese bosses were "cheap" they were underpaid while forced to work long hours in bad conditions. Both groups noted that their relations were only "money relations" and as such had no "human feeling."[125]

In only one case was there a significant, qualitative change in the practices of a Taiwanese WFOE. The change in this firm's labor practices coincided with its decision to pursue a longer-term investment plan and to win a significant proportion of the domestic market for office equipment.[126] In the initial period of its PRC investment, this Taiwanese firm experienced labor conflict when a "gang" of Taiwanese managers was transferred from the firm's calculator factory in Thailand. Their authoritarian labor management style upset the Chinese workers who had a "strong sense of their human rights."[127] As the firm began to make its transition from export production to domestic market penetration, it hired a Taiwanese industrial relations expert trained in the United States. The firm had also made major investments into staff housing in order to retain workers and had firm plans for localization of management in the short term.[128]

According to managers, the firm wanted to establish a corporate reputation in the PRC. For this reason the firm made substantial investment into human resource management, provided substantial benefits for skilled workers and managers (such as housing) and opportunities for advancement. Unionization, however, was avoided on the basis that it only increased local governmental interference. Their experience reiterates the opinions found in larger surveys of Taiwanese investors. In a survey of Taiwanese firms in China it was found that "the majority of Taiwanese firms in China are endeavoring to strengthen worker-management relations . . . through improved communication between workers and management (also between superiors and subordinates), and worker-oriented initiatives such as promotions and training programs."[129] When it comes to the question of worker organization, however, most Taiwanese investors reject it entirely and rely instead on direct managerial control of the workforce.[130]

There is reason to believe that small domestic firms increasingly mimic the strict labor practices of overseas Chinese. As the union (and party) structures weaken in many collective and state firms, despotic labor practices and authority relations spread to these other firms and indeed are often justified by the pressure of competition with foreign and private companies.[131] These publicly owned firms are often competing against FIEs for export markets and reform their mode of labor control accordingly. For the Hebei rural collective it meant stripping away older and more experienced workers who might complain about working conditions or the lack of benefits. For the urban collective it meant granting enterprise managers increased autonomy and restructuring the traditional mass organizations out of existence. Organizations that represent workers' interests in these firms are increasingly marginalized.

CONCLUSION

The emergence of a new regime of labor practices based on managerial control, insecure employment, and subjugation of workers organization in China came without a political transformation or even with large-scale privatization. In the absence of political transition, China's trade unions have gone in the same direction as those in the post-socialist world: toward further marginalization and weakness.[132] In fact, the weakness of postsocialisst labor may indicate that socialist worker organizations were uniquely unprepared to resistance the onslaught of global capitalism.

Labor practices at the firm level are varied and diverse, reflecting not only sectoral and regional variation but also vastly increased managerial autonomy and decision-making power in setting labor practices. The state's withdrawal from its previous role as administrator of labor allocation and employment has granted enterprises a great degree of power in setting labor practices. Attempts to balance this withdrawal with greater attention to laws and regulations as a means of regulating managerial power have been mostly unsuccessful. Developmentalist local governments have neither the capacity nor the will to implement constraints on capital. The strengthening of worker organizations as a means to mitigate the unequal relationship between firms and individual workers has also not been achieved. Despite some legislative attention to collective contracts, collective bargaining, and an enhanced role for the trade union, in practice Chinese trade unions are marginalized or co-opted by management. Even in firms where the trade union is well established, its existence is closely tied to management goals.

China's transition to capitalism in the absence of political change is intimately related to an economic reform program that emphasized trade and investment liberalization with regional decentralization. Convergence with free-market labor practices was part of a dynamic process of external liberalization and internal competition for the investment brought by liberalization. The state's attempts to mitigate the excesses of capitalism through increased legislation and unionization drives have met with less success. Policies intended to preserve some of the stability and security of socialism are in implementation shifted to favor management and its demands for flexibility and autonomy.

CHAPTER FIVE

"Use the Law as Your Weapon!"

FDI AND THE LEGALIZATION OF LABOR RELATIONS

"THE LABOR LAW IS A WEAPON to protect the rights of workers," reads an excerpt from a page in the official workers' newspaper heralding the second year of the law's implementation. The page details new regulations, shows pictures of child workers in a Yunnan mine, has a write-in advice column for disgruntled workers, and provides information about a legal aid center for workers. Exhorting workers to "use the law as a weapon" is an apt and ironic phrase for this new emphasis on legal institutions. It reflects both the new importance that the state places on law as well as the increasingly contentious and even violent state of labor politics (which require the need for a weapon).[1] In the past several years labor disputes in China have risen at an exponential rate. (See figure 5.1.)

In 1994, 19,098 disputes occurred, rising 73 percent in 1995 to 33,030. The year-on-year rate jumped again by 45.6 percent in 1996, 48.6 percent in 1997, 31.3 percent in 1998 to 93,649, and in 2003 labor disputes reached an all-time high of 226,000.[2] This phenomenon took place in tandem with rapid changes in industrial relations, an FDI boom, several important legal reforms and renewed commitment to state enterprise reform by the central leadership. In this context increasing contentiousness is not a complete surprise. Yet in a country with very weak legal institutions and with a regime that is not wholly committed to the rule of law, it is puzzling that workers turned in increasing numbers to China's newly developed legal infrastructure for the resolution of labor disputes. Moreover, this phenomenon also seems at odds with current analysis of the Chinese legal system as weak, easily corrupted, and subservient to CCP political rule.

This new emphasis on legal institutions to structure and mediate labor relations and the resulting explosion in labor disputes is directly related to the role of FDI in China's economy and its increasing significance in the 1990s. First, concerns about FDI led the state to rely on the rule of law as a way both to encourage foreign investment and to control its adverse effects, particularly its effects on labor relations. Labor laws and regulations, in particular the National Labor Law of 1995, were promulgated as a response to the increasing complexity of labor-management relations.[3] Second, the legalization of labor relations had the effect of in-

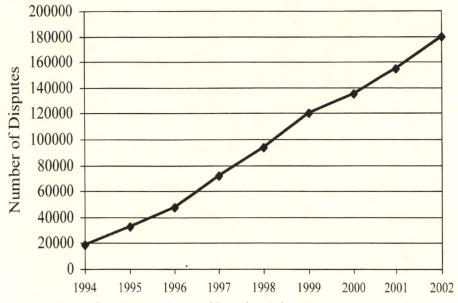

Figure 5.1. Labor Disputes Accepted by Labor Arbitration Committees, 1994–2002. *Source: China Labor Statistical Yearbook,* various years (Beijing: China Statistical Publishing House.

creasing labor disputes, particularly within foreign enterprises by opening an officially sanctioned channel for discontent outside of the enterprise. The Chinese government was not inclined to allow the settlement of labor conflict to rest in the hands of management, particularly in the hands of foreigners. Unlike Taiwan, whose experience I also examine briefly in this chapter, the PRC government was not content to allow its burgeoning nonstate sector to settle labor conflict directly. Instead the government has opened up new legal and administrative channels through which workers demand redress for their grievances. This has drawn labor conflict out of the firm and toward administrative and legal channels. These disputes are more likely to occur when foreign capital is involved and in regions where FDI is dominant. Moreover, labor disputes in FIEs are not only more frequent, they are also more likely to be collective, to include more workers, and to lead to strikes, slowdowns, and general social instability.[4]

As other chapters have shown, foreign capital has become more integrated into the domestic economy through foreign acquisition of state and collective firms and through measures to increase foreign equity share and managerial control in existing joint ventures. Firm-level practices across all types of ownership are becoming more similar and converging with

FIE practices. As foreign ownership of enterprises increases and as domestic Chinese firms increasingly mimic foreign practices, labor disputes across all types of ownership continue to rise rapidly. This chapter examines the increase in labor disputes in light of China's legalization of labor relations. FDI played an important role as a reason for legalization and the effect of this legalization, an increasing number of labor disputes, is particularly significant in foreign companies. As restructuring and ownership reforms occur more regularly in state and collective firms, however, labor disputes are now increasing in these sectors as well. Labor dispute rates are also increasing quickly in China's domestic private companies.

My focus in this chapter is on the increase in labor disputes (*laodong zhengyi*) as measured by the number of cases filed at local Labor Arbitration Committees. These figures are recordings of formal filings of a labor conflict and as such do not include many kinds of labor conflict, such as informally resolved disputes. In addition, it is often reported that the government takes over the handling of large collective disputes in order to mitigate the social and political consequences of large-scale demonstrations and strikes.[5] Thus there are many instances of labor conflict that are not recorded as "labor disputes" and therefore are not included in this analysis. While it is almost certainly the case that labor conflict more generally has risen in concert with the number of formal filings, my interest here is in documenting how new processes of dispute resolution were created as a reaction to reports of abuse and exploitation in China's foreign-invested sector and as an attempt to offer clear rules for management in the event of a labor dispute. These processes stand in sharp contrast to previous methods of dispute resolution that mainly relied on internal enterprise mediation and to methods employed in Taiwan during a similar period of rapid industrial growth and political authoritarianism. These new legal weapons are far from perfect, but imperfections and problems notwithstanding, they have opened up new avenues for workers to lodge grievances against their employers.

The first section of this chapter is a general discussion of China's turn toward the rule of law and the development of a legal infrastructure. It shows why laws are important in a reforming socialist economy despite the continuing authoritarian nature of Chinese politics. The second, third, and fourth sections examine the development of legal institutions, specifically labor contracts and the National Labor Law, to manage labor conflict. Reform followed the dual but contradictory demands of foreign investors and the concerns of the state about foreign capital's exploitation of workers. In the 1990s, as the increasing competition from the nonstate sector overwhelmed failing state firms, these legal reforms were gradually expanded to include the domestic state sector. The fifth section introduces the process of labor dispute resolution and places the increase in PRC labor disputes in comparative perspective through analysis of PRC and Taiwanese labor dispute rates. Through this comparison, we are able to gain a better comparative sense of the rate of labor disputes in the PRC. The sixth section is an analysis of trends in PRC labor disputes. The major trends in labor disputes are an increase in frequency, an increase in size, and an increase in intractability. These trends are particularly evident in foreign-invested firms but are no longer isolated there. As ownership has blurred, legislation has become less ownership specific and foreign-invested enterprises more difficult to treat separately. Moreover labor practices in SOEs and collectives are no longer easily differentiated from those of private and foreign firms.

China's Turn to the Rule of Law

The development of China's legal system and infrastructure has resulted in a wide-ranging debate regarding the nature of law in China, the relevance of law in an authoritarian state, and finally the contribution, if any, a more developed legal system will have toward more democratic politics in China. As a general statement the majority of Western legal scholars are pessimistic regarding the rule of law in China.[6] The dominant concern is the CCP's unwillingness to submit to legal regulations and strictures that may reduce its political power. Others point to the vast and awesome difficulties of implementation and enforcement of laws in China's vast, diverse, and often independent-minded regions. Both of these are significant barriers to the achievement of a less arbitrary, rule-based polity. They are not, however, reasons to ignore the development of Chinese law. In fact, the strengthening of China's legal institutions is directly related to the Chinese state's interest in holding on to power. While pessimists might argue that the CCP will never willingly submit to laws that limit its power, the development of rule of law may have unintended consequences for their hold on political power. The Party-State might gamble that rule through law and the added benefits of increased legitimacy both at home and abroad are worth the risk of activating social forces and enlarging space in which new interest groups make their voices heard. In the absence of any organized, cross-regional worker uprising, it seems that so far the formalization and legalization of labor relations has "mutually empowered"[7] the state and workers. The state garners greater legitimacy and workers have an arena for controlled but real conflict.

But why has the Chinese state turned to the rule of law in the first place? Legitimacy has been mentioned above as one reason. It is itself an important reason for the state's emphasis on the rule of law. After the chaotic and despairing years of the Cultural Revolution, the CCP leaders specifically emphasized legalization most famously with the phrase coined by Deng Xiaoping: "There must be laws for people to follow, these laws must be observed, their enforcement must be strict, and lawbreakers must be dealt with."[8] Official support for the "rule of law" was often couched in terms of opposition to "rule of men." Moreover, with economic reform, the CCP's main foundation of socialism has withered away, leaving the party to search for new justifications for its rule. Although most of this justification has been found in China's rapid and sustained economic growth over the last twenty years, the state has also found increased legitimacy through the construction of more durable and predictable political institutions. These include the election of rural leaders, the development of the rule of law, and China's participation in international institutions as a status quo, not revolutionary, state.

Although the gain in legitimacy is undoubtedly of some importance, the Chinese state's turn to the rule of law is at its foundation an instrumentalist and pragmatic choice. If economic growth brought increased legitimacy, sustained economic growth was achieved through opening and integration with the outside world. Opening to the outside world through FDI required the development of a legal system. Importantly for China, however, this was not the only way to establish links to global capital. China was also able to utilize the familial and cultural ties between Mainland China and overseas Chinese communities in Hong Kong and Taiwan. These ties were especially important during the 1980s and early 1990s when legal development was in its infancy and Chinese law lacked sophistication and breadth. Over time, however, as China's economy and society grew more complex the legal system has developed and matured. Since 1978, 350 national laws have been passed along with 6,000 regulations.[9] Legislation activity has been particularly active since 1992 with many important laws and regulations passed including the Law on Lawyers, the Labor Law, and a revised Criminal Procedure Law. In 1997 the Fifteenth Congress of the CCP incorporated the rule of law into party doctrine and also made the development of a rule of law a top priority.[10]

Legal reform helps to accomplish the state's major goals, including integration into the world economy. A second and equally important instrumentalist goal on the part of the Chinese state is to control and manage domestic social change through laws. In a reforming socialist economy, the transformative role of law is central to the state's mission to reform the economy.[11] The state itself is an agent of change.[12] Rule through laws yields more efficient and acceptable control of individuals and social groups that threaten to destabilize the CCP's hold on political power. These "deployments of legality" on the part of authoritarian states are often part of a move away from overt repression.[13] That the state often undertakes this transformative mission with a sharp eye to the maintenance of its political power does not negate the fact that many of these laws, which are often crucial to economic efficiency and development, have potentially corrosive side effects for state power. This makes it necessary to separate empirically the stated goals of the state from the actual results of a law's implementation. Authoritarian states may enact laws that are potentially dangerous to their hold on power because of other important state goals.[14] The unintended effects of laws can have wide ramifications on the broader state-society relationship. It is a process that forms legal institutions into both "makers of hegemony and a means of resistance."[15] Law becomes a "double-edged sword," capable of empowering others beyond the state.[16] Unlike much work on the connection between law and power, the focus here is on mass-level labor disputes rather than the study of disputes involving dissidents that generally contest civil and political rights enshrined in the constitution. Labor disputes are mainly concerned with economic relations, particularly the economic and social rights of workers against the economic rights and responsibilities of enterprises. While the protection of the civil and political rights of intellectuals and dissidents is extremely important for the possibility of political liberalization, this focus on mass-level economic and social rights is equally significant. Despite their economic goals and content, changes in and clarification of workers' rights and employers' responsibilities have political ramifications.

LABOR AND LEGAL INSTITUTIONALIZATION

One needs not to attribute lofty or liberal goals to the Chinese state in order to show the effect of labor laws on the state-society relationship. These laws were seen by the state as crucial both to attract FDI and to control the exploitation of workers in FIEs.[17] By the mid-1990s, the expansion of the laws' jurisdiction was also seen as necessary to improve the competitiveness of state and collective firms. These laws were instrumental in channeling disputes and conflicts toward officially sanctioned resolution processes, so in this sense they contributed to the state's ability to maintain control over workers despite rapid economic and social change. At the same time the rapid increase in all types of labor disputes, the increasing size of collective disputes, the massive explosion of disputes in foreign and then later in private companies, and the declining efficacy of dispute mediation all point to increased societal conflict and rising rights consciousness, especially among workers.

Due to China's reliance on FDI, the role of law is particularly important in China's restructuring of the economy and its gradual integration with the global economy. In developing economies the decision to woo foreign investors provides the impetus to develop laws more fully and in accordance with international practices. This is a general phenomenon, but it is exacerbated in the Chinese context for several reasons. First, one of the legacies of Maoism was the almost complete absence of legal institutions, lawyers, and laws by the end of the Cultural Revolution. Foreign investors are an infamously skittish herd and prefer investment environments that are predictable, transparent, and stable. China in the late 1970s, recovering from the excesses and institutional decay of the Cultural Revolution, lacked these attributes. Thus the development of laws was foremost in the leadership's mind as a source of control and as reassurance to foreign investors that China was a reliable place for investment:

> The application of Chinese law to foreign investment projects was central to the joint venture policy not only because it was considered the central mechanism for protecting China's sovereignty, but also because it was the specific means for defining the legal status of joint ventures and for seeing that joint ventures met the myriad concerns of the leadership. Because post-Mao China did not have a well-developed code of commercial law, a central task of the reformers was to develop such a code to govern foreign involvement in China's economy.[18]

China began to develop quickly a body of law focused on FDI because the state strongly desired that foreign investors be subject to China's laws. In order to control FDI through laws, China needed laws. As Potter has pointed out, the leadership in China has needed law both to control and to attract FDI. This "dilemma of state control" has meant an increasing reliance on law and an increasing expansion of law as the economy has grown more complex.[19] The new laws and regulations on labor management in foreign-invested companies were an important subset of the new legal regime created to structure foreign capital's relationship to the Chinese domestic economy and society. FDI, more than other indirect sources of overseas capital, directly affects and interacts with domestic institutions. Labor laws and regulations were particularly important in the Chinese case because of the reliance on FDI over other types of foreign capital. Moreover unlike many other developing economies China did not limit the share of foreign ownership of an equity joint venture except in strategic industries. Foreigners could own from 25 percent to 99 percent of the joint venture, allowing foreign investors to have controlling stakes in their enterprises and a deciding say in enterprise management. In 1986, moreover, China legalized the entrance of wholly foreign owned subsidiaries, firms that had absolutely no domestic ownership share. Thus particular emphasis was placed on how to control and manage the behavior of enterprises because it was at the enterprise level where the impact of foreign capital was felt. "The level of the enterprise was the point at which the tension between the desire to attract and control foreign capital was most evident."[20]

China passed the Equity Joint Venture Law (EJVL) in 1979, the first law designed to attract foreign direct investment into China. Underlining the critical importance that labor management played in both attracting investors and controlling FDI, the EJVL was followed twenty-six days later by "Provisions of the People's Republic of China for Labor Management in Chinese-Foreign Joint Ventures."[21] This was the first law to tackle the new and important issues of labor management in firms that were not state-owned. For foreign managers the implementation of labor contracts granted enterprise autonomy that was heretofore unknown in PRC industrial relations.[22]

THE LABOR CONTRACT SYSTEM

The principles of the labor contract system (LCS) include: (1) a contract detailing the terms of employment that is signed between the employee and the employer and is approved by the local labor bureau. The contract details the length of employment, workday and vacation length, welfare benefits, wages, insurance, punishments for disciplinary infractions, and the terms for changes, renewal, and cancellation of the contract; (2) the contract is voluntary and renewal of the contract is dependent on the agreement of both parties;[23] (3) the contract can be broken. An employee may terminate the contract with thirty days advance written notice. The enterprise may abrogate the labor contract if the company is under duress as stipulated by article 27 of the National Labor Law.[24] It should be noted that this right to terminate the contract was not recognized until 1995, when the Labor Law was finally passed. Throughout the 1980s it was extremely difficult for enterprises to fire workers even with the existence of a labor contract. The actual meaning and effect of labor contracts has changed over time. At this early stage, it was more significant as a move away from administrative assignment of lifelong employment than as a means for employers to reduce staff. Foreign firms had more choice in hiring than they had in firing those workers once they were employees. The right to fire and lay off came more gradually than the right to hire freely.

The adoption of the LCS was a crucial first reform. It signaled the move away from China's state-socialist tradition. This tradition was characterized by very low labor mobility, low and strictly regulated rural-to-urban migration, lifetime employment for state-sector workers, and enterprise-provided welfare benefits. Compared to even other state-socialist economies, China's system of "work-unit" socialism was extreme in the ties of "organized dependence" binding worker to firm.[25] For these reasons, the introduction of the LCS and labor laws based on contractual employment was all the more radical. Their implementation would mean the gradual undoing of the institutional foundations of China's urban industrial system.

The LCS was first instituted in the SEZs of southeastern China, Shenzhen and Zhuhai.[26] These areas were created in the early stages of reform to attract FDI, particularly from overseas Chinese in Hong Kong. Regulations and taxes were relaxed, and the Chinese state seemed ready to tolerate capitalism on its soil as a trade-off for the transfer of management skills and technology. They also served as the laboratories of reform. Potentially destabilizing reforms were tried there first as a way to measure their impact and gauge their success. Reformist leaders also hoped that the success of the SEZs would soften bureaucratic and public resistance to urban industrial reforms in general.[27] Insofar as the SEZs were successful, SEZ policies, including contract labor, could receive some of the credit, and the extension of those policies to other areas and other sectors would be justified. The early implementation of the LCS in the SEZs and in Sino-Foreign joint ventures fits the use of laws and regulations as described above. The LCS granted (at least on paper) foreign investors control over employment and the terms of such employment. At the same time, it allowed the state some degree of supervision over internal enterprise behavior and practices. Through the use of relatively long contracts (two to five years) at this early stage of reform, it also guaranteed some basic employment stability to these new FIE workers.

The LCS was not a universally accepted concept. Its implementation was first restricted to these new foreign-invested sectors of the economy, sectors that were extremely small and isolated and themselves politically controversial. The Chinese state began to tinker with labor contracts outside of the SEZs and foreign firms in 1983, and from that time until the early to mid-1990s labor contracts expanded only gradually; their implementation was subject to the same "relax-retrench" cycles of economic reform in general.[28] Opposition to the LCS was substantial on political, economic, and ideological grounds. Much of this opposition is related to the history of contract labor in China prior to the reform period.[29]

Soon after the CCP came to power in 1949 the state began a process of curtailing rural-to-urban migration. After several decades of war, dislocation, and economic chaos, the cities were not able to handle the employment and social control demands of such migration. By the 1960s, there was a clear rural-urban divide embodied in the *hukou* (registered permanent resident) system.[30] Urban *hukou* holders were a minority and an elite. Rural labor, when needed, was used on a temporary "contract"

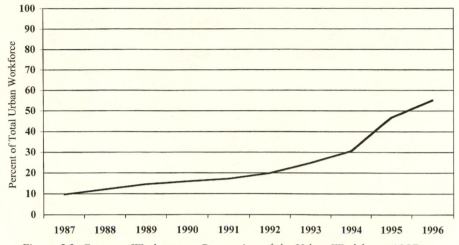

Figure 5.2. Contract Workers as a Proportion of the Urban Workforce, 1987–1996. *Source:* Compiled from *China Statistical Yearbook,* various years. Beijing: China Statistical Publishing House.

basis. These contract workers were discriminated against in pay and benefits at the factory; it was partly their dissatisfaction with the contract system that fueled conflict during the Cultural Revolution.[31] To an urban worker, a contract worker signified someone who was weak, held a tenuous employment position, and was not a full member of the enterprise.[32]

On an ideological level, the labor contract system was uncomfortably close to the capitalist wage-labor system. Some leaders and academics feared that it gave up the ideal of socialist enterprise and sacrificed the socialist notion of full employment for an undue emphasis on increased efficiency.[33] State-owned managers and workers also worried about the divide it would create in the firm. State-owned managers were especially unenthusiastic to grant skilled workers and technicians some ability to leave the firm. Nor did managers want the chance of increased conflict between permanent and contract workers to damage an already weak morale on the factory floor.[34] The contract system was finally expanded to all newly hired workers in the SOE sector in 1986.[35] But for nearly eight years the system expanded only gradually and growth was particularly flat after the suppression of the Prodemocracy Movement of 1989. As figure 5.2 demonstrates, the proportion of contract workers to the total urban workforce grew very slowly from 1987 to 1992.

Many problems contributed to this slow rate of implementation, and several of the anticipated conflicts, ideological and political, as well as practical snafus in implementation became roadblocks in the further development of the LCS. At the enterprise level, strong opposition to the LCS meant that contract workers were treated as permanent workers—very few firings occurred and most contracts were extended when they expired. Under the soft budget constraint, managers still had little incentive to alienate workers or to cut the workforce to save money. Capital for investment and wage and bonus increases continued to flow from the state banks. Hiring practices did seem to adjust more quickly in that managers were given more autonomy in choosing workers, but once a worker was hired, his contract status made it only marginally easier for him to be fired.

The institutional foundation of China's industrial system was also ill-prepared for contract labor. The enterprise-centered welfare system tied the workers not to the state directly, as in Eastern Europe, but to the enterprise work-unit. Enterprise control over housing, in particular, made contract labor difficult and unpalatable. China also had yet to implement comprehensive social insurance and unemployment insurance programs. There was no safety net to protect workers who would be unemployed, no private housing market for contract workers to enter, and no clear way for a worker to maintain pension or medical benefits after switching jobs.[36]

Thus labor reform moved slowly.[37] The LCS was caught up in a process typical of reforming socialist states. Typically, apart from the liberal reformers and technocrats at the top, "political constituencies for reform policies are hard to find."[38] Reforms were pushed forward by their supporters at the top, but the top was rarely unified and conservative opponents blocked and slowed the pace of reform. Implementation was tentative so as not to alienate further the opponents of reform. New problems and contradictions sprang up during implementation, which conservatives used ably to slow down reform.

Yet in China, as in other places, this has not been only a cyclical process of reform and conservative backlash. There is a dynamic effect from the reforms that remains even during the retrenchment period. Two steps forward are followed by one step back. The implementation of the labor contract system typifies this dynamic process of reform. Thus despite the slow, halting, and gradual implementation of the LCS in SOEs, the use of labor contracts spread throughout the 1990s. The ideological debate among the leaders at the top also shifted quite radically as Deng Xiaoping reiterated support for reform in his "southern tour" in 1992. Liberal proponents of a labor market based on contracts won the day, and the socialist misgivings regarding contract labor that were still extant in the 1980s faded from the mainstream. In firms that had already implemented contracts but found them weak sources of enterprise autonomy, these changes help strengthen the effect of contracts.[39]

This dynamic effect originated mostly from outside the public sector in which the LCS met opposition from both workers and managers alike. Specifically, dynamism sprung from the rapid expansion of FDI in the early-to-mid 1990s and from the huge increase in domestic nonstate sector firms. These two phenomena placed new and disparate demands on China's labor force and created new problems for the state's ability to manage capital and labor. First, there was the visible increase in firms with horrific labor conditions (both FIEs and domestic private firms) including the lack of benefits and insurance, no job security, dangerous working conditions, and nonpayment of wages. These firms were concentrated in the coastal development zones and in labor-intensive manufacturing. They were most often owned by Asian investors searching out new production locations with lower wages and less participatory politics.[40] Employment was unregulated, chaotic, and destabilizing since many of these firms preferred to hire rural migrants. Many smaller foreign firms, while nominally required to sign contracts, avoided doing so in order to maintain extreme levels of labor flexibility. Labor contracts and the codification of the labor contract system into law offered the prospect of better control and supervision over these abusive firms.[41]

Second, complaints by foreign investors that Chinese labor was too rigid, too passive, and too tightly controlled threatened to scare off investors from the United States and Japan who could not rely on cultural or linguistic connections to bypass onerous personnel regulations.[42] Despite the fact that all workers in FIEs were contract workers, these employers found that contract workers were also difficult to lay off or fire (although it had become increasingly easier to not re-sign contracts upon expiration).[43] This increased tendencies on the part of foreign investors to hire illegally without contracts and to use migrant workers who had no legal recourse to complain if fired due to their uncertain residential status. Local governments had an interest in promoting contracts if it would help boost local employment and decrease the illegal use of rural migrants by foreign firms.[44] More regularized hiring through the labor contract system also increased the fees that local governments could collect, including fees on hiring migrants.[45]

Third, growing chaos in the emerging labor market was beginning to affect the ability of SOEs to hire and retain skilled workers. The expansion of employment opportunities and the declining fortunes of the SOE sector made nonstate sector employment increasingly attractive. SOEs that were losing skilled workers and managers to foreign firms began to look to contracts as a way to retain their core workforce or to be compensated for their losses when these workers left.[46]

As these problems arose, the parameters of the LCS debate changed. The state no longer focused on the socialist debate of employment versus efficiency. Unemployment (and very substantial underemployment) was acknowledged openly in the media. Laid-off workers became a hot social topic and the "right to choose your work" replaced the socialist idea of a "right to work." The unspoken assumption of the new "right to choose" statement is, of course, that the state will no longer find you a job. Efficiency, competitiveness, and productivity became the order of the day. State policy turned to the practical problems of crafting an institutional foundation for contract labor: a real housing market, funding of unemployment insurance, and schemes to minimize the socially destabilizing effects of large-scale unemployment.

With the passage of the National Labor Law in 1994, the permanency and growing universality of the LCS was no longer in doubt. The implementation rate increased very gradually throughout the 1980s and immediately following the Tiananmen Incident, but rose more quickly as FDI increased and SOE reform deepened. As early as 1996, before the Fifteenth Party Congress that announced the acceleration of SOE reform, the Beijing Labor Bureau reported that 380 SOEs had stopped production, an increase of 23.7 percent over 1995. Moreover, the bureau expected that many of the failing SOEs would choose not to re-sign labor contracts with their employees. Just a few years earlier this ability to let SOE workers go by allowing their contracts to expire was nearly unheard of.[47]

THE NATIONAL LABOR LAW

The LCS expanded gradually, but by 1994 the Chinese state showed its commitment to radical reform of socialist labor with the passage of the first national labor law in PRC history. This law is significant for two reasons. First, it enshrined the basic rights of all Chinese workers, erasing some of the legal differences between permanent, contract, seasonal, and migrant workers—differences that had long existed and shaped the enterprises' treatment of workers.[48] It set certain basic standards for all kinds of workers. Second, the law was comprehensive. It did not discriminate between different types of enterprises based on ownership (public or private) or nationality (Chinese or foreign). It set a basic standard for all enterprises and it guaranteed all enterprises a significant degree of autonomy in deciding personnel and labor matters.[49] With this autonomy, however, came new responsibilities. For the first time in the reform era, collective contracts and collective bargaining were set out as primary measures for wage setting and other issues of employment in all types of firms.[50]

The content and the timing of the National Labor Law are closely connected with the flow of FDI and the new strains in labor-capital relations in FIEs. In the early-and-mid 1990s, FDI boomed to previously unimaginable proportions. This boom highlighted two major problems. First, labor relations in FIEs were bad and growing worse. Ministry of Labor officials and union officials were pushing for greater supervision and jurisdiction over the management practices at foreign firms. Second, the boom in FDI highlighted the continuing failure of SOE reform and the rapidly declining competitive position of SOEs. State managers began clamoring for greater enterprise autonomy and a level playing field with these new foreign and nonstate enterprises. This increased pressure on lawmakers to make the law comprehensive; to include the regulation of SOEs with foreign and private firms under one law. Both of these reasons were specified as important to the passage of the Labor Law in 1994 by Zhang Zuoji, the Vice-Minister of Labor, in a speech in 1994. He notes that passage of the law failed in 1983 and again as late as 1991 but passed in 1994 after such abuses as excessive overtime, corporal punishment, and the nonpayment of salaries were found in China's nonstate sector.[51]

Attention to the rising labor unrest and less than ideal working conditions in FIEs rose dramatically in the early 1990s. Although it is almost certain that problems were evident in the 1980s, the rapid growth of FDI and of foreign-invested enterprises in the early 1990s drew greater attention to this problem, particularly from China's domestic media and human rights groups and unions based out of Hong Kong. The sharp rise in Asian FDI, especially from Japan, Taiwan, and Korea, also helped draw attention to the problems of labor because much of this investment was concentrated in labor-intensive light manufacturing and assembly.

In early 1993 Japanese firms in the southern SEZs of Zhuhai and Shenzhen and Taiwanese firms in Guangdong were besieged by wildcat strikes and work stoppages. Eight hundred of the one thousand workers at a Canon factory in Zhuhai went on strike for three days, demanding a 30–50 percent pay increase.[52] Another two thousand mostly women workers struck at the Japanese firm, Mitsumi Electric, in May, also demanding higher pay and better benefits.[53] This strike was followed a few days later by a strike in the Japanese company, Sanmei Electromechanical Plant, also in Zhuhai. Here again the issues revolved around higher pay in light of a new minimum wage regulation set in Zhuhai.[54] A few months later in September, Korean factories in the Tianjin Economic Development Area (TEDA) were lambasted in the domestic press for their abysmal treatment of workers and widespread labor abuse. The unusual report went into great detail. Workers were kicked for working too slowly; a woman employee was forced to eat seven steamed buns and seven eggs for taking too long at lunch; and workers were forced to kneel as Korean managers slapped and beat them.[55] As international and domestic media coverage of these conflicts increased, foreign investors expressed concern about stability while China's domestic media expressed anger at the treatment of

Chinese workers by foreign bosses. The Vice-Minister of Labor stated bluntly that unless labor legislation was quickly introduced, the strikes would only increase.[56]

Strikes and protests continued throughout 1993 and 1994, particularly in Guangdong, where FDI is highly concentrated, and strikes in one plant often lead to copycat tactics in nearby factories. In May 1994 trade union officials reported that one hundred joint ventures had strikes in 1993. In 90 percent of the strikes, workers were not organized by the official trade union. Several aspects of this spike in industrial action increased the pressure on the state to respond to labor problems in FIEs. First, the copycat syndrome of strike after strike in one area or development zone gravely threatened the ability of regions to attract FDI.[57] Second, the ability to organize strike action without the presence of the official union meant that some kind of worker organization was supplanting official unions in foreign-invested enterprises. Without a firmer hold on workers in FIEs, the CCP faced a new threat from underground, illegal workers' organization.

As the market penetrated and labor conditions deteriorated (intensity of work, working conditions, and job security), the state began enacting regulations to rein in exploitative labor practices. It set labor standards for working conditions and safety, outlined an expanded role for the official union to defend and protect workers' legal rights through collective contracts and limited collective bargaining, and set up a system of dispute resolution and government inspection of labor practices.[58] These regulations were given extra weight with their codification in the labor law.

The flip side to these concerns about how to retain and control FDI was the state's concern about a level playing field for state firms. The decision to allow FDI and expansion of the nonstate sector while maintaining state ownership as a key sector in the economy meant that the state had to consider the competitive threat from these new sectors, which were now exposed as sectors that reaped profits and gained efficiency through abusive management, meager wages, and extreme labor flexibility.[59] A successful state sector would require some degree of fairness in social welfare benefits and enterprise decision-making autonomy. The state had granted "enterprise autonomy rights" to firms in the 1988 Enterprise Law, but many of these rights remained elusive, particularly those that affected the job security of state workers.[60] The National Labor Law was not ownership-specific, and through its implementation the state hoped to create a more equitable system for SOEs by relieving them of the burdens of socialist enterprise.[61]

The Labor Law in its inclusiveness signaled support within the state for bringing the practices of state and nonstate firms closer together. State firms would be relieved of their duty to act like a *"xiao shehui"* (little society) while nonstate, especially foreign firms, would be compelled to treat workers better and to take responsibility for longer term employment issues, such as medical benefits, pensions, maternity leave, and workers' compensation. These were responsibilities that many FIEs had preferred to evade because they increased labor costs and extended the potential term of employment for workers.

The ultimate effects of the Labor Law will be apparent only in the longer term. The actual content of the law is quite vague and serves as a broad template for future laws and regulations. Supplementary laws will need to be much more detailed, outlining the proper implementation of the broad principles in the Labor Law. Many of the supplementary laws in planning or at the drafting stage have been delayed by internal disagreements between ministries.[62] This is a testament to the sensitivity of the Labor Law and also a warning sign that there is real and significant disagreement within the government on how or even whether to implement some of the principles outlined in the law.[63] The eight most important supplementary laws were in the drafting or planning stage as of 1998, with the Labor Contract Law, the Employment Promotion Law, the Labor Safety and Health Law, all to be passed by 1999. The remaining laws, the Collective Contract Law, the Salary Law, and the Law on Settlement of Labor Disputes were to be passed by 2000.[64] By 2003, only two supplementary laws had been passed: the Work Safety Law and the Occupational Health Law. The delay in the supplementary laws indicates that these laws are now caught in the same bureaucratic wrangle that delayed the passage of the National Labor Law itself throughout the 1980s until the rise of labor strikes and exploitation in foreign-invested companies gave impetus to its passage.[65]

Despite the real problems that continue in the implementation of individual and collective contracts, and labor laws more generally, the codification of rules and principles has expanded the space for legitimate disputes to take place. The passage of rules for labor dispute resolution has widened the jurisdiction to include more employment issues. It has clarified the procedures of the resolution process. Moreover the basic principle of the Labor Law is that the position of workers in the employer-employee relationship is inherently weak and requires greater legal protection.[66] The state through the state-controlled media has actively encouraged workers to make use of the new laws and regulations. Although large-scale national or regional worker uprisings have occurred only sporadically (most likely due to the repressive measures of the Chinese state when it comes to organized, large-scale labor protest), there is a steady and inexorable rise in labor conflict mediated through these new legal institutions.

RISING CONFLICT: LABOR DISPUTES IN THE 1990s

The development of labor dispute guidelines evolved in much the same way that labor law has evolved in general in the PRC. To summarize, the state briefly attempted in the early 1950s to develop a code of labor laws that fit China's new commitment to socialism and, at the time, a vibrant trade unionist history of struggle against capitalism and imperialism. In November 1949, the newly established CCP government passed temporary measures to handle labor-capital relations and by the next year had passed guidelines for the resolution of labor disputes. But by the mid-1950s these moderate measures were abandoned in favor of more radical industrial policies pushed by Mao Zedong. In 1956 the handling of labor disputes became an administrative process, with disputes settled by an enterprise's CCP leadership. Workers who were dissatisfied and sought justice from above did so by "writing letters or visiting" (laixin laifang) CCP or government bureaucrats to beg for intervention. Legal measures to regulate labor relations were cast aside.[67]

The development of labor laws and dispute guidelines would not begin again until 1979 with the Equity Joint Venture Law and in 1986 with the renewal of the labor mediation process. In 1987 the government passed "Temporary Guidelines for the Handling of Labor Disputes in State-run Enterprises." But because this document was specific to the SOE sector, the great majority of disputes, which were disputes between contract workers and nonstate (collective, rural, and foreign) firms, could not be resolved easily. This problem was not resolved until 1993, when the state issued "Regulations on the Handling of Labor Disputes in the PRC." These regulations were unprecedented in that they were not ownership-specific and applied to foreign and private firms as well as public and collective ones. This change was followed and reiterated the following year when the Standing Committee of the National People's Congress passed the Labor Law. This broad law also sets out the framework for the resolution of labor disputes in all firms.[68]

China has a three-step formal process of dispute resolution under the Labor Law: firm-level mediation, local-level arbitration, and finally civil-court litigation.[69] Firm-level mediation is different from the previous informal negotiation between worker and management/party in that it requires that a three-sided mediation committee undertake the dispute. This committee is made up of representatives of the workers, firm, and the firm's trade union. It must have an odd number of representatives and should be chaired by a trade union representative. As some trade union activists have pointed out, this is an unusual and awkward use of the trade union representative who must act as mediator between workers and management.[70] Because China's trade union is subservient to the CCP and is weak generally within the enterprise vis-à-vis management, this mediation process unfairly privileges management over workers. The role of the trade union in the mediation process represents the contradictory and difficult position of the trade union in general.[71] In the 2001 Trade Union Law (a revision of the existing law first promulgated in 1950 and then revised in 1992), the union's task is to safeguard the "legal rights and interests" of the workers.[72] Yet article 80 of the Labor Law provides that union representatives serve as middlemen caught between the competing interests of the worker and management. Thus in the firm-level mediation process, the worker's only true representative is himself.

Local-level arbitration is the next step. Parties who are dissatisfied with the mediation decision can apply for arbitration proceedings. Importantly, however, workers may also bypass mediation completely and apply directly for arbitration. Local Labor Arbitration Committees (LAC) are made up of representatives from the local labor bureau, representatives from the local office of the trade union, and representatives from the local organization of enterprise managers or other relevant units. This design places the labor bureau representative as the intermediary with the union standing in for the worker, although the worker may also have legal representation.[73] In practice most labor dispute cases are processed by local labor bureau staff members without direct involvement of the trade union or other organizations.

The LAC has two main modes of settlement: arbitrated mediation (*zhongcai tiaojie*) or arbitral judgment (*zhongcai caijue*).[74] Arbitrated mediation is a form of mediation, but unlike enterprise-level mediation, it includes active participation of the LAC. Mediation is almost always attempted first before proceeding to the more formal arbitral judgment. Arbitral judgments must decide who is at fault and then issue any required compensation. Arbitral judgments in China are not binding. Either side has the right to appeal the judgment in civil court. The court may uphold or overturn the arbitration decision. The civil-court process also involves the right to appeal. In the 1990s, few arbitration cases went to court and in most cases the court upheld the arbitration decision.[75] In the past few years, however, the number of labor disputes adjudicated in courts has risen sharply. In 2001 Chinese courts heard over one hundred thousand labor disputes, a 33 percent increase from the year before and a marked increase from the mid-1990s.[76] Labor arbitrators in China's largest cities, including Beijing, Shanghai, Tianjin, and Guangzhou report that between 50 to 70 percent of arbitrated cases are now appealed in civil court.[77]

The cost of arbitration in China is fairly low but not inconsequential for a low-paid worker. For example, in 2003 in Shanghai the arbitration fee was 300 RMB, which was 20 percent of the average monthly salary in the city. The cost of court appeals was 50 RMB for each appeal. These costs do not include the costs of legal representation, which is increasingly common for both sides in labor disputes.[78]

One of the most significant aspects of the National Labor Law and the regulations for the resolution of labor disputes (1993) is the range of options available to workers who wish to lodge a suit against their employer. The 1993 PRC regulations allow either party to bypass enterprise-level mediation and proceed directly to local-level arbitration. Because the worker's position within the enterprise is quite weak and the role of the union is as middleman rather than worker representative, workers have very strong reasons to go straight to arbitration. It also makes it more likely that the worker can use the local arbitration committee's power to obtain enterprise documents as evidence to support his case.[79] Finally, if the dispute is regarding or has already led to the worker's dismissal or resignation, the worker is not compelled to resolve the dispute within a company he has already left.[80] At the arbitration level, the worker is more likely to use outside legal representation or, as stipulated in the legal regulations, legal aid provided by the local trade union bureau or non-government legal aid centers.[81]

Since the passage of these regulations, dispute resolution methods have shifted toward higher levels of arbitration and litigation. Enterprise mediation has suffered across the board and is no longer the principal method to resolve labor conflicts. Dispute resolution of labor conflict has become increasingly legalized as disputes have shifted from the firm to the local government, and especially in the last few years, to the courts.

LABOR DISPUTES IN COMPARATIVE PERSPECTIVE

As figure 5.1 demonstrates, there has been a rapid increase in labor disputes from 1995 to 2002. While it is apparent from the national statistics that labor disputes have risen quickly in China, there is less certainty about what this increase signifies. Due to the lack of legal regulation of labor prior to the reform era, the rate of increase is from an extremely low base point. Could it be that the increase itself is only due to catch-up from an unnaturally low number, which itself was the result of the repression of overt societal conflict under socialism? If this is the case, then the rapid increase signifies that social conflict, while on the increase in China, remains low despite rapid economic growth and social change.

One method of getting at the significance of labor disputes is to place China in comparative perspective. In this section, China's rate of labor disputes to labor dispute figures for Taiwan prior to democratization are compared.[82] It finds that labor disputes in the PRC are significantly higher than were Taiwan's during a comparable period of rapid economic development and authoritarian rule. Both Taiwan and PRC labor laws include multistep methods for dispute resolution, including firm-level mediation and local-level arbitration. In practice, however, these laws have been implemented very differently, with Taiwan putting much greater emphasis on internal enterprise settlement, thus limiting the number of disputes that reach arbitration. In the PRC, enterprise-level mediation has been deemphasized in favor of external modes of resolution, first arbitration and then litigation. PRC labor law encourages workers to lodge complaints outside of the enterprise first as an arbitration claim and then as a civil court case. Taiwan's labor laws under authoritarian rule relied primarily on enterprise-level settlement and managerial control to suppress labor conflict.

There are several reasons to compare China to Taiwan including the shared cultural and historical background. Many Chinese and Western scholars alike have argued that the major schools of thought in Chinese philosophy eschew legal rights of individuals and rule-based behavior in favor of modes of behavior that promote mediation, compromise, and nonlitigiousness.[83] By comparing across these two Chinese cultures, we control for cultural preferences for mediation and nonlegal dispute resolution processes.

Second, the labor codes in China today and Taiwan under the authoritarian rule of the Kuomintang (KMT) are similar and related to each other.[84] Taiwan's labor law were brought from the mainland and left mostly untouched because "substantial amendment of the laws ideologically was unacceptable as it would have compromised the KMT's claim that it was the legitimate government of all of China."[85] From 1949 to 1978 mainland China did not have a national labor law, preferring to rely instead on administrative regulations for state and collective industries, which made up the vast majority of China's industrial enterprises. Thus when China returned attention to the passage of a national labor law in the 1980s, the last existing laws were those from the pre-1949 era and the very laws that Taiwan had used under authoritarian rule. Labor lawyers involved with the consultative process of China's first national Labor Law reported that these pre-liberation laws were used during the drafting process.[86] The end product of this drafting process differed, however, in some crucial ways including the modes of dispute resolution as mentioned above.

Third, comparing modern-day China to authoritarian (pre-1987) Taiwan also captures some of the other similarities of the two systems. Taiwan, like the PRC, was an authoritarian state run by a Leninist-style party. Both have used state corporatist ties with labor to control workers and prevent the rise of an independent labor movement. Finally, both economies are heavily integrated with the global economy through production for export and therefore are dependent on efficient production and manufacturing. Ties to the global economy create a dual challenge for authoritarian developmentalist states. The state must maintain political control and political demobilization of labor while at the same time realizing high levels of efficiency and economic mobilization. This situation often leads to repressive and abusive factory regimes, which are different from the modes of control employed in China's pre-reform state socialist factories. These factories maintained political control of workers but under much less pressure to realize high rates of productivity, which led to factory labor regimes that were often lax and inefficient.

Table 5.1 examines the rate of labor disputes in Taiwan in four different years. In 1977 and 1980 Taiwan was still under martial law and the KMT ruled in an oppressive and authoritarian manner. In these years, labor disputes in Taiwan were extremely low although on the increase. In 1977 for every 100,000 employees there were only 6.5 labor disputes. In 1980 this figure increased to 10.5. The final year of martial law, 1986, marked the beginning of the end of KMT's monopoly on political power. The mid-1980s were heady years for Taiwanese opposition leaders and activists, with the rise of many new social movements organized around ideas of social justice, protection of the environment, and democratization. By 1986 labor disputes had jumped to 21 per 100,000 workers. Finally in 1998 labor disputes in Taiwan reached an all-time high of 4,138 or 44.9 disputes per 100,000 employees. By this time Taiwan was a functioning democracy, with active and fierce competition between the KMT and other political parties as well as a free and vibrant press.

From table 5.1 and table 5.2 we can see the very low rate of labor disputes in Taiwan under authoritarian rule in comparison to PRC rates. Although there are many reasons for this low rate, a major explanation is the repressive nature of the political and economic system and the nature of Taiwanese labor law. Under authoritarian corporatism, workers had little independent power to press for their interests nor were there viable channels through which workers could make their grievances heard. As Cooney found in his study of Taiwan labor law: "Workers made few attempts to invoke the legal system to resolve conflict with their employers. Disputes over working conditions, particularly those occurring in small-scale enterprises, were settled within the enterprise or through local community networks. Prevailing social attitudes discouraged litigation, and institutional obstacles reinforced this sentiment."[87]

Individual workers were weak vis-à-vis management, and organized labor associations were under the thumb of the KMT. The rise of labor disputes followed the process of democratization, rising steadily as political opening and liberalization took place. By the 1990s Taiwanese labor politics were much more diverse and antagonistic than they were under

TABLE 5.1
Labor Disputes in Taiwan

Year	Labor Force (millions)	Disputes	Disputes Per 100,000 Workers
1977 (Authoritarian rule)	5.7	380	6.5
1980 (Authoritarian rule)	6.6	700	10.5
1986 (Final year of martial law)	7.7	1,622	21
1998 (Democratic rule)	9.2	4,138	44.9

Source: Compiled from *Yearbook of Labor Statistics,* Taiwan Area, ROC, 1998 (Taipei: Council of Labor Affairs, Executive Yuan, 1999); *Republic of China Statistical Yearbook,* ROC Year 88 (Taipei: Executive Yuan Statistical Office).

martial law. Strikes increased rapidly and unionization rates rose steadily. In 1989 over 60,000 workers took part in strike actions. Unionization rose from 23 percent in 1984 to 49 percent in 1994.[88] Subsequently labor disputes increased and have remained at historically high levels.

Table 5.2 shows the obvious difference between the PRC and Taiwan. Despite similar cultures, laws, and modes of repression and control, the rate of labor disputes in the PRC are much higher than Taiwan's were under authoritarian rule. In fact PRC rates of labor disputes are closer to

TABLE 5.2
Labor Disputes in the PRC

Year	Labor Force* (millions)	Disputes	Disputes per 100,000 Workers
1994	288	19,098	6.6
1995	301	33,000**	10.9
1996	310	47,951	15.4
1997	274	71,524	26.1
1998	291	93,649	32.1

Source: Compiled from *China Statistical Yearbook,* various years (Beijing: China Statistical Publishing House); *China Labor Statistical Yearbook,* various years (Beijing: China Statistical Publishing House).

*These figures are based on the reported number of employed persons (*cong yue renuan*) in urban enterprises and rural collective enterprises.

**The first PRC Labor Law went into effect January 1, 1995.

Taiwan's rates under full democracy. By 1998 labor disputes in the PRC had reached a rate of 32.1 per 100,000 workers. This figure is especially impressive because it counts both urban employees and employees of rural township enterprises, even though these employees are often less educated and organized, and information about labor laws and dispute processes is spotty at best in rural areas. In fact if we look only at labor disputes among urban workers, the rate of disputes per 100,000 workers climbs to 52.9, *higher* than the rate of Taiwanese disputes in 1998.[89]

This section has used a comparison of labor disputes under authoritarianism in Taiwan to demonstrate that China's labor dispute rate is high relative to a country with a similar cultural, legal, and institutional context. The rate of PRC labor disputes are significantly higher than the rates of labor disputes in Taiwan under martial law: in fact PRC rates are more similar to Taiwan's rate of disputes under full democracy. This comparison is not used to suggest that workers in the PRC are less repressed under continued authoritarian rule than Taiwanese workers in a functioning democracy. The difference in rates of legal labor disputes does indicate, however, the degree to which the PRC government has been active in opening up administrative and legal avenues outside the enterprise through which workers can lodge complaints, proceed through arbitration, and in the end be heard in a court of law. One major difference between the mainland and Taiwan is in regard to the range of legal options ceded to workers in the event of labor conflict. Taiwanese labor law put much greater emphasis on enterprise-level mediation and granted managers a greater degree of autonomy in dealing with labor problems at the firm level. PRC labor law, on the other hand, does not require workers to process their claims first through firm management. Instead these laws permitted workers to bypass the firm and appeal directly to the local government and then, if still dissatisfied with the decision, to proceed to civil court.[90] This process ensures continued government involvement in labor dispute resolution, which allows the government to be notified of and to intervene in disputes that may impact political or social stability. On the other hand, it has led to increased legal mobilization of workers and dramatically increased the number of workers seeking redress at higher levels. As we see in the following section, this inclination to use the law is particularly strong among workers in foreign-invested firms.

The development of Chinese labor law, in particular the opening up of these new avenues for dispute resolution outside the enterprise, is closely related to China's economic reforms, which have relied on creating a dynamic nonstate sector through liberalization of foreign direct investment (FDI) and, more recently, on nurturing domestic private industry. By the mid-1990s the nonstate sector had become a sizable presence in Chinese coastal cities and development zones. Large-scale strikes and well-publicized

abuses of workers had already occurred in many foreign and private factories.[91] Leaving labor relations to the firm as was done in authoritarian
Taiwan was clearly untenable as strikes threatened social stability and the
investment environment.[92] Labor arbitration at the local level opened up
new channels for dispute resolution and was intended to ensure the government's continued involvement in the resolution of labor conflict.

TRENDS IN PRC LABOR DISPUTES

As seen above, the labor dispute rate in China is significant for a developing country that is still ruled by an authoritarian state with weak and
nascent legal institutions. There are other trends, beyond the rapid increase, that are both significant and puzzling, but seem to point to increased societal conflict and rising rights-consciousness among Chinese
workers. These trends include a rapid increase in the rate of collective disputes and larger collective disputes, a high rate of disputes in foreign-invested enterprises and increasingly in the nonstate sector in general, and
the failure of mediation at the firm level, with many more workers going
directly to arbitration. At the arbitration level, mediated settlements are
also decreasing; most disputes now end with an arbitrated decision or
award. In addition, worker-initiated disputes constitute the vast majority
of all labor disputes, and the success rate of workers has increased over
time.[93]

Collective Disputes

As tables 5.3 and 5.4 show, there has been a rapid rise in collective disputes as well as a slower increase in the average size of those disputes.[94]
The latter is surprising despite a change in the legal regulations that reduced the number of workers required to file a dispute from ten to three.
That might be expected to increase the likelihood of many more small disputes, yet the average size of collective disputes grew until 1998. Because
strikes or slowdowns often accompany collective disputes, this trend gives
some indication of the deterioration of labor relations.[95] Collective disputes are also more common in the FIE sector and tend to be larger there.
In 1996, the average size of a collective dispute in a foreign-invested firm
was forty workers, while this figure was only twenty-four workers in
SOEs. Also in 1996, the last year in which foreign firms were separated
out from overseas-Chinese invested firms, collective disputes made up
twenty-four percent of all disputes in overseas Chinese factories but only
8.6 percent of all disputes in foreign-invested firms.[96] This somewhat surprising statistic shows that even within foreign-invested firms, some kinds

122 • Chapter Five

TABLE 5.3
Collective Disputes, 1996–2002

Year	Collective Disputes	Workers Involved	Average Size of Dispute (person)
1996	3,150	92,203	29.2
1997	4,109	132,647	32.2
1998	6,767	251,268	37.1
1999	9,043	319,241	35.3
2000	8,247	259,445	31.4
2001	9,847	286,680	29.1
2002	11,024	374,956	34.0

Source: *China Labor Statistical Yearbook,* various years (Beijing: China Statistical Publishing).

of firms have much higher rates of collective disputes. Overseas Chinese-invested enterprises are highly concentrated in labor-intensive, export-oriented sectors. These firms seem to rely extensively on labor practices that are repressive, arbitrary, and abusive.[97] There is very likely a connection between this mode of labor management and a higher incidence of collective disputes.

By 1999, the average size of collective disputes was becoming more similar across different kinds of firms. This seems to indicate that as SOE reform intensified after the Fifteenth Party Congress in 1997, workers in SOEs became more inclined to use the dispute process as a way to resist restructuring and reform. The average number of SOE workers involved in collective disputes jumped from 24.3 in 1996, to 30.8 in 1997, to 40 workers in 1998, compared to an average of 45 workers per collective dispute in FIEs.[98] In 1999, there was a slight decline in the average size of collective disputes across foreign and state firms with foreign firms averaging 40.8 persons per dispute and SOEs averaging 31 persons per dispute. The gap in size of collective disputes between foreign and state firms has narrowed over time.

Some regions also seem to show a more marked tendency toward collective labor disputes. In 2001 the top five provinces for collective labor disputes were Guangdong (2,397), Jiangsu (974), Shanghai (612), Hubei (607), and Shandong (556). The average number of workers nationally in 2001 was about 29, but several provinces varied from this considerably. They include Fujian (45.4 workers on average) and Shandong (45.2). In some provinces the predominance of collective disputes is quite striking. In Guangdong and Fujian nearly three out of four workers in a labor dispute are involved in a collective dispute. The rate is two out of three in

TABLE 5.4
Collective Disputes by Firm Ownership, 1997–2002
(as a percentage of total disputes)

	1997	1998	1999	2000	2001	2002
All	5.7	7.2	7.5	6.0	6.3	5.9
State-owned enterprises	5.2	6.1	6.7	6.7	7.5	7.5
Urban collectives	5.7	5.8	8.2	5.4	6.7	7.0*
Rural collectives	3.9	9.2	7.6	4.6	5.7	
Foreign-invested enterprises***	6.9	8.3	9.7	7.5	6.2	5.2
Private enterprises (siying)	5	8.9	9.4	7.1	5.3	6.0
Joint-owned or stock-holding enterprises	7.2	5.0	8.0	6.9	6.2	5.5**
Individually owned enterprises (geti)	4.7	7.0	5.7	3.9	3.0	4.0

Source: China Labor Statistical Yearbook, various years (Beijing: China Statistical Publishing).

*aggregated percentage for number of labor disputes in urban and rural collectives

**aggregated percentage for number of labor disputes in share-holding joint ownership enterprises

***After 1996 the State Statistical Bureau stopped publishing statistics on labor disputes that disaggregated foreign-invested enterprises from "Hong Kong, Macao, and Taiwanese-invested enterprises." This makes it impossible to trace the then markedly higher proportion of collective disputes in overseas Chinese-invested enterprises.

Liaoning and Shandong, and over four out of five in Jilin and Jiangxi.[99] In China's most developed cities (Beijing, Shanghai, Tianjin, for example) one sees a more balanced distribution between individual and collective disputes. In areas where labor-intensive manufacturing is quite high or SOE restructuring is quite difficult, one sees a marked rise in collective disputes without the same happening for individual labor disputes.

Since the 1997 decision to speed up SOE reform and the related rise in unemployment, the government has become more proactive in the handling of collective labor disputes, often intervening and settling a conflict through government fiat so as to minimize the impact on social and political stability.[100] This may explain the decrease in collective dispute size since 1998 as well as the general leveling off of collective disputes. The by-passing of the administrative and legal procedures for dispute resolution makes it difficult to interpret the statistical data presented by the Ministry of Labor and Social Security. The decline in the official statistics in labor disputes may reflect more the government's instrumentalist and interventionist approach to law than a real improvement in the state of labor relations. This statistical decline may in fact be a result of the state's (especially local governments) inability to handle effectively the explosion in labor disputes since 1995, leading to a concerted official attempt to thwart the increasing numbers of Chinese workers lodging official grievances against their employers. Direct government settlement of labor disputes has been concentrated in the areas most prone to high levels of instability and anger, including disputes involving migrants, disputes over social insurance, and large collective disputes.[101]

Ownership and Labor Disputes

Different types of firms continue to have varying rates of labor disputes. As seen in table 5.5, foreign-invested enterprises have much higher rates of disputes compared to any other type of firm, *with 456 disputes for every 100,000 workers in 1999*. Private enterprises, with 159 disputes per 100,000 workers in 2000, also have a high rate of disputes, four times higher than the rate in SOEs. This does not indicate, however, that disputes are high only in nonstate firms. Publicly owned firms that are currently undergoing significant restructuring and reform also tend to have higher labor disputes.[102] Disputes in SOEs have climbed from 24.5 disputes per 100,000 workers in 1998 to 40.4 disputes in 2000. Urban collectives have the third highest rate of labor disputes after foreign and private firms, reaching 154.6 disputes for every 100,000 workers in 1999. Over the past ten years, urban collectives have undergone significant restructuring measures and new methods of operation, including leasing or contracting the factory out to private or foreign investors. While these measures do not change the ownership of the firm, they also can lead to radical changes in labor management and to an increase in disputes and conflict. Joint-owned and stockholding companies had a rate of 108 disputes per 100,000 workers in 2000. These firms are still state owned but have issued stocks to sell to workers, individual investors, and other institutions. Often the state remains the dominant shareholder, but the management of the firm is often overhauled and labor restructured. This process tends to lead to labor disputes as workers protest restructuring that takes away their job security, reduces their wages, or increases the degree of labor discipline within the firm. Some of these disputes also probably involve the forced purchase of shares, a problem that has dogged the implementation of the shareholding system.[103]

Despite the relatively high rates of disputes in collective, shareholding, and private firms, the rate of disputes in foreign-invested firms still stands out. In 2001 labor dispute rates in foreign firms were still more than twice the rate in private firms and nearly six times the rate in SOEs. These figures demonstrate not only the tense and antagonistic labor relations that

TABLE 5.5
Labor Disputes per 100,000 Employees, by Ownership Type, 1998–2001

Type of firm	1998	1999	2000	2001
State-owned enterprises	24.5	31.2	40.4	56.1
Urban collectives	69.2	106.2	154.6	197
Foreign-invested	384	456	327	300.6
Private enterprises	110	132	159	156.6
Rural collectives	9.6	7.9	3.1	1.8
Joint-owned and stock	81	66.5	108	199
Individually owned (geti)	7.0	10.2	19.1	30.1

Source: *China Labor Statistical Yearbook,* various years (Beijing: China Statistical Publishing House).

exist at many foreign firms; they also demonstrate the increasing boldness of workers to file suit against foreign managers.

The Failure of Mediation

The growing complexity of labor disputes and the deterioration of worker-management relations has also meant a sharp decline in firm-level mediation success and in the decline of mediation success through the local-level arbitration committees.[104] This is seen in figure 5.3.

From 1987 (with the restoration of mediation guidelines) until the early 1990s, the vast majority of labor disputes (over 90 percent) were settled at the firm level. As mentioned above, this process is extremely unfavorable to the worker. The weak union position in the firm translates to a lop-sided mediation committee: union and management versus the worker. With the freedom to apply directly for arbitration codified in the 1993 regulations, many workers now bypass the mediation process completely. The proportion of disputes settled through mediation has now sunk from a high of over 95 percent to below 50 percent.[105] This phenomenon shows that workers feel local government intervention is more likely to yield results than intra-firm negotiation. More and more workers are pressing their claim past mediation to the arbitration stage where they are more likely to be fairly treated.[106]

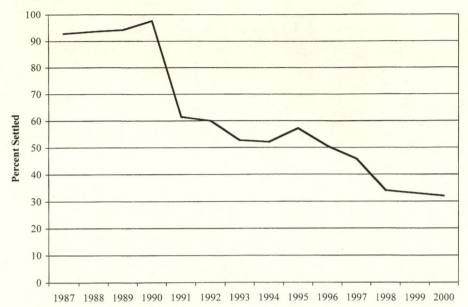

Figure 5.3. Labor Disputes Settled by Mediation, 1987–2000. *Source:* Compiled from *China Labor Statistical Yearbook*, various years. Beijing: China Statistical Publishing; and Shoichi Ito, "Changes in Labour Markets, Labour Law, and Industrial Relations in Modern China," paper presented at 1996 Asian Regional Conference on Industrial Relations.

Table 5.6 also shows the declining success of enterprise-level mediation. The number of mediation committees grew after the passage of the Labor Law, from 127,669 labor mediation committees in 1995 to 153,904 in 1996. It fell to 127,039 the next year. Even more worrying is that the number of cases accepted have fallen each year since the passage of the law, as have the number of cases actually mediated by the committees. These figures indicate the increasing difficulty in settling disputes at the enterprise level. Ironically, the declining efficacy of mediated settlements comes at a time when the state is pushing for the use of this very process.[107] Mediation is seen as a way to reduce the caseload at the local level and to keep disputes within the enterprise where they are less likely to affect other cases or give rise to copycat suits.[108] Local governments are, however, constrained in their ability to compel enterprises to set up mediation committees given the increase in firm autonomy. In an atmosphere that is increasingly contentious and tense, local officials report that it is also very difficult to encourage workers to mediate in situations where they feel completely in the right.[109] This movement away from mediation toward arbitration and litigation reflects workers' rising rights conscious-

TABLE 5.6
Labor Dispute Mediation Committees in Enterprises, 1995–1997

Year	Number of Labor Dispute Mediation Committees	Number of Labor Diputes Accepted by Committees	Number of disputes Mediated by Committees
1995	127,669	93,578	78,761
1996	153,904	86,037	74,538
1997	127,039	72,594	47,528

Source: China Labor Statistical Yearbook, various years (Beijing: China Statistical Publishing House).

ness and some limited ability for workers to press the state for expanded workers' rights and better enforcement of the labor laws that safeguard these rights.

As seen in figure 5.4, the decline in mediation has occurred in enterprises across the board, but the drop has been the sharpest in foreign-invested enterprises. In 1996, a year after the passage of the National Labor Law, nearly 55,000 disputes were still mediated in FIEs, but this number declined precipitously in the following years to a low of 104 cases in 2001. In other ownership sectors, the decline was more gradual; but by 2001 it seemed that firm-level mediation was nearly abandoned as a mode of resolution.

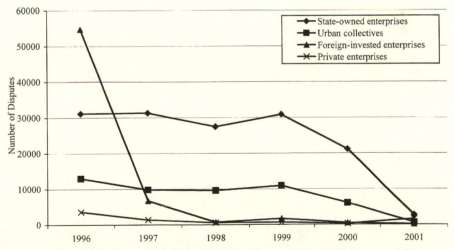

Figure 5.4. Labor Disputes Mediated by Employer, 1996–2001. *Source: China Labor Statistical Yearbook,* various years. Beijing: China Statistical Publishing.

Worker-Initiated Disputes and Rates of Success

Worker-initiated disputes are by far the great majority of labor disputes in the PRC.[110] This proportion has continued to stand as the number of disputes has increased over time. Interestingly, however, in SOEs management is increasingly likely to initiate a dispute.[111] In 1999, for example, SOE managers initiated 5 percent of the total number of disputes while in disputes in foreign-invested firms, employers lodged only 2.3 percent of disputes. This trend partly reflects SOEs' inability to retain skilled workers as workers break their labor contracts and turn to employment opportunities in the foreign and private sectors. The rate at which workers win disputes outright has also been changing. From 1986 to 1990 workers won fewer than 40 percent of all labor disputes, but by 1997 this figure had increased to over 50 percent. Combined with decisions in which "both sides partially win," workers meet some success in over 75 percent of all disputes.[112] Workers' growing rights-consciousness and reliance on legal measures may continue to increase if this trend lasts, although these statistics say little about the quality of the implementation of arbitration decisions.[113]

Labor Disputes and the Right to Strike

With the movement away from the planned economy, the superficial harmony of that period has passed. The diversification of interests and the clarification of positions are two results of market reform and this had led to rapidly increasing rights consciousness on the part of firm managers and workers.[114] The withering away of the planned economy and the introduction of contractual arrangements and efficiency has reduced the efficacy of mediation. The state has sought to move closer toward a regulatory role and has strengthened China's legal infrastructure. With the entrance of private and foreign firms the characteristics of labor disputes have changed. There is now a "confrontational" (*duikang xing*) atmosphere caused in part by the exploitative tendencies of many FIEs and private firms.[115]

As changes in property rights have complicated firm ownership, higher rates of disputes, which in the early 1990s seemed to be concentrated in the foreign-invested sector, have now appeared in other kinds of firms. Despite the absence of widespread privatization in China the walls dividing state ownership from nonstate and foreign ownership have been eroded. The quasi-privatization schemes like "responsibility contracts," leasing out factories and workers to entrepreneurs, and the grafted joint venture structure have complicated the labor relationship between employer and employee.[116] When changes have been extreme or influenced by corruption, large-scale strikes and violence have been the result.[117]

As the inevitability of strikes begins to dawn on government officials, there is a growing discussion within the state and bureaucracies to legalize and regulate industrial actions.[118] This would reverse the 1982 removal of the right to strike from the Chinese Constitution, a move that sought to reverse the tendencies of the Cultural Revolution to glorify and support mass uprisings against authority, both against the CCP and the state, and in enterprises, against management. Throughout the 1990s support for the right to strike has grown among researchers and government and trade union officials.[119] Once again the rationale for legal change is the ownership change pushed forward by reform, specifically ownership of firms by foreign investors. In 1994 this rationale was based on the fact that most of the strikes already occurring were in FIEs in which, as one Chinese scholar stated, "the degree of pressure and exploitation that workers are already suffering from goes beyond Western countries and even goes beyond what occurred here before liberation."[120] By 1999, the link between strikes and foreign capital was still apparent, but exploitation at the hands of foreigner bosses now implicated the state sector as well:

> Some state-owned companies are losing money badly, so their higher authority sells the company off to foreign merchants, it is not discussed with the workers beforehand, moreover the sale price is too low, and the workers haven't been settled, so the buyer just dismisses them. When workers strike because of this problem, they often earn the sympathy of society. I believe that the basic nature of these strikes does not oppose the policies of the state, rather it should be clearly recognized that (these strikes) represent very positive support for the party's and state's anti-corruption policy.[121]

If strikes are legalized in China, there is likely to be greater tolerance for strikes that involve foreign capital. But as in the example above, when "the higher authority sells the company to foreign merchants," foreign capital "exploitation" can no longer be neatly separated from Chinese state "corruption."[122] Moreover, the actual regulations and laws guiding and limiting industrial actions cannot be ownership-specific and thus risk the possibility that legal strikes will occur just as regularly in domestic state and nonstate firms.[123] In 1997 some interviewees expressed support for the legalization of strikes only in foreign companies, but when asked about this again in 1999, with WTO accession looming, government officials laughed and shook their head: "That would be impossible."[124]

LABOR CONFLICT AND FOREIGN INVESTMENT

FIEs continue to outpace other kinds of firms in the number and intensity of labor disputes. But in general there seem to be more areas of convergence than divergence. Labor disputes are increasing rapidly in private firms and in firms that have been restructured and reformed, including stockholding companies and urban collectives. With the implementation of the labor contract system in SOEs and the deepening of SOE reform, labor disputes are increasingly common in that sector as well. Although there are many reasons for the lower rates in SOEs, one major factor is that through the process of restructuring, privatization, or foreign-capital infusion, the SOEs with the greatest possibility of labor conflict are reassigned into another statistical category. Labor practices in FIEs may have been on the cutting edge of change in the 1990s, but as discussed in chapter 4, differences between types of ownership are fading.

Certain characteristics of FIE labor relations, however, may contribute to a higher rate of labor disputes in this sector even in comparison to other nonstate firms. These include the role of China's domestic media and the use of nationalism rather than class as a rallying point. China's domestic media has in general been much more free to report on labor abuse and labor disputes in FIEs than in domestic Chinese firms.[125] This had led to the perception both within China and abroad that the worse labor abuse occurs in foreign-invested factories. The 1993–94 spate of strikes in Korean and Japanese factories was widely reported in the Chinese media, as were other smaller incidents of labor abuse and humiliation of Chinese workers at the hands of foreign bosses. In fact, while conditions at many foreign-invested factories are horrific, there has yet to be any reliable study that compares labor conditions across different types of firms. Labor conditions in TVEs and private enterprises are unlikely to be significantly better than those in FIEs. As detailed in chapter 6, the Hebei TVE employed exactly the same methods of labor control and discipline as foreign firms. Some research into certain sectors has found evidence that labor practices in SOEs are growing more despotic and repressive.[126] Moreover, given the restructuring and subsequent massive layoffs that begin in the 1990s, one would expect that labor disputes regarding contract termination, job change, and new forms of compensation would also have led to a very rapid climb in the dispute rate. But state and collective firms are often protected by their close ties to local governments and are thus able to avoid media scrutiny and public attention. There also may be more pressure from within public sector firms, especially from the party committee or union, on workers to resolve disputes informally or not lodge disputes at all.[127]

The domestic media's greater attention to and greater freedom to report on labor problems in FIEs is also related to the role that nationalism plays in these disputes. The abuse of workers at the hands of foreign bosses is presented as potential or actual reenactment of national humiliation, something that the CCP eradicated with liberation in 1949. This interpretation allows greater media attention and public anger. Casting labor conflict as a problem between Chinese workers and foreign managers is also at times used effectively at the firm level by some trade union chairmen who define their role as defending Chinese interests against foreign ones.[128] Foreign managers in interviews also tended to frame labor problems as related to cultural misunderstanding or historical events. In the firms interviewed for this study, American managers were most likely to view labor conflict as a cultural misunderstanding, while Japanese managers often framed labor issues against the larger backdrop of Sino-Japanese history, including Japan's invasion and colonization of parts of China.[129] In the fall of 2003 two events, a prostitution scandal involving Japanese businessmen and an anti-Japanese riot in Xian, both of which were widely reported on and discussed virulently on the Internet, caused enough anti-Japanese sentiment in other cities for Japanese companies included in this study to describe their labor relations as "unstable"; they also refused another round of interviews.[130]

CONCLUSION

The implementation of a labor contract system and the development of a growing body of labor laws and regulations were state-initiated reforms to attract FDI. China's labor force had to be rationalized, formalized, and commodified in order for another "East Asian miracle," led by export-oriented manufacturing, to occur on PRC soil. Foreign investors' emphasis on controlling costs and minimizing extra-wage burdens led them to press continuously for clear regulations and a more flexible and short-term employment relationship. Aware from the beginning of the deleterious effects of FDI on labor and, in turn, on its own legitimacy, the state was equally concerned with building legal institutions that would help control foreign capital but not chase it away.

The iron rice bowl of SOE workers remained in place as these changes occurred in FIEs. It took longer to break despite support within the central leadership for more inclusive labor reform even in the mid-1980s. Labor contracts had a marginal effect on SOE workers in the 1980s. The majority of SOE workers did not sign them, and signed contracts were rarely enforced. Why the change then in the 1990s? Why did labor reform in SOEs so long delayed and so long ineffectual suddenly speed up?

By the 1990s, the divisions in regulations and in practices between China's state and nonstate sectors became increasingly untenable. Many state firms continued to build up massive debts while remaining inefficient. The problem of vast underemployment in a significant number of state firms had yet to be tackled. The number of FIEs was increasing dramatically, grabbing up managers and skilled labor as they went. China's economy was growing quickly, but the leadership's most treasured core, the state sector, lagged behind.[131] Reflected in the light and success of the new nonstate sectors, its failings were all the more glaring. As integration increased and discussions of GATT and WTO membership increased, the lack of competitiveness of many SOEs, even within their own domestic economy, intensified the need for a level playing field.

The passage of labor laws and regulations that are no longer specific to different kinds of ownership is one sign of the state's commitment to capitalist reforms, essential in order to provide that level playing field. To state firms it signals greater autonomy and new, lower expectations for worker welfare beyond wages and insurance. To foreign and private firms, it signals a bit more attention to labor conditions and workers' rights. To workers, it signals a switch from state-mediated labor relations to contract-based employment relations. Contracts have supplied a foundation on which disagreement, protest, even violence can rest. However, the state has also been active in its construction of a legal framework that encourages conflict to rise above the level of the firm. Unlike Taiwan, the PRC government has not been content to allow labor conflict to be settled informally by powerful managers. This has directed labor conflict into officially sanctioned channels, first to the local arbitration commissions and increasingly to the courts. The state supplied laws and legal institutions as part of a project of global economic integration and domestic social change. Labor law and labor dispute resolution procedures have developed as a dual response to the demands of foreign capital and to the fear that labor exploitation in foreign firms would create social instability. The imperfections of China's labor laws, in particular the problems of implementation and enforcement, have in part led to the huge increase in labor disputes. Workers have responded not only to the legalization of labor relations, but also to the huge gaps in what the law promises and what they actually receive. They have taken the state at its word "to use the law as a weapon."

CHAPTER SIX

From State-owned to National Industry

> The international operation of these [multinational] corporations is consistent with liberalism but is directly counter to the doctrine of economic nationalism and to the views of countries committed to socialism and state intervention in the economy.
> —Robert Gilpin, "The Multinational Corporations and International Production"[1]

FDI AND THE COMPETITION IT CREATED between regions and firms affected the way state leaders thought about state ownership, leading to a radical reformulation of one of the key debates of socialist transition: the role of public ownership in a global, market economy. In other reforming socialist economies, the debate over public ownership leads to mortal divisions both within the Party-State and between state and society. A decision to abandon public ownership and privatize signals the death of socialism—for what is socialism if not a commitment to public industry for the improvement of the entire economy and the protection of the working class? Transitions from socialism generally begin with a struggle to allow a limited role for the private economy in the hope that it will contribute to a general improvement in economic conditions and lessen some of the negative attributes of the plan—shortages, lack of consumer goods, and low-quality goods. In the 1980s, however, in most reforming socialist economies, the plan continued to falter, while the private (or mixed) economy spawned greater subversion and increased corruption, and led to decreasing legitimacy of the regime. Thus in the debate over public versus private, public ownership's standing continuously fell and further contributed to the dissolution of socialism in the USSR and Eastern Europe.

What we see in China is, empirically speaking, not entirely different. The SOE sector of the economy has lost out repeatedly under reform. Many SOEs have shown themselves to be immune to reform and still operating under incentives from the socialist era: problems of corporate governance and control, continuing state support for failing firms, irrational investment, and politically determined personnel appointments.[2] The nonstate economy, including the foreign-invested sector, has time and time again shown itself to be more efficient, more dynamic, and more capable of bringing widespread benefits like increased employment, rising exports, better goods and services, and higher levels of technological accomplishment.[3] In the earlier stages of reform, the debate between public and private ownership, while intense at times, could continue without resolution because the dual-track system allowed both to continue side by side, the nonstate sector in success and the state sector in (often hidden) failure. Resolution of the debate was postponed as the party and the state tinkered with various attempts of state-owned enterprise reform in an increasingly desperate attempt to justify public ownership. By the mid-1990s, it had become clear that SOE reform without privatization had reached a dead end. By the Fifteenth Party Congress in 1997, when the regime finally signaled its willingness to privatize large swaths of Chinese state industry, this debate was reformulated into one over Chinese national industry versus foreign industry. The Chinese regime has retained its legitimacy by refashioning the debate into one of Chinese industrial survival amid ever increasing foreign competition. Privatization ("letting go") is necessary so that Chinese "national industry" can be enlivened and strengthened to meet its global competitors. A nationalist perspective has replaced a socialist perspective and shielded the Chinese leadership so far from accusations that it has sold socialism down the river.

This reformulation of the ideological debate away from private versus public and toward Chinese industry versus foreign industry marks China's leaders continued attachment to state-led developmentalism without a concomitant attachment to socialism. At the central level, capitalist developmentalism means improving China's global competitiveness and building strong Chinese "national champions."[4] State-owned industry is maintained at the "commanding heights" of the economy in order to reach this goal of global competitiveness. The economy remains state-led but state-owned industry is no longer burdened with the goals of socialism.[5] This developmental model mixes aspects of both the Taiwanese and Korean development paths. As in Taiwan, the CCP continues to preserve an important role for the public sector at the top while allowing small and medium firms to go private. Admiration for some aspects of the Korean chaebol system has led to the encouragement of mergers between large SOEs so that they form the foundation for large business conglomerates in the hope that they will become internationally competitive.

This shift at the top away from socialism to capitalist developmentalism has contradictory consequences for those below. Despite the central government's emphasis on China's national economy, for local governments developmentalism has only increased the importance of foreign investment because even as the state "grasps" the large firms, it now allows the "letting go" of the vast majority of SOEs. Thus at the local level, developmentalism is translated into the large-scale privatization of small and medium failing state firms and a renewed drive to attract FDI to buy up state assets. In the latter half of the 1990s these developmentalist local governments have also turned toward building up the local private economy.[6]

At the firm level, this developmentalism requires further increasing workers' sense of insecurity and competition with other workers. This new drive for increased efficiency is justified as the only way to compete with the more efficient FIEs or as a way to attract foreign partners. At each level the notion of competition is visible and integrally related to foreign capital: as the challenge to China's national economy, as the savior of failing firms, and as the harbinger of a new managerial ideology at the firm level.

Previous chapters have accounted for changes in economic structure, firm practices, and legal institutions, so why is it necessary to examine changes in ideology? The quotation from Robert Gilpin above gives a hint as to why ideology or beliefs might matter. Gilpin argued during an earlier stage of economic globalization that the international production of multinationals is compatible with liberalism, but "directly counter to the doctrine of economic nationalism." Had the Chinese state undergone a transformation from socialism to economic liberalism, ideological changes might not matter. We would expect the changes that spring from economic integration and FDI inflows to be compatible with a transformation to liberalism. Instead, in the Chinese case, there is only uneasy coexistence between a liberal FDI policy and developmentalism. Examining ideological change is necessary because it demonstrates so convincingly the contradictions between China's open FDI policy and its overall developmentalist ideology.

As argued in chapter 2, China's use of FDI did not weaken the state's capacity. In fact, opening to FDI gave the Chinese state more room and time to implement difficult and politically destabilizing economic reforms. But is also apparent that this path has costs as well. By sequencing FDI liberalization before the development of domestic private industry and before deep and effective reform of state-owned industry, the importance of FDI has been heightened. State-led capitalist developmentalism at the center must coexist with heavy dependence on FDI among local governments and firms. In breaking the social contract with urban workers, the state has subjected workers to a new market ideology of competition and individualism. Its ideological justification has been, however, the threat of foreign competition and the need for strong national industry. FDI is liberally utilized to bring about economic growth and change; at the same time, however, the threat of foreign competition and economic domination is used to justify the state's developmentalist policies.

As we also know from chapter 5, labor conflict and societal protest is more frequent when foreign capital is involved. Opening to foreign capital has granted the regime time to implement these difficult restructuring reforms, but it has also led to a rapid increase in labor conflict, particularly in firms with foreign investment. This phenomenon raises questions about the long-term use of foreign investment and global economic competition more generally as "change agents" in China's domestic reform process. While the use of foreign pressure to speed up internal reform was also tried in Japan, China's use of foreign competition to speed painful internal reform and restructuring is unprecedented and politically risky. In Japan foreign pressure (*gaiatsu*) was used to encourage structural changes in Japan's domestic economy, in particular to make it more open to foreign competition and investment. This kind of pressure was often political, transmitted by foreign leaders and businesspeople. In China some forms of "foreign pressure" are similar to this—for example, when China acceded to the WTO. But there is also a form of foreign pressure that springs from China's relatively open economy. This foreign economic competition (from outside China's borders or from within in the form of foreign-invested enterprises) is then used to push forward internal reform.

Giving Up on Socialism

The transformation from socialism to state-led capitalist developmentalism was a reaction to domestic and international changes during China's first decade of reform. Because socialism itself has a strong developmentalist component to it, this transformation should be seen as a change in orientation; a change in how development was pursued rather than an abandonment of state-led development. Domestic factors include the way in which early reforms were sequenced and implemented. International factors include the rise of China's capitalist neighbors and the decline and demise of socialist models of economic development and reform. The East Asian newly industrialized countries (NICs) attracted attention in China because they offered a path to economic development and modernization that incorporated a large role for the state. As will be seen below, China's growing interest in an East Asian model of development continued even after the Asian Financial Crisis in 1997 spurred a widespread skepticism in the West toward an "Asian model of development."

Domestically, the sequencing of reform and the strong decentralizing aspect of China's FDI policy constrained the central leadership's choices in the later reforms of the 1990s. The sequencing of reforms in urban areas placed liberalization of FDI first, the development of a domestic private industry second, and SOE reform and privatization last. This early sequencing of reform narrowed and constrained the choices for later reform. By the end of the 1990s, China was increasingly integrated into the global economy, but its competitive position was hampered by the lack of a strong private sector and a failing, debt-ridden state sector.[7]

Due to the lack of state support and political commitment to the development of a real private sector, China's domestic private economy was weak and small-scale, with private firms finding it difficult to expand out of their localities.[8] Not only were firms discriminated against in finding markets and paying taxes and fees; private firms found it difficult to receive state bank loans. The vast majority of state bank credit was doled out to support failing SOEs. As Huang argues, the discrimination against private domestic firms coupled with the long-term protection and subsidization of SOEs dramatically increased the importance of FDI:

> First, much of the export-oriented FDI mainly originating from ethnic Chinese firms in Hong Kong and Taiwan materializes because of the severe liquidity constraints on the part of export-oriented Chinese firms. These liquidity constraints arise not because export-oriented Chinese firms are inefficient but because they are private. . . . Private firms have no choice but to raise financing in the only way they can: selling their claims on future cash flow to foreign firms. FDI rises as a result.[9]

In addition, the delay of SOE reform and the concomitant accumulation of high levels of SOE debt, millions of redundant workers, and a high rate of nonperforming loans to SOEs posed significant problems for the future of China's economy. While this delay of SOE reform put off politically destabilizing unemployment, it also severely hampered the state's attempts to pursue greater integration with the world economy and to build a more sophisticated financial system.[10] Continuing commitment to socialist goals, in particular the goal of continuing state ownership of large parts of the economy (based on the belief that state ownership was superior) was untenable. Such commitment risked the survival of the entire economy because of the large debt burden of Chinese state banks and the increase in foreign competition that came with WTO membership.

In sum, the early sequencing of reform has constrained China's leaders at this critical juncture. The lack of support for the development of a domestic private sector early on increased the importance of FDI. FDI acted as a substitute for domestic private industry. Also the delay of deep SOE reform and the general failure of tinkering reforms in profit retention and corporate governance narrowed the state's options. The state would have to pick and choose which state firms would remain and receive government support. The remainder would be let go.

China's development strategies have also been shaped by its relatively recent inclusion into the global economic and political system. China is a late industrializer and a developing country, but one with a socialist past. China is also surrounded by and increasingly integrated with states that have championed a development model that varies from the prescriptions of classic Western political economy and liberalism. China's neighbors, namely Japan, Korea, and Taiwan, developed their economies under heavy state guidance and corporatist societal relations but with strong export-oriented economies. This development model was made possible in no small part by their security relationships with the United States.

China's development strategies attempt to borrow from the developmental trajectories of its neighbors, but China faces distinct problems. It must negotiate a transition from socialism, thus radically renegotiating the social contract between the state and urban society. In addition, it must operate in a more open and competitive global economy in which export markets are no longer freely opened without a return demand for reciprocal access to China's large domestic market. Thus China's current attempt to adopt many of the developmentalist institutions of its neighbors is tempered by differences in current global and domestic conditions.

China's transformation from socialism to developmentalism is manifested differently at the central, local, and firm levels. First, at the center, the debate centered on the question of ownership and competition. It has led eventually to less and less emphasis on state ownership of industry and much greater emphasis to the development of China's "national industry" in general. At the local level, implementation of this developmentalist policy underscores the contradictory nature of a developmentalist strategy that utilizes FDI. The local level's main focus becomes industrial restructuring and the management of unemployment. This need to restructure increased the importance of FDI. It further spurs competition among localities and firms for foreign capital investment in (and even acquisition of) local state firms. Finally at the firm and individual worker level, this transformation is reflected in a changed managerial ideology. Global competition and economic insecurity are used as justifications for layoffs, unemployment and intraworker competition. Workers are asked to accept this new moral economy so that China might become stronger and more competitive. This collectivist ideology, however, differs markedly from socialist collectivism. While socialism was based on the belief that equality and development could and should co-exist, this new managerial ideology justifies domestic inequality for national development.

The thread that connects these macro and micro levels is the presence of FDI and the competition that foreign capital presented both to central leaders at the top, local officials in the middle, and firm managers at the bottom. In fact at all these levels, the notion of competition is the key justification for developmentalism with competition linked to FDI and, increasingly as WTO accession has become a reality, to global competition more generally. The central state rallies around national development and the threat of global competition in order to justify massive privatization.

Massive privatization, implemented locally, means greater foreign capital investment and control. Heightened competition at the firm level and growing economic insecurity further divide workers and alienates workers who are left behind.

DEVELOPMENTALISM IN PRACTICE: FROM THE CENTER TO THE FIRM

One of the critical changes from socialism to state-led capitalist developmentalism is the change in the perception of and expectations placed on state-owned industry. What are SOEs for? What are they supposed to do? For the country? For workers? Under socialism and during the period of early reform, the SOE was seen as an institution that, while economic in nature, guaranteed the social and political rights of the working class. Under early reform, economic productivity became more important but productivity was not placed above other broader goals, like the supply of social welfare benefits, full urban employment, and the ideological supremacy of workers and state ownership. Leaders wanted SOEs to be more efficient and to produce higher-quality goods. Leaders wanted to harden the soft budget constraint and make managers more accountable for firm performance. It was thought then that this could be done without changing the ownership structure and without changing the basic employment structure. The changes in employment relations that did occur, limited contracts and greater use of material incentives, occurred as means to improve productivity and grant managers some tools to improve workers' performance. These were not reforms meant to undo the socialist enterprise.[11]

As we saw in chapter 3, the perception of SOEs changed in the 1990s as they continued to fail and the tinkering reforms of the 1980s failed to yield the needed results. Most SOEs continued to be in heavy debt. By 1996 over half of China's state firms were reporting losses.[12] With the simultaneous boom of FDI in the early 1990s, the failure of state enterprise began to be placed in a comparative and inherently competitive perspective. SOE managers and reformist state leaders began to examine the performance of SOEs from a different vantage point. How did SOEs perform against China's burgeoning nonstate sector? Would China ever produce globally competitive industrial firms? Interestingly, SOEs were not often compared against rural Chinese firms, or at least most township village enterprises (TVEs) were not acceptable as *models* for future SOE reform.[13] Despite the fact that TVEs were growing rapidly in the early 1990s, these firms were considered too rustic and unruly to copy. They were also not considered to be examples of "modern" or "scientifically managed" firms. Rather, state managers complained that TVEs earned profits through unfair and underhanded business practices, such as disorderly competition, shoddy goods, and exploitative labor practices that were often based on familial or clan relations.[14] Most often, the Chinese urban state firm was placed in a comparative and competitive perspective against foreign companies.[15] SOEs faced unfair advantages against FIEs as well, but FIEs were *considered* to be examples of modern industrial management and more fitting as aspirations for Chinese urban firms.[16] While this was reflected generally in the search for "national champions" that could go toe-to-toe with large MNCs, adoption and imitation of foreign enterprise practices extended to increasing use of piece rates, new salary compensation systems, and other "rational" systems of enterprise management.[17] Guthrie argues in fact that imitation is a critical stage in China's transition, finding that "Chinese firms mimic the examples of market actors that they view as being the most market-savvy, namely, foreign investors."[18]

As this competitive challenge from nonstate firms grew, the central leadership redefined the meaning of state-owned industry. State ownership of the economy was still to be "dominant" but the definition of dominance was changed. The state began to define dominance not numerically, but strategically. This change was the turning point for ownership structure in China. It meant that state ownership was no longer essential for socialism. As Jiang Zemin proclaimed in 1997, all forms of ownership that contributed to growth and employment "can and should be used to serve socialism."[19] State ownership was justified for developmental and competitive reasons but China could remain "socialist" (and ruled by the CCP) without a large and dominant state sector. By 1997 the "diversification of ownership," which meant large-scale privatization in practice, was actively promoted by the central leadership. The change was contained in the "Hold the Large, Let Go the Small" policy that was announced at the Fifteenth Party Congress in 1997 but had been in various stages of implementation at the provincial level since at least 1994. This policy approved the sale, merger, acquisition, or bankruptcy of tens of thousands of small-to-medium state firms. Ownership by the state would now be concentrated at the "commanding heights" of the economy, the large state firms. These large firms would be further concentrated "to become flagship enterprises within China and internationally."[20] Thus this period began the leadership's promotion of industrial transformation directly based on the developmental trajectories of other East Asian economies.[21] Through mergers and acquisitions state firms would be transformed into huge, diversified enterprises along the lines of the Korean chaebols.[22] Jiang Zemin announced at the 1997 Party Congress that "we will establish highly competitive large enterprise groups with trans-regional, inter-trade, cross-ownership, and transnational operations."[23]

The Asian financial crisis enlivened the debate about the future of Chinese enterprise reform and the wisdom of following a model that seemed to be in trouble. In general, however, the central leadership continued to support consolidation among large SOEs through mergers and acquisitions and the privatization of smaller SOEs. The most significant lesson that leaders and managers seemed to absorb from the Asian financial crisis was not to overdiversify but to concentrate on several core industries.[24] An article in a journal from the Ministry of Foreign Trade and Economic Cooperation (now the Ministry of Commerce) for example, continued to support the development of general trading companies in China modeled after the experiences of Japan and Korea:

> Since the East Asian financial crisis, the Japanese and South Korean general trading company has been questioned, which has put unprecedented pressure on China's general trading company pilot program. We hold that, since the problems exposed in and lessons learned from the crisis countries are profound, with their causes being diverse, disclosing as soon as possible the flaws in their system design and development difficulties will undoubtedly be a good thing.[25]

The Tangshan SOE was an example of this state-directed merger and acquisition activity.[26] As Zhu Rongji had made clear in an earlier speech at the Conference on the Reemployment of State Enterprise Employees, "we will standardize bankruptcies, encourage mergers. In order to realize the guiding policy of many mergers and few bankruptcies, the state will increase its promotion of the policy that superior companies merge with inferior companies."[27] The Hebei Province government encouraged a Tangshan SOE to merge with another cement company in Qinhuangdao City. This company, QX Cement, was the oldest cement company in China, established in the nineteenth century, and by the reform era possessed all the characteristic problems of an SOE. It was old, its equipment was decrepit, its workforce was too large, and it had heavy debts. Its brand name, however, was widely known throughout China, and its distribution networks were well established. The Tangshan SOE, on the other hand, was established in the early 1980s, had newly imported equipment from Germany, a relatively low debt burden, and a productive and disciplined workforce.[28] These mergers are seen as a safer alternative to widespread plant closings and bankruptcies. The Tangshan SOE took over the debts of QX Cement and also took on the responsibility of settling its four thousand workers. Fifty percent of these workers were let go: "settled" through early retirement and through reemployment in Tangshan SOE's subsidiaries where they earned lower wages and received fewer benefits than the core workforce. [By 2003 these subsidiaries had begun their own layoffs and labor contract buyouts. The road to unemployment for QX workers was a long and gradual one.] It is too early to tell if these large-scale mergers will be economically successful, but in the short term these mergers have decreased the number of unemployed workers and delayed and probably reduced social instability. Continuing with the merger and acquisition path for larger state firms, despite the Asian financial crisis, allowed the Chinese state to continue its commitment to national industry while winnowing down its commitments to the vast majority of SOEs. In this new globally competitive environment, this model was touted as China's only chance to do battle in the global marketplace:

> Experts point out that mergers and acquisitions are presently underway in many industries with powerful multinationals as major players. If China joins the World Trade Organization, mergers and acquisitions will become inevitable as many industries would be exposed to tougher competition from multinationals. . . . [T]he anticipated merger and acquisition wave will produce China's own conglomerates, improve its industrial structure, optimize the allocation of resources, and sharpen the competitive edge of the nation's economy.[29]

The managers of the Tangshan SOE certainly framed their development strategy in this competitive light. Moreover, this competitive outlook had strengthened dramatically between 1997 and 1999. This was partially due to the Asian financial crisis, which cut Tangshan SOE's exports from a high in 1996 of one-third of total output to zero in 1998. Domestic competition grew more intense as export markets shut down. It was also a result of the natural expansion of FIEs and TVEs in the cement industry. The Tangshan SOE found itself in intense competition between a recently established Sino-Japanese cement joint venture in Qinhuangdao, numerous TVEs operating in the surrounding countryside, plus an onslaught of competition from neighboring Shandong Province. Much of the competition, they believed, was unfair and consisted of "disorderly competition, underselling, and harassment (*saorao*)."[30] What their complaints signified in economic terms was the breakdown of local protectionism and long-established production contracts between SOEs and their customers. The increasing ability of nonstate firms from nearby provinces and cities to steal traditional customers was clearly creating new challenges for SOEs. The merger between this Tangshan SOE and QX Cement was one response to this challenge. The managers at the SOE believed that their competitive position would be strengthened in the long term if they consolidated production and expanded into other cities and nearby markets. They also planned to further consolidate by absorbing smaller companies, including TVEs. In this way, they would be better poised to compete with the foreign-invested cement firms, firms that by establishing joint ventures in several regions could overcome local concern over new protectionism in a way that traditional SOEs could not. By 2003 this competition was palpable among the managers as large MNCs from both France and Taiwan began to invest in the region.[31]

A somewhat different restructuring process took place in China's camera film industry, a process that attempted to make use of FDI as a way to build strong Chinese national industry. This example neatly demonstrates the state's commitment to "national industry" and its justification to utilize FDI to build China's own globally competitive firms. It also demonstrates the underlying, fundamental ambivalence of the Chinese state toward FDI.

China's camera film industry had been ravaged by the earlier opening to foreign film and large-scale smuggling of film into China's borders. Kodak (United States) and Fuji (Japan) dominated the market, despite their lack of on-the-ground productive capacity. China's production had fallen, debts had risen, and the factories were badly managed. The industry had avoided large-scale joint ventures, choosing instead to import high-tech equipment that the firms were unable to use properly. China's industry was losing out to foreign firms and showed no sign of a turnaround.

In 1995, after three years of negotiations, Kodak was allowed to buy out three SOEs in the film industry. These firms were radically restructured and absorbed into Kodak's multinational operations. Of the 5,978 total workers in all three plants, Kodak retained only 1,771, or about 30 percent. The remaining workers were sorted out in different ways depending on their age and ability. Eleven hundred workers retired; 919 accepted a one-time payment and handled their own reemployment; 496 took company stock in lieu of continued employment. Another 1,094 workers had their labor contracts bought out, a controversial practice that is being used more widely now as a way to cut staff who have signed long-term labor contracts.[32] The remaining 600 either entered into state-run reemployment centers or "found their own means." What is interesting and important about the Kodak experience with regards to labor is that this restructuring process had great effects on other firms, even firms that had no connection with Kodak or the acquisition. The state, in a bid to transform the firms that had remained solely state-owned *extended the preferential policies reserved for foreign firms to all firms in the film industry.* This included more flexible labor policies and the right to lay-off and fire redundant staff. The state justified the extension of these policies to state firms as a way to allow them "to enjoy the same policies as those firms involved in the joint ventures, and creating an environment of fair competition for their development."[33]

Above all the Kodak experiment was an attempt by state planners to turn around state firms by subjecting them to the restructuring and management overhaul that comes with foreign investment. By extending Kodak's practices to firms that remained state-owned, it demonstrates how state leaders hope to utilize FDI to make China stronger. As a report by the State Development Planning Commission stated:

> The photosensitive materials industry's successful use of foreign capital to implement industry reorganization and reinvention is a valuable exploration for other state owned enterprises using foreign capital to stimulate reform, reorganization, and reinvention. . . . So now we want to combine our opening up to the outside with self-reliant development to form an organic whole, and explore the new path by which China's industry will move from weakness to strength. . . . After the photosensitive materials industry has "cut the cord" with Kodak, this will objectively create conditions for reorganization of enterprises.

This pragmatic policy and the hope that sooner or later China's national firms would "cut the cord" with Kodak exposes the deep developmentalist roots of China's FDI policy.[34] Kodak first introduced labor reforms and the end of socialist labor practices but the Chinese state allowed SOEs to follow suit in a bid to improve their global and domestic competitiveness. In the end, the state envisions a turnaround of the remaining SOEs in the film industry and a "self-reliant" Chinese national industry. Unfortunately by 2003, the Chinese camera film industry was no closer to cutting the cord. Instead Kodak became one of the first foreign investors to take advantage of the new rules allowing foreign purchase of state shares. It acquired a 20 percent stake in its main domestic competitor, Lucky Film, with the acquisition likely to be only the first step in a series of acquisitions. At the time of the purchase, Kodak held 50 percent of China's domestic film market with Lucky holding 20 percent.[35]

Jiang Zemin's enthusiastic embrace of the East Asian development model in 1997, although inconveniently timed just prior to the collapse of the Korean economy, signaled the end of socialist ownership in China. State ownership of firms would continue in a limited way, but its mission was redefined as a developmental one. The vast majority of state firms that were not included in the "commanding heights" of the economy were given up to various kinds of privatization. In 1997 the leadership saw this as an economic imperative (and actually a fait accompli in many coastal provinces). China was increasingly integrated into the global economy, WTO accession talks had already begun in earnest, and FIEs continued to boost market share and ownership control in China's domestic economy.

The irony is, of course, that the "letting go" policy would only further increase foreign investment and control within the domestic economy.

China's private sector is weak and endemically short of capital due to the monopoly of state bank funds enjoyed by the state sector. One entrepreneur in Shenyang, in northeastern China, who helps turn around state firms in order to attract foreign buyers maligned the difficulty that domestic Chinese entrepreneurs face in getting loans. "If only I could get banks to lend to me, I would not just be a tiger but a tiger with wings."[36] Foreign investors were in a much better position to take advantage of the bargain basement prices for many small-to-medium state firms.[37] Local governments, responding to the policy change from above, simply looked for capital where it could be found. The mayor of Shenyang toured Europe to find buyers for 18 Shenyang SOEs with a total workforce of 309,436.[38] In total, 3,000 SOEs in Shenyang were put up for sale. In 1998 the deputy mayor of Shenyang stated that of its 232 large SOEs only 16 were to remain state-owned, "eventually coalesc[ing] into 5 large diversified groups that might be modeled on Korea's chaebol."[39] As chapter 3 shows in greater detail, grafted joint ventures and various modes of foreign participation in stockholding firms increased dramatically in the late 1990s. You Ji, writing on Liaoning Province's use of grafted joint ventures, calls it "using capitalism to save socialism." As he notes, other provinces quickly began to adopt similar measures:

> What Yue (the governor of Liaoning Province) did was simple: he encouraged the factories to offer their land and facilities fairly cheaply to foreign investors and transform themselves partly or wholly into joint ventures. On the basis of this "grafting" the joint ventures would be further transformed into joint stock companies. . . . As the profit rate of the province picked up visibly, the Liaoning experiment has been seen as the "dawn light" for China's state sector and followed by other provinces.[40]

Indeed the experiment of Liaoning was seen in other provinces as well, including Fujian, Guangdong, Tianjin, Chongqing, Shandong and others.[41] The dawn light of reform in 1994 was no longer so bright by 1999, when layoffs and unemployment in Liaoning and its neighboring rust-belt provinces had reached levels of over 30 percent of the total workforce.[42] While investors who acquire SOEs often agree at the onset to take on the burden of the state firm's employees, the use of short-term contracts allows the firm to begin to downsize fairly quickly. Some cities and regions allow the acquirer to buy out the workers for a one-time sum, with the worker forfeiting any pension or additional support in the future. Shenyang, the capital of Liaoning, reported the use of these severance packages for employees as a way to entice foreign investors to come in and invest without the added headache of state firm employees.[43]

This state-led capitalist developmentalism is reflected in the ideological debates and policy changes that take place at the top. At the local level, however, as SOEs and their local government owners find their mission redefined and their economic surroundings undergoing rapid change, these policy changes are manifested differently. Local governments and state enterprise managers are developmentalist too, but in their local context; this means beating the competition by joining it, which included finding foreign investment, restructuring and selling of firms, and laying off workers.[44] Like Taiwan, China's leadership places great political importance on state ownership of strategic sectors of the economy. Like South Korea, it hopes to build large, diversified conglomerates but also to avoid the problems of overdiversification and heavy bank debt. Like both Korea and Taiwan, China finds rapid growth through export markets and global integration. Unlike the other East Asian NICs, however, China allowed foreign investors to exploit China's domestic market and invest directly into the Chinese economy. The importance of this decision was only enhanced with the "let go" policy as thousands of SOEs were "freed" from their state ties and told to sink or swim.

Within Chinese firms, state managers were attentive to the debate at the center about what was wrong with state ownership and what options were available to change the internal workings of the state firm. They were also aware of the growing competition from nonstate sectors as they watched their monopolies erode and their products go unsold on stores' shelves that were also lined with flashy foreign brands. Moreover, they were acutely aware of the preferential policies granted to firms with foreign investment and the greater flexibility that foreign firms had in internal management decisions. Notions of unfair competition that touched on labor relations revolved around several issues, including the welfare and employment burdens of SOEs, the salary controls on SOE managerial and skilled staff, and the ability of FIEs to buy state assets at low, bargain-basement prices yet avoid taking on the personnel burdens of the acquired firms. Proponents of deeper SOE reform argued that this institutionalized unfair playing field not only turned FIEs into successful exporters but also beat out SOEs on their turf, in China's domestic market.[45]

Firms were driven by the knowledge that in regard to labor issues state firms had the heaviest burden. Unlike other issues of corporate governance, firms were relatively clear about how to improve the labor problem: use employment contracts, control salary and welfare increases, lay off noncore workers, hire younger workers, and hire migrant or rural workers for low-skilled positions. These were all practices that FIEs had employed from the beginning. A report by the Chinese Academy of Social Sciences stated that "if SOEs' welfare payments were brought in line with private or foreign-invested enterprises, many more would be profitable."[46] And internal study by the Labor Science Research Institute, a government organization affiliated with the Ministry of Labor, also reached the same conclusion:

> There is a long way to go in the reform of labor and social security system to meet the demands of establishment of market economy [sic]. As things stand now, the backwardness of labor and social security reform seriously conditions the state enterprise reform. . . . Especially with the nonpublic economy becoming stronger and stronger, more and more foreign products (including foreign invested enterprises' products) pouring into China's market, the competitions between state enterprises and nonpublic enterprises, the domestic enterprises and foreign enterprises are becoming white-hot. Now the greatest problem faced by state enterprises is poor competition capacity.[47]

The poor competition capacity of SOEs and some of the underlying reasons have been well known within China for some time. However, analysis of SOE constraints was increasingly placed in a comparative perspective, with greater attention on SOE profitability vis-à-vis competition from FIEs and the need for a level playing field.

Changes at the firm level were driven by several other factors besides the unfair competitive position of FIEs versus SOEs. First, firms that had already absorbed foreign investment implemented reforms as dictated by the foreign managers. They took for granted that foreign managers knew best how to reform and restructure an enterprise.[48] If anything, the Chinese managers were there to make sure the reforms did not go too quickly and alienate the workers completely.[49] State firms were also driven to reform their managerial practices to accord with foreign practices because it increased the likelihood that they would attract foreign capital into their firm. The investment hunger that drove state firms and local governments alike to attract FDI cannot be underestimated. Foreign investment not only brought cash, equipment, and knowledge, it also brought political prestige, economic independence, more flexible policies, and even some ability to expand across regions: something that Chinese state and rural firms have great difficulty doing due to levels of local protectionism in China's provinces.[50] Douglas Guthrie has argued that FDI has an impact that goes beyond each individual company's investment. In Shanghai, he shows that "firms both mimic the practices of their foreign partners and adopt formal rational bureaucratic structures to attract new partners."[51] Guthrie's choice of wording is instructive. Mimicking is the adoption of practices that have been effective in a different context with the connotation of blind imitation.

Reinhard Bendix's work on ideologies of management in Russia, England, and the United States is useful as a way to characterize the changes at the firm level, changes that reflect the larger macro debate about the meaning of firm ownership and the nature (and target) of competition.[52] Bendix defined these ideologies of management as "attempts by leaders of enterprises to justify the privilege of voluntary action and association for themselves, while imposing upon all subordinates the duty of obedience and the obligation to serve their employers to the best of their ability."[53] In Chinese SOEs, the managerial ideology that prevailed under socialism has been replaced by a developmentalist ideology. This developmentalist ideology is different in its rationale from the previous socialist ideology but it is also different in many ways from managerial ideologies that prevail in market economies. Socialist managerial ideology was a collective ideology that espoused the dominant rule of the CCP and the subordination of enterprise management to the CCP's leadership. Workers, as the elite class in whose name the party rules, were empowered by this definition as long as they too could claim to be faithful followers under the party's leadership. This struggle over political credentials was, of course, the reason for the intense politicization of the Chinese factory under socialism. Legitimacy and power were granted from above in recognition of party allegiance, not economic performance.

Managerial ideologies in market economies are again different from developmentalist ideologies. These ideologies justify dominant-subordinate relations through the glorification of the individual and through the assumption of meritocratic attainment of position. Managerial ideologies have changed over time, of course, as the economy has matured in most market societies. In the post–World War II period in the United States, enterprises incorporated methods of human resources management and corporate training and culture to inculcate a sense of belonging as firms became bureaucratized. More recently, with the growth of high technology and information industries there has been the rise of managerial ideologies that glorify work as creative and (therefore) all consuming. With the rise of globalization and a strong economy in the United States, both employee and employer are perceived to be cutthroat. Workers leave for better pay or more interesting positions. Companies lay off at the earliest sign of an economic downturn or a dip in stock price.

The developmentalist managerial ideology in China retained some socialist ideals while incorporating much of the market ideology familiar in the United States. China has also learned from the experiences of its neighbors as states that were able to inculcate a sense of collectivism at the firm level that yielded rapid growth with social stability. This developmentalist ideology employs a sense of collectivism, as did socialism. Unlike socialism, which was a collectivism that was predicated on a high position for workers in the firm and in society, this developmentalist collectivism builds on a feeling of economic nationalism and economic insecurity at the global level. It justifies the contractualization and commodification of labor in SOEs on the dire position of state firms in the national and global economy and more generally, on China's weak competitive position. This ideology, in fact, blames the workers for the dire position of the factory and asks that the workers make sacrifices so that state firms can survive. While workers were asked to sacrifice under socialism as well, accepting low wages and consumer shortages, their own employment security and compensation were not linked to firm performance. Under the current capitalist developmentalism, however, workers are asked to do badly so that the factory can do well.[54]

Borrowing from market ideologies, this developmentalist ideology employs practices from foreign firms that extol meritocratic achievement, individualism, and internal firm competition. Using these practices, workers that fare the worst are responsible for their own failure. This individualism of course goes hand in hand with a market ideology that is presented as natural and infallible. The inevitability of the market is itself used as further justification for labor restructuring. A worker fails the market; the market does not fail the worker. This ideology of the market's hegemony and inevitability is reflected both in the state-controlled media and in the practices that state firms have adopted in order to compete.[55]

The media and state managers alike criticize state workers for their passive dependency on their work units. "Waiting, relying, demanding" (*deng, kao, yao*) is a popular label in the media, used to demonstrate the passivity and arrogance of state workers who continued to assume their previous employment relationship with the state. Managers echo this criticism, sometimes genuinely surprised that workers have not realized that the rules of the game had changed. A manager in Tianjin laughed when asked about the redundant workers in his collective, and said, "Don't these workers know? Wait? Nobody comes. Rely? No one's there to support you. Demand? They have nothing to give you."[56] His comment typifies the popular belief that unemployment and redundancy are unavoidable because neither the state nor firms are willing to continue to support workers at the risk of delaying reform even further. The message from the state through the media is at times almost refreshingly honest: workers are no longer protected from the market and those who continue to wait passively for the state to distribute new jobs lose out in this new economy. Newspapers herald laid-off workers who find new employment on their own and chastise those workers who refuse to accept work they consider to be "beneath the status of state employees," for example, employment in rural areas, in foreign or private enterprises, or in the service sector.[57] Sounding not unlike critics of welfare in the United States, the state embraces individual responsibility and a hearty work ethic:

We should pay attention to fostering and giving wide publicity to typical examples of vigorous efforts among laid-off workers and staff members; we should guide them in doing away with the idea of "waiting for, relying on, and asking for assistance" and help them foster a correct concept of obtaining employment; and we should help them understand that within the limits permitted by state policies and laws, there is neither lowliness nor nobleness in any work one does, and any occupation in which one is engaged is glorious.[58]

The Shenyang Daily ran an article by a union cadre that was more direct in its suggestions for Chinese workers. In a city with an unemployment rate that surpassed 30 percent the last line is particularly ironic:

The party and the government cannot forget the unemployed, but the market economy doesn't pity the weak. Facing up to unemployment, what should Chinese workers do? Straighten up one's back, become one of the strong! As long as one is willing to endure hardship, the ground will be beneath your feet. As long as you use your head, work isn't hard to find.[59]

The official trade union newspaper, the *Workers Daily,* has also been active in promoting the idea that the main problem of unemployment and reemployment is the outlook of the workers. A 1997 front-page editorial proclaimed:

The enterprise is the source of workers' employment, but the enterprise itself also must rise or fall by the market, it is a life or death problem, so workers should stay or go, be hired or be laid off according to that [the market]. Under these conditions, if a worker acts according to the past, looking for the factory (*gongchang*) not for the market (*shichang*), [if he] only waits for the upper level to arrange, but doesn't understand the demands of the market, then it will be very difficult to realize reemployment. . . . The core is that the worker fits the market, not that the market fits the worker.[60]

This message of "blame the victim" used the market as justification for the reforms and for the hardships encountered by SOE workers. It placed these hardships secondary to the hardships that the nation as a whole encountered in its bid to compete in the global economy. Competition in a global context meant both achieving Chinese economic strength abroad through the development of Chinese MNCs as well as making Chinese state firms competitive within the domestic economy. Workers were asked to accept these changes in state goals from socialism to competitive developmentalism as a matter of course. When they did not accept it—for example, when they failed to find new jobs on their own, or refused to work in another sector that did not supply benefits, or stayed in their factory-supplied housing living on subsidies—they were disparaged.

The changing managerial ideology of Chinese firms was reflected in new practices, often borrowed from foreign companies, which brought competition down to the individual worker. The vocabulary that firm managers used to describe implementation of these competitive practices demonstrates the vast difference between the present system and the previous socialist one. Socialism justified hardship through a sense of collective sacrifice. Now state managers spoke of increasing each individual worker's "sense of crisis" and of "opening the wage distribution," which meant distributing salaries that varied widely between individual workers and could even vary widely from month to month for each individual worker.[61] For these managers, "scientific management" became a mixture of Taylorist work arrangements and rules that emphasized individual achievement and interworker competition with a collectivist ethos directed at external competition.[62] Managers in Tangshan spoke of a new ideology modeled after images of Western firms. We have a "spirit of dedication like GM or Toyota."[63] But to achieve collective dedication within the factory, managers increasingly relied on divisive managerial techniques. The Tangshan SOE personnel manager boasted of a newly instituted hundred-point wage system that ruthlessly deducted points for infractions that were common under socialism: being late, eating sunflower seeds on the jobs, reading the newspaper, or doing one's wash in the factory bathrooms. Although the actual rules seemed normal enough, the penalties amounted to 30 percent of a worker's annual wage.[64] Moreover, the worker who reported the infraction was rewarded. In a Sino–Hong Kong joint venture in Tangshan, the managers used labor competitions to improve workers' "zeal." These competitions were cutthroat attempts to increase competition between workers. In each competition the workers with the two lowest scores would automatically lose their bonus regardless of how well they actually did. This joint venture, the Tangshan SOE, and the rural collective in Tianjin all used a reporting system that rewarded workers for finding mistakes in other workers' work or in the work of maintenance workers.

Internal factory relations were further changed with the increased use of "the confidential wage system." Confidential wages were first implemented in China's special economic zones, then later adopted by Shanghai SOEs, and in the 1990s this system was included within enterprise management textbooks as an acceptable form of wage distribution. Under this system, the wage of each worker is decided upon through "discussion" between the worker and management. Workers are then forbidden to discuss their salary with other workers or any other person; to do so is considered a violation of the labor contract. SOE managers consider it an effective way to hinder the traditional egalitarian thinking and "red-eyed disease," or the jealousy of other workers. Under socialism and partial reform, bonuses were distributed equally among workers without regard to individual performance to imbue workers with a collectivist ethos and, more realistically, to insulate management from workers' disagreement about equitable distribution. Union officials who have publicly disapproved of "confidential wages" point out that confidential salary practices dramatically increase the power of management over workers.[65]

While it is difficult to gauge how prevalent this practice is, it seems to be quite widely used by a range of different companies, including urban collectives, some smaller SOEs, rural collectives, and many FIEs. Combined with the widely reported practices of information sharing (regarding prevailing wages and benefits) between firms in the same locality, workers are severely hampered in their ability to determine what their wage should be.[66] It also makes collective action nearly impossible if sharing information is a violation of the labor contract and a threat to employment. Workers are already fragmented along many different lines in Chinese factories: older "permanent" workers, younger contract workers, female production-line workers, male maintenance and supervisory workers, local workers and rural migrants. Increasingly these workers work side by side and under similar conditions of competition and job insecurity. Yet this system effectively makes collective wage discussion impossible.

Several factories included in this study employed a separate system of wage distribution called "vague distribution" (*mohufenpei*). The Tangshan SOE, the Sino–Hong Kong joint venture, and one of the Sino-Japanese joint ventures used this system. The rural collective used a combination of piecework with a complicated point system for quality control that borrowed from the vague distribution system. The actual rules of distribution are unclear and change month to month and there is also variation between workers as to how much of the monthly wage is subject to variation. Variation can depend on objective measures of performance, like piecework, hours worked, and the quality of the goods. But there is also a complicated system of wage deductions based on various infractions, such as improper uniform, incorrect position at the machine, breaks for the bathroom or meals that are too long, or simply a "bad attitude." The official Chinese Trade Union opposes these policies but to no avail. Since egalitarianism is a bigger problem in SOEs than inequality, the Ministry of Labor argued, it supported the continuation of these practices in 1994.[67] Their prevalence in firms in 1997 and 1999 seem to indicate their proliferation across other firms and regions.

Media messages that blamed the victim and firm practices that intensified competition between workers and a general feeling of crisis were responses to the new goals of state-led development as set by the central leadership. Local governments, eager to find foreign buyers for state firms and to manage growing unemployment as best they could, also promoted this new ideology of competition and insecurity.

CONCLUSION

Bendix poses a critical question: "[O]n what terms will a society undergoing industrialization solve the problem of incorporating its newly recruited industrial work force within the economic and political community of the nation?"[68] China's experiment with socialism means that the incorporation that is taking place now is a dual process of exclusion and reincorporation. Urban workers must give up the benefits they enjoyed under socialism and be incorporated into a new moral economy of capitalism and competition. Moreover, this incorporation of the working class is not only into the political community of the nation but also into a global economic order, an order that the CCP had rejected and vilified from 1949 to 1978. The state's relationship with the working class was founded on this rejection of capitalism. The state interpreted development within a socialist, and basically autarkic, context, particularly after the Sino-Soviet split in 1960. Therefore this reincorporation of the working class into a national community and a new global economic order is rife with contradictions. At the central level, a developmentalist state gives up socialism to improve its competitive position in the global economy. At the local level, firms and officials, left to find their own lifeline, go out in search of foreign investors who will take on the burden of turning these companies around and turning the workers away. At the firm level, workers are asked to accept the economic insecurity that accompanies this new competition.

In a review essay of works on developmental states in East Asia, Ziya Onis writes "the power of the developmental state has depended on the formation of political coalitions with domestic industry and on the destruction of the left and curtailment of the power of organized labor."[69] The exclusion of labor from the corporatist-style politics of developmental Japan is also well noted in the literature, as are the repressive labor politics of predemocratic Korea and Taiwan.[70] The ideology and policies of state-led capitalist development adopted in China since the 1990s have brought this mark of developmentalism home. The marginalization of labor has been achieved in part through the expansion of the workforce through new ownership types and greater rural-to-urban migration. As this chapter has also shown, however, these structural changes have been accompanied by rapidly changing ideological justifications for state ownership and a radical shift in the state's relationship to the urban working class. Competition, insecurity, and individual responsibility are the new slogans of the state in its attempt to remake workers to fit the market.

The Contradiction of "Reform and Openness"

> The wolves are at the door, the more time passes, the more they come.
> —*Will Foreign Capital Swallow Up China?*[1]

VIEWED IN A COMPARATIVE PERSPECTIVE, China's gradual reform path is often characterized as a success story or as "reform without losers".[2] It may be more accurate to say that China's reform process has been a success story, so far, in spite of the losers. The pain of the economic transformation of the urban state sector was delayed, sparing workers the unemployment and displacement that shook Eastern Europe and Russia. The sequencing of the Chinese reform process has meant a gradual and correspondingly less painful reform process for China's urban workforce. Reforms were introduced first at the margins, in the newly created sectors, as opposed to the entrenched core of socialism: the urban state and collective firms. The roles of FIEs as a competitive pressure for state firms, as a laboratory for difficult labor reforms, and as an ideological justification for deeper reform pushed reform forward without first endangering those who benefited most from the previous system. The opening to FDI created an entirely new sector with which to experiment with the development of labor markets, salary and benefit changes, and new management techniques.

Growth in the size and importance of the nonstate sector, including FIEs, increased competitive pressure on state firms. State firms competed with FIEs for market share and skilled workers, and they also competed among themselves for FDI in order to boost capital investment and technological capacity. This competition for FDI was heightened by regional competition for FDI flows. Thus, liberalization of FDI had a dynamic effect on the state sector by spreading capitalist labor practices across firms of different types of ownership. As competition with foreign firms grew, the state used this new sense of competition and economic insecurity to justify deeper and more painful reforms of China's beleaguered state industry. In order to achieve developmentalist goals of national economic competition, these deeper reforms rejected socialist goals of state-owned industry in exchange for strategic state ownership of industry. The "letting-go" policy approved the privatization of most state firms and further expanded FDI in China's domestic economy. Thus, the delay of urban restructuring strengthened the political position of the CCP vis-à-vis urban society by allowing economic growth to take place while protecting the core, politically important sectors long into the reform process. The delay of SOE reform, however, has had an economic cost; China's SOEs now face their most drastic reforms, which include the liquidation of firms as well as the wholesale acquisition of firms by foreign and private investors, in a much more competitive and open economic environment.[3]

This delay in the restructuring also brings with it political risks. The "white-hot competition" from FIEs and the competition that accompanies China's accession to the World Trade Organization serve as the impetus for deeper reform and privatization.[4] However, due to the weak position of China's private industry, privatization and restructuring of the state sector themselves involve increased foreign participation.[5] The rapid increase in labor disputes and conflicts are directly related to the restructuring process and have been on the rise throughout the 1990s. The rate of labor disputes is highest in FIEs, where workers seem to find greater political space and legitimacy in opposing foreign capital.[6] A recent example of this phenomenon occurred in August 2000 when six foreign managers were taken hostage at an American WFOE in Tianjin. This company, originally an SOE, had formed a JV with an American company in the 1990s. With the acceleration of reform and the subsequent increase in cross-border mergers and acquisitions, it had recently been acquired by a second American company and turned into a WFOE. Following the logic of competitive liberalization, this company then decided to consolidate its four factories in Tianjin and move to TEDA, the development zone thirty miles away, in order to reap the benefits of the zone's preferential tax policies. The firm then divided the workforce by age, asking workers thirty and under to accompany the plant to the new location and offering the older workers a one-time severance package. When six managers went to the factory to post the closure notice, seventy workers took them hostage for over forty hours.[7] Although such extreme action is rare, less dramatic variations of this dynamic are frequent and becoming only more so as foreign investors continue to participate actively in the restructuring process.[8]

With China's accession to WTO in December 2001, the acceleration of reform and restructuring is directly related to foreign capital and China's integration into the global economy. Workers may increasingly resort to nationalist, rather than class-based rhetoric, to voice their opposition to the reforms and their loss of job security and benefits. This ability to use nationalism as a way to challenge economic reform will open greater political space for workers because it exploits the contradiction between a developmentalist ideology and global economic integration. As we know from the development trajectories of China's neighbors, the developmental state, despite many internal variations, is defined by its commitment to nationalist economic development and the related abilities to "insulate the domestic economy from extensive foreign capital penetration."[9] As Meredith Woo-Cumings notes, "[T]his state form originated as the region's idiosyncratic response to a world dominated by the West. . . . today state policies continue to be justified by the need to hone the nation's economic competitiveness and by a residual nationalism (even in the contemporary context of globalization)."[10]

The developmental state is also defined by the ability to co-opt and/or exclude important social forces. Labor, in particular, is a critical social force that in the developmental state model is subordinate to the overwhelming nationalist project of rapid growth.[11] There was substantial variation in the mode of labor exclusion among the developmental states of East Asia. Postwar Japan achieved relatively harmonious labor relations through an employer-dominated system of enterprise unions, lifetime employment for core workers, and labor market segmentation.[12] Taiwan relied on the suppression of independent unions, labor market fragmentation through the subcontracting system, and a paternalistic management style in its many small-to-medium firms.[13] Korea, with the most antagonistic labor relations among the East Asian NICs, also suppressed independent unions through repression under authoritarian rule. Even after the democratic transition in Korea, labor relations have remained a flashpoint in Korean politics.[14] Despite this variation, none of these states achieved labor subordination with simultaneous foreign capital penetration.

Can nationalist economic development coexist with FDI and globalization more generally as a competitive catalyst for reform without creating a political backlash directed at foreign capital but by extension implicating the entire reform program? Utilization of FDI has improved the state's ability to implement reform and reduced demands for political change from an increasingly fragmented and diverse urban workforce. This reform path, however, now presents significant challenges to the Chinese state, particularly as China's accession to WTO requires even further opening and competition in the domestic economy. First, it must continue with the implementation of a developmentalist policy that uses FDI to make China stronger. Under this policy, FDI is extremely critical to the reform process, particularly for local officials and managers who must deal with the huge majority of state firms that have been "let go." There is a need to balance utilization of FDI against the threat of dependence on foreign capital and the disappearance of "national champions" into global production networks. There is a political challenge as well. The presence and growing importance of foreign capital coexists uneasily with the emphasis on nationalist economic development. Nationalist rhetoric is not only a tool of the state to justify reform; it is also a tool of workers who feel the brunt of economic change. The very presence of foreign capital creates an opening for greater societal conflict and protest. Nolan's speculation on China's large firms after WTO captures this predicament well: "[A] large fraction of China's "national champions" face the prospect of, at best, takeover by the multinationals, followed by drastic downsizing and absorption into the production system of the global firm. Many of them will face bankruptcy. There are almost ninety million people employed in China's state-owned enterprises. It is an open question how many of these will lose their jobs if China's state-owned enterprises are forced to compete rapidly on the 'global level playing field.'"[15]

In China's dual transition from state socialism and to a market economy, the transition processes have been dynamic and interlocking, with early reform cycles circling forward to shape the next wave of liberalization. The dual nature of China's transition, with the state's *withdrawal* from the key welfare and surveillance duties of socialism and its *embrace* of market principles and tools to regulate labor, makes for difficult analysis. It forces the observer to look for both the "institutional stickiness" of socialist institutions and the transformative power of the market with its liberal concepts of contractual obligations and individual rights. The staying power of socialism is revealed in the resistance of China's urban workers to this new moral economy of competitive capitalism and insecurity. There is also the strengthening of new institutions like labor contracts and dispute resolution processes that place greater emphasis on individual rights and equal representation. These institutions, despite their different emphases, work in tandem to create a new mode of resistance among workers: workers use new legal institutions to oppose the demise of the old institutions of socialist equality and employment guarantees.[16]

Up to now, openness to FDI has enhanced the staying power of the CCP. Integration into the global economy did not mean the withering away or "eclipse" of the state. Instead, integration offered the regime a political opportunity. Reformists in the central leadership viewed the institutions of socialism (such as lifetime employment, extensive welfare benefits, and little labor mobility) as obstacles to growth and to economic reform. Reform of these institutions if done directly, however, posed political risks and therefore were done halfheartedly throughout the 1980s, characteristic of the "tinkering" reform undertaken by most socialisst states.[17] FDI liberalization granted the regime space to withdraw from the social contract of socialism and to whittle away at these institutions. The institutions of a market economy are gradually coming into place and are founded in a profoundly different ideology of competition, contractual obligation, and freedom of movement.

Yet this story of how FDI played a key role in China's domestic institutional change is not a tale of the market's triumph over socialism and the freeing up of Chinese workers through capitalism. The Chinese state continues to resist the dual liberalization of the economic and political sphere. It attempts instead to square the circle of development by continuing with strong state-led development and authoritarian subordination of labor in conjunction with a heavy reliance on FDI and global economic integration. Under this system, legal institutions do not protect workers rights well nor does the trade union structure offer effective interest representation of labor.

From the evidence of increasing labor conflict, however, this is also not a story of the enslavement of the Chinese workforce through capitalism. The institutionalization of market ideologies and a contractual legal framework can have unintended effects on state-society relations by legitimating the discontent of the weak. The ideology of capitalism, in particular, its emphasis on the employment relationship as a contractual obligation, can be a powerful motivator of "rightful resistance."[18] As shown by the rapid increase in labor disputes and the deteriorating labor-management relations at many firms, workers are increasingly likely to use these new institutions to press for the protection of their rights and interests.

Firms and Interviews

I CONDUCTED THIS RESEARCH from August 1996 to July 1997 and then again in the summer of 1999, the summer of 2001, and the fall of 2003. In addition to firm-level interviews, I also conducted interviews with labor lawyers in Beijing and Shanghai, trade union officials in Beijing, Tianjin, and Shanghai, Ministry of Labor officials and researchers in Beijing, local level labor bureaus in Tianjin and Shanghai, and development zone administrators in Tianjin and Hebei Province. The book also relies on primary source materials including internal reports from the Ministry of Labor, the ACFTU, and other government and academic organizations, as well as many public sources of information.

The firms included were varied by ownership type including a stock-holding SOE (interviewed five times), an urban collective (twice), a rural collective (once, then it went bankrupt), three Sino-Japanese joint ventures (three times, twice, once), one Sino–Hong Kong joint venture (three times), three wholly owned Taiwanese firms (three times, twice, twice), two Sino-U.S. JV (both once) and one wholly owned American firm (twice). The visits were spaced out between 1997 and the fall of 2003. The firms were located in Tianjin, Shanghai, Jiangsu, and Hebei. Despite some variation across industrial sectors and products, the entry skill level of the average production worker was constant across all the firms, except for the American firms, which had higher entry-level requirements. The interviews at the firm were structured but open-ended and were conducted in Chinese, unless the manager was a foreigner. I interviewed the same managerial positions across all the firms when possible. These positions included the enterprise general manager, the human resource manager, the trade union chairman, and the highest-ranking Chinese manager. Informal interviews were conducted with other personnel when possible, for example, other top managers, secretaries, and production-line workers. In all cases except at the urban collective where I interviewed at the general offices, I was able to see the factory floor, the general working conditions, and the mode of work organization.

Interviewees were asked about the general structure of the firm, its products, markets, main competition, financial situation, and future plans. The remainder of the questions revolved around issues of labor management, including characteristics of the workforce, hiring methods, firing methods, implementation of individual labor contracts, collective labor contracts, salary system, insurance, and benefits. The structure of workers' organization was also examined, including questions about the trade union, the Communist Party cell, the Workers Representative Council, and the settlement of labor disputes. The interviews in 1999 and 2001 returned to these questions and also asked new questions about the impact of the Asian Financial Crisis. More abstract questions about the nature of labor relations, the existence of conflict, tension between foreign managers and Chinese workers, and managerial attitudes toward workers were also explored. Individual interviews ranged between one to three hours.

These firms were not randomly selected. I was introduced to these firms through personal acquaintances. I asked to be introduced to firms that were involved in manufacturing, that employed at least two hundred workers, and that had a moderately low skill-level entry requirement. I did not go through any official procedures or approvals to attain the interviews.

A small number of firms limits one's ability to generalize. When I do make general arguments about what I believe to be the general tendency in Chinese labor relations, I also employ other kinds of data to support these points. In chapter 4 where I discuss the trends in labor contracts and unionization, I use the firm-level data to illustrate general phenomena. Under better research conditions and with a less sensitive topic, survey research would have allowed more room for generalizing. Despite the small number of firms studied, however, there are at least four reasons to believe that these firms reflect individually some of the prevalent issues of contemporary labor relations in China.

First, because the Chinese government did not select the firms or approve the interviews in any way, I did not study handpicked "model" firms. Admittedly, any firm with horrific labor conditions would not have let me in to do research. These kinds of firms do exist in China, but it is extremely difficult for anyone, foreign or Chinese, to gain entry. My focus therefore has been not to investigate the very worst labor conditions that exist in China but rather to see how firms in the middle and upper-middle range structure labor relations.

Second, I visited these firms more than once (with the exception of a Sino-Japanese JV in Tianjin that refused further interviews, two Sino-U.S. JVs that were only interviewed late in 2002 and 2003, and the rural collective, which went bankrupt by the summer of 1999 after only two years in operation). Thus I was able to gain some sense of familiarity with the firms and managers. The ability to study the firms' development over time was particularly helpful in tracing changes in labor practices as the firms adjusted to internal reforms or external shocks such as the Asian Financial Crisis. Had I chosen to pursue one-time visits to many more firms over the same years, I would not have had the same insight into these longitudinal issues. Even survey research with its superior methods of sampling and range would have been deficient in this respect unless conducted multiple times.

Third, the variation across nationality, particularly inclusion of Japanese and overseas Chinese-invested firms, makes this sample of firms more representative of the general makeup of China's FDI inflows, in which large amounts comes from overseas Chinese and other Asian countries. There is no bias toward American and European firms, which would present, I believe, a too optimistic view of labor trends in China today.

Fourth, I have compared the data compiled from these interviews with information found in other interviews, extensive primary research of Ministry of Labor internal publications, Trade Union surveys and internal materials, scholarly research in English, Chinese, and Japanese, and articles in the Chinese media. I point out when the practices of the firms in the sample seem unusual in light of the other documentary research.

Given the constraints of small-n research, my focus in the book is to examine general trends as manifested at the firm level. Therefore in chapter 5, I examine how the labor contract system and the requirement for ACFTU monopoly representation are reflected in firm practices. I make no attempt to compare wages, benefits, productivity, or other quantitative measures across these firms because such a comparison would not be able to adequately resolve possible causation. For example, the American-invested firms that I visited had higher wages than the Taiwanese firms that I visited. The Japanese firms that I interviewed had lower wages and benefits than the American firms but were still higher than those in the Taiwanese and Hong Kong firms. This corresponds to the general impression of Chinese workers who almost uniformly believe that work conditions and compensation are best in American and European firms, adequate in Japanese firms, and far below adequate in Hong Kong, Taiwanese, and some other Asian-invested firms. However, I avoided focusing on this kind of comparison within my study because I had no confidence that national origin was the most important variable in producing the results that I gathered. The American and Japanese firms that I visited were also more capital-intensive, more concerned with the domestic market and their reputation in it, and more likely to be producing name-brand goods that could be tarnished through association with substandard labor conditions. These problems of multicollinearity cannot be controlled for given the small number of firms in the study. The variations that I do observe in labor contract practices and modes of worker representation are discussed at length in the text, with the firm-level observations backed up by other sources. I use the firm level data to provide greater detail and richness to these general trends.

Notes

1. The concept of a "social contract" or "social compact" in which workers in socialist states were politically quiescent in exchange for extensive welfare benefits and a lax workplace was developed by Alex Pravda, "East-West Interdependence and the Social Compact in Eastern Europe," in Morris Bornstein, Zvi Gitelman, and William Zimmerman, eds., *East-West Relations and the Future of Eastern Europe* (London: Allen and Unwin, 1981), 162–90. See also Valerie Bunce, *Subversive Institutions: The Design and Destruction of Socialism and the State* (Cambridge: Cambridge University Press, 1999), 33–34.

2. See Bunce (1999), 21–22.

3. "Iron rice bowl" is a term used to describe the system of lifetime employment and social welfare benefits enjoyed by China's urban working class. These benefits were distributed through the work unit rather than from the state directly.

4. Nicholas Lardy, "Economic Engine? Foreign Trade and Investment in China, *The Brookings Review* 14:1 (Winter 1996); Yanrui Wu, *Foreign Direct Investment and Economic Growth in China* (Cheltenham, UK: Edward Elgar; 1999). Lardy found that while contributing greatly to China's export boom, FIEs did not provide many backward linkages to the domestic economy nor did the presence of FIEs contribute to the reform of SOEs given their still-continuing protection. His FDI data for the article ends in 1994, so the analysis misses the later boom years in FDI and their effects. Yanrui Wu and others find links between FDI and economic growth, but show that the linkage is not a one-way causal relationship between FDI and GDP. See especially Jordan Shan, Gary Tian, and Fiona Sun, "Causality between FDI and Economic Growth," in Yanrui Wu (1999): 140–56. Yasheng Huang discusses some of the negative effects of China's dependence on FDI in *Selling China: Foreign Direct Investment during the Reform Era* (New York: Cambridge University Press, 2003).

5. This argument is promoted by policy analysts, business executives, and academics who argue that greater engagement with the outside world, mainly through trade and economic investment, has a liberalizing effect on Chinese domestic politics. While most treatments of this question readily admit the presence of negative effects, the overwhelming conclusion is that interaction with global capitalism has liberalizing effects on politics and society. For example, Douglas Guthrie, *Dragon in a Three-Piece Suit: The Emergence of Capitalism in China* (Princeton: Princeton University Press, 1998); and "Transition to a Market Economy: The Transformation of Labor Relations in China's Global Economy," paper presented at the Annual Conference of the Association of Asian Studies, Chicago, March 2001; Michael Santoro in *Profits and Principles: Global Capitalism and Human Rights in China* (Ithaca: Cornell University Press, 2000) addresses the pos-

itive and negative effects of MNC investment in China while trying to lay out a way for investment to have "moral integrity."

6. Anita Chan, *Chinese Workers under Assault: The Exploitation of Labor in a Globalizing Economy* (New York: M. E. Sharpe, 2001); Greg O'Leary, ed., *Adjusting to Capitalism: Chinese Workers and the State* (New York: M. E. Sharpe, 1997).

7. This is not the criticism that it may seem to be. China is a large and complicated country; in order to be good and careful, research must be limited. The criticism leveled here is at broad generalizations that have narrow empirical foundations. Guthrie's positive conclusions on the effects of FDI and marketization in general are drawn from research in Shanghai. Chan's analysis of labor exploitation looks mainly at industries that are labor-intensive, export-oriented, very cost sensitive, and located in China's southeastern coastal regions where overseas Chinese investors are dominant. Shanghai, on the other hand, attracts FDI from a more diverse group of investors including Japanese, American, and European investors.

8. Interview, Chinese Enterprise Management Association, March 1997.

9. Interview, Tangshan SOE general manager, July 1999.

10. Interview, Tangshan SOE personnel manager, May 2001.

11. Interview, Hebei rural collective general manager, July 1997.

12. Jung-Dong Park, *The Special Economic Zones of China and Their Impact on Its Economic Development* (Westport, Conn.: Praeger Publishers, 1997), 5.

13. Interview, Tianjin urban collective, manager, General Affairs Office, March 1997.

14. Interview, Tianjin urban collective, manager, General Affairs Office, July 1997.

15. The political connotation of calling a Communist Party Secretary "just like a landlord" should not be underestimated. Interview, Korean-contracted SOE worker, Tianjin, March 1997.

16. I date large-scale privatization as starting in 1997. In some regions, privatization had already begun.

17. Ronald McKinnon, "Gradual versus Rapid Liberalization in Socialist Economies: The Problems of Macroeconomic Control," in Michael Bruno and Boris Pleskovic, eds., *Proceedings of the World Bank Annual Conference on Development Economics, 1993* (Washington, D.C.: World Bank, 1994); John McMillan and Barry Naughton, "How to Reform a Planned Economy: Lessons from China," *Oxford Review of Economic Policy* 8 (Spring 1992). Anders Aslund lists several reasons for why Soviet and Chinese reforms had to differ. He includes the role of FDI, in particular overseas Chinese capital, as crucial to China's economic success. His analysis, however, is quite different; as he notes, "In a way, overseas Chinese represented an émigré civil society, making up for the lack of one within Chinese itself." The analysis here presents a much different role for FDI and overseas Chinese capital. Anders Aslund, *How Russia Became a Market Economy* (Washington, D.C.: Brookings Institution, 1995), 16.

18. Lawrence Lau, Yingyi Qian, and Gerald Roland, "Reform without Losers: An Interpretation of China's Dual-Track Approach to Transition," *Journal of Political Economy* 108 (February 2000).

19. I try to account for why Chinese economic reforms, particularly reforms involving urban workers, have not led to widespread political instability and demands for political liberalization. These demands, had they appeared, may or may not have led to a process of democratization. Therefore, this argument falls short of explaining the failure or success of democratization, but rather focuses on an arguably prior social condition: demands for political change from society.

20. See Kathryn Sikkink, *Ideas and Institutions: Developmentalism in Brazil and Argentina* (Ithaca: Cornell University Press, 1991). On China's developmentalist local governments see Marc Blecher and Vivienne Shue, "Into Leather: State-Led Development and the Private Sector in Xinji," *China Quarterly* (2001); and their earlier book on the same county, *Tethered Deer: Government and Economy in a Chinese County* (Stanford, Calif.: Stanford University Press, 1996); and Marc Blecher, "Developmental State, Entrepreneurial State: The Political Economy of Socialist Reform in Xinji Municipality and Guanghan County," "in Gordon White, ed. *The Road to Crisis: The Chinese State in the Era of Economic Reform,* (London: Macmillan, 1991), 265–91. See also Jonathan Unger and Anita Chan, "Inheritors of the Boom: Private Enterprises and the Role of the Local Government in a Rural South China Township," *China Journal* 42 (July 1999) 45–74.

21. Gordon White and Robert Wade, "Developmental States and Markets in East Asia: An Introduction," in Gordon White, ed., *Developmental States in East Asia* (New York: St. Martin's Press, 1988), p. 1.

22. The East Asian development model has served as an alternative model for Chinese leaders since at least the late 1980s. Its attractiveness lies not only in the economic success of many East Asian economies in the post–World War II era, but also in its rejection of both state socialism and neoliberal capitalism. Like socialism, the East Asian "developmental state" retains the primacy of a strong central state directing economic growth. Moreover, democracy is not a prerequisite of East Asian economic success. Unlike socialism, the East Asian developmental model entails integration into the global economy and has yielded high rates of economic growth for long periods of time. On East Asia see Gordon White ed., *Developmental States in East Asia* (Basingstoke, UK: Macmillan, 1988). On the application of developmentalism in China see Joseph Fewsmith, *China after Tiananmen: The Politics of Transition* (New York: Cambridge University Press, 2001), 77.

CHAPTER 2: CONTAGIOUS CAPITALISM

1. Joseph A. Schumpeter, "Capitalism in the Postwar World (1943)," in Harry F. Dahms, ed. *Transformations of Capitalism: Economy, Society, and the State in Modern Times* (New York: New York University Press, 2000), 154.

2. See Lau, Qian, and Roland (2000).

3. Works on labor that draw attention to the declining status of urban state-sector workers as well as the abysmal working conditions of migrant and rural workers include Anita Chan, *China's Workers under Assault: The Exploitation of Labor in a Globalizing Economy* (New York: M. E. Sharpe, 2001); "Chan Globalization, China's 'Free' (Read Bonded) Labour Market and the Chinese Trade

Unions," *Asia Pacific Business Review,* special issue on Globalization and Labor Market Regulation (2000); Ching Kwan Lee, "From Organized Dependence to Disorganized Despotism: Changing Labour Regimes in Chinese Factories," *China Quarterly* 157 (1999); and Dorothy Solinger, *Contesting Citizenship in China: Peasant Migrants, the State, and the Logic of the Market* (Berkeley and Los Angeles: University of California Press, 1999).

4. Barry Naughton, *Growing Out of the Plan: Chinese Economic Reform, 1978–1993* (New York: Cambridge University Press, 1995), 329.

5. I am dating FDI liberalization from 1979 with the decision to form Special Economic Zones (SEZs). Development of the private sector began in the 1980s, in particular the rise of the "Wenzhou model" which popularized the development of private businesses in coastal Zhejiang. The national development of the private sector, however, occurred after 1992. SOE reform has occurred since the early 1980s; however, most of these reforms were of the "tinkering" variant, to use Kornai's definition. Significant reform of the SOE sector should be dated from 1992 with limited privatization recognized by the central government in 1997 at the Fifteenth Party Congress. See Barbara Krup and Hans Hendrischke, "China Incorporated: Property Rights, Networks, and the Emergence of a Private Business Sector in China," *Managerial Finance* 29:12 (2003). On the later privatization of rural collective industry, see Susan H. Whiting, *Power and Wealth in Rural China: The Political Economy of Institutional Change* (New York: Cambridge University Press, 2001).

6. Other works have also focused on China's liberalization to foreign trade and investment as a dynamic process in which domestic and external interests were important in pushing forward reform. They include Jude Howell, *China Opens Its Doors: The Politics of Economic Transition* (Boulder, Colo.: Lynne Reinner Publishers, 1993); Dali Yang, *Beyond Beijing: Liberalization and the Regions in China* (New York: Routledge, 1997); and David Zweig, *Internationalizing China: Domestic Interests and Global Linkages* (Ithaca: Cornell University Press, 2002). Howell's book also examines the effect on labor politics, but does not explore in detail the effects of openness on domestic firms.

7. Peter Evans, "The Eclipse of the State? Reflections on Stateness in an Era of Globalization," *World Politics* 50:1 (1997), 65. The globalization debate is wide-ranging and contradictory. The strand that I question here is, however, one of the most powerful subthemes within the globalization debate and unites both neoliberal proponents of globalization and neo-Marxist critics of global capitalism with the assumption that globalization reduces state power. For a summary of the globalization debates see David Held, Anthony McGrew, David Goldblatt, and Jonathan Perraton, *Global Transformations: Politics, Economics, and Culture* (Stanford, Calif.: Stanford University Press, 2001), 2–20.

8. Seymour Martin Lipset, "Some Social Requisites of Democracy: Economic Development and Political Legitimacy," *American Political Science Review* 53 (March 1959).

9. For a recent review and in-depth analysis of the relationship between democracy and development see Adam Przeworski and Fernando Limongi, "Modernization: Theories and Facts," *World Politics* 49 (January 1997); and Adam Przeworski, Michael Alvarez, Jose Antonio Cheibub, and Fernando Limongi,

Democracy and Development: Political Institutions and Well-Being in the World, 1950–1990 (New York: Cambridge University Press, 2000). Przeworski et al. find that the causal link posited by modernization theories is not strongly supported by the empirical evidence.

10. Held et al. divide this "hyperglobalist" thesis into neoliberal and radical/neo-Marxist camps. There is of course much disagreement on the normative implications of convergence, particularly the debates on the fate of the social welfare state and the implications of globalization on the environment and labor. David Held, Anthony McGrew, David Goldblatt, and Jonathan Perraton, *Global Transformations: Politics, Economics, and Culture* (Stanford, Calif.: Stanford University Press, 1999), 3–5.

11. Susan Strange, *The Retreat of the State: The Diffusion of Power in the World Economy* (Cambridge: Cambridge University Press, 1996).

12. Joel Hellman, "Winners Take All: The Politics of Partial Reform in Post-communist Transitions," *World Politics* 50:2 (January 1998), 203–35.

13. I use Yang's "competitive liberalization" here but the concept is also similar to Zweig's "segmented deregulation." It could be argued that Zweig's definition is more comprehensive because the notion of deregulation focuses attention on the power and rents that accrued to "gatekeepers" of the deregulation process. Despite these differences of emphases, I use these terms in this chapter more or less interchangeably to convey the notion of uneven liberalization across regions. See Zweig (2002); Yang (1997).

14. Recombinant property is defined as "novel forms of interorganizational ownership that blurred the boundaries of public and private, as well as the boundaries of the enterprises themselves." David Stark and Laszlo Bruszt, *Postsocialist Pathways: Transforming Politics and Property in East Central Europe* (New York: Cambridge University Press, 1998), 143.

15. SOEs competed increasingly with the nonstate sector generally for profits and market share. I focus here specifically on competition for skilled labor and managerial talent. On competition for labor, especially skilled labor, and the SOE sector's declining labor monopsony, see Margaret Maurer-Fazio, "Labor Reform in China: Crossing the River by Feeling the Stones," *Comparative Economic Studies* 37:4 (Winter 1995): 111–23 and Xiao-yuan Dong and Louis Putterman, "China's State Owned-Enterprises in the first Reform Decade: An Analysis of a Declining Monopsony," *Economics of Planning* 35 (2002): 109–39.

16. Gabriella Montinola, Yingyi Qian, and Barry Weingast, "Federalism, Chinese Style: The Political Basis for Economic Success," *World Politics* 48:1 (1996), 50–81.

17. See note 13.

18. For variations on this argument, which has become an increasingly important part of an explanation for China's reform success, see Zweig (2002); Yang (1997); and Montinola, Qian, Weingast (1996).

19. Zweig (2002).

20. Some of the initial consequences emanating from ownership changes were noted by Barry Naughton, "Implications of the State Monopoly over Industry and Its Relaxation," *Modern China* 18:1 (January 1992), 14–41. Naughton focuses on the fiscal consequences of the growing nonstate sector. This is an important early article on ownership liberalization.

21. Dorothy Solinger (1999), chaps. 5–6. For estimates of labor mobility and the hiring of migrants, see *China in the World Economy: The Domestic Policy Challenges* (Paris: OECD, 2002), 551. They find that nonstate urban firms are more than five times more likely to hire migrants than are SOEs.

22. Robert Weller and Jiansheng Li,. "From State-Owned Enterprise to Joint Venture: A Case Study of the Crisis in Urban Social Services," *China Journal* 43 (January 2000), 83–99); Feng Chen, "Industrial Restructuring and Workers' Resistance in China," *Modern China* 29:2 (April 2003), 237–62; X. L. Ding, "Illicit Asset-Stripping in Chinese Firms," *China Journal* 43 (January 2000).

23. Edward Gu, "Foreign Direct Investment and the Restructuring of Chinese State-Owned Enterprises, 1992–1995: A New Institutionalist Perspective," *China Information* 12:3 (1997–98); Shu-Yun Ma, "Foreign Participation in China's Privatization," *Communist Economies and Economic Transformation* 4 (1996); Yasheng Huang, *Selling China: Foreign Direct Investment during the Reform Era* (New York: Cambridge University Press, 2003), 130.

24. An analysis of the logic of institutional breakdown in socialist states is Valerie Bunce, *Subversive Institutions: The Design and the Destruction of Socialism and the State* (Cambridge: Cambridge University Press, 1999). See also Andrew Walder, ed., *The Waning of the Communist State: Economic Origins of Political Decline in China and Hungary* (Berkeley and Los Angeles: University of California, 1995).

25. Shaomin Li, Shuhe Li, and Weiying Zhang, "The Road to Capitalism: Competition and Institutional Change in China," *Journal of Comparative Economics* 28 (June 2000): 269–92. This article is a large, quantitative study of firms using China's industrial census. It does not focus on the particular effects of foreign-invested firms but generally finds that cross-regional competition leads to market-conforming behavior by managers of SOEs and collectives.

26. Articles in the national media as well as more scholarly articles on the problems of reform hammered away at this point of an "unequal playing field" between SOEs and FIEs. These articles focused on the heavy employment burden, the gap in managers' salaries, and the inability of SOEs to retain skilled workers. "Should one take a yearly salary of hundreds of thousand RMB?" (*shubaiwanyuan nianxin gaibugai na*) *Nanfang Zhoumo*, December 20, 1996, 2; "How can SOEs retain people?" (*guoqi zenyang liuzhuren*) *Renmin Ribao*, November 19, 1996, 10; (*qiangzhanshichang bixu guimo jingying*) *Zhongguo Gongshang Shibao*, April 22, 1997, 7; "Establish a Consciousness of Talent, Perfect the Two Mechanisms," (*shulirencaiyishi jianquan liangge jizhi*) *Workers Daily*, April 8, 1997, 7. The two mechanisms include the collective contract system (to make it more difficult for workers to leave) and the incentive wage system (to improve skilled workers' wages). "Skilled Workers Call for Policy Help," (*jishugongren huhuan zhengce fuzhu*) *Workers Daily*, December 13, 1996, 3; "Perfect the Adjustment Mechanism for the Distribution of Individual Salaries," (*wanshanqiyegerenshouru fenpei tiaokongjizhi*) *Zhongguo Gongshang Shibao*, May 5, 1997, 3; "The Rights and Interests of Enterprises Must Also Be Protected,"(*qiyequanyi yebixu weihu*) *Jingji Ribao*, October 9, 1996.

27. Barry Naughton uses this word, "disarticulation," to describe the relation-

ship between the foreign-invested sector of the economy and the rest of the Chinese economy. Naughton (1995).

28. These statements are based on the author's observations while doing field research in firms from 1997 to 2003. In joint ventures, management positions were often filled by former SOE employees (often the partner of the foreign firm), but production positions were almost exclusively filled by young urban residents or young rural migrants. In all of the foreign-invested firms except the Sino-American JVs, migrant workers were used for production positions. In the Japanese JVs, the American WFOE, and the Hong Kong JV migrants made up an increasing part of the workforce (new hires were predominantly migrants). In the Taiwanese companies, all of the production workers were migrants. Woman workers make up the vast majority of the workforce in the electronics industry and other relatively labor-intensive industries. See Ching Kwan Lee, *Gender and the South China Miracle: Two Worlds of Factory Women* (Berkeley and Los Angeles: University of California Press, 1998), 68–70.

29. In a speech at the National Conference of Labor Dispute Resolution, an SOE manager complained of the inability of SOEs to retain workers as they left in droves for the private and foreign sectors. Chen Quansheng stated, "presently SOE workers fire the enterprise more than SOEs fire workers." "Speech of Chen Quansheng at the National Conference of Labor Dispute Resolution," *Handling and Research of Labor Disputes*, (laodong zhengyi chuli yu yanjiu) (January 1996). Carrie Lee, "Industry Frustrated by Job-Hopping, *South China Morning Post*, August 9, 1997.

30. Mary Gallagher, "Why Labor Laws Fail to Protect Workers," *China Rights Forum* (Summer 1997), 12–15.

31. This schematic depiction of legal convergence is borrowed from an article explaining how to reduce staff in Japanese-invested enterprises in China. In an interview in 1999, one of the authors (a Japanese lawyer representing Japanese-invested enterprises in China) described how important the convergence of labor laws was in determining changes in enterprise behavior. In Hiroaki Tsukamoto et al., "Restructuring FIEs in China and Procedures to Cut Staff (*chugoku niokeru gaisho taishi kigyo no resutora oyobi) International Commercial Law Journal* (kokusai shoji ho) 27:5 (1999) 1–20; Interview, Japanese labor lawyer, Shanghai, July 1999; interview, Chinese labor lawyer, Shanghai, July 1999.

32. See articles in Gary Jefferson and Inderjit Singh, *Enterprise Reform in China: Ownership, Transition, and Performance* (New York: Oxford University Press, 1999); World Bank, *Bureaucrats in Business: The Economics and Politics of Government Ownership* (New York: Oxford University Press, 1995). There still remains considerable debate as to whether state-owned enterprise inefficiency is a result of differences in pure ownership or policy differences, especially political or social obligations of state firms. For the political and policy causes of SOE sector inefficiency see John Waterbury, *Exposed to Innumerable Delusions: Public Enterprise and State Power in Egypt, India, Mexico, and Turkey* (Cambridge: Cambridge University Press, 1993), 107–34.

33. Problems of the SOE sectors are detailed in Edward Steinfeld, *Forging Reform in China: The Fate of State-Owned Industry* (Cambridge: Cambridge Uni-

versity Press, 1998) and Jiagui Chen, *Research on the Development of China's State-Owned Enterprise Reform* (*zhongguo guoyou qiye gaige fazhan yanjiu*) (Beijing: Economic Management Press, 2000) On the larger impact of the SOE problem, see Nicholas R. Lardy, *China's Unfinished Economic Revolution* (Washington, D.C.: Brookings Institution, 1998.).

34. The debate over public versus private industry, while already apparent in the 1980s, was minimal because of the state's continuing adherence to the primacy of the state sector and to the continued faith among the leaders that the state sector could be turned around without fundamental changes in property rights. The debate changed in the 1990s as the private sector grew rapidly, FDI inflows surged, and China's integration into the global trading regime deepened. For a discussion of the intellectual and elite debates that surfaced during this time see Joseph Fewsmith, *China since Tiananmen: The Politics of Transition* (New York: Cambridge University Press, 2001).

35. Janos Kornai, *The Socialist System: The Political Economy of Communism* (Princeton: Princeton University Press, 1992), 433.

36. Aslund argues that Russia's mistake was not in diverging from the Chinese path but from following it too closely when their objective differences (in the labor supply, level of industrialization, length of time under communism, etc.) were so stark. Anders Aslund, *How Russia Became a Market Economy* (Washington D.C.: Brookings Institution, 1995), 13–17.

37. Anders Aslund, *Gorbachev's Struggle for Economic Reform* (London: Pinter Publishers, 1991).

38. On the lack of success in labor reform see Michel Korzec, "Contract Labor, the Right to Work, and New Labor Laws in the People's Republic of China," *Comparative Economic Studies* 30:2 (Summer 1988): 117–49.

39. Xueguang Zhou, "Unorganized Interests and Collective Action in Communist China," *American Sociological Review* 58 (February 1993). Zhou argues that under state socialism "state monopoly of the public sphere fosters and reproduces large numbers of individual behaviors with similar claims, patterns, and targets." Extending this argument to all state socialist countries, it is plausible that exclusive and primary reform of the state sector would intensify the reactions of urban workers affected by such reforms, leading to greater likelihood of mobilization and resistance.

40. Akos Rona-Tas, "The Second Economy as a Subversive Force," in Andrew Walder, ed., *The Waning of the Communist State: economic origins of political decline in China and Hungary* (Berkeley and Los Angeles: University of California Press, 1995), 79.

41. Ibid., 78.

42. Hungary's reforms in the early 1980s led to the gradual loss of control over enterprises as managers grew more powerful and, with the help of the growing private economy, spun off state assets into privately controlled commercial entities. Roman Frydman, Andrzej Rapaczynski, and Joel Turkewitz, "Transition to a Private Property Regime in the Czech Republic and Hungary," in Wing Thye Woo, Stephen Parker, and Jeffrey Sachs, eds., *Economies in Transition: Comparing Asia and Eastern Europe* (Cambridge: MIT Press, 1997), 53.

43. Ibid, 51.

44. For example, Barrett McCormick and Jonathan Unger, eds., *China after Socialism: In the Footsteps of Eastern Europe or East Asia* (New York: M. E. Sharpe, 1996).

45. The top ten firms in Korea accounted for 63.5 percent of country's GDP in 1987, showing the very large dominance of the chaebols within the Korean economy. In Taiwan, however, the ten largest firms, four of which were state-owned, made up only 14.3 percent of GDP. Most of Taiwan's growth came from the small-to-medium, ethnically Taiwanese private firms. Gary Gereffi, "Big Business and the State," in Gary Gereffi and Donald Wyman, eds., *Manufacturing Miracles: Paths of Industrialization in Latin America and East Asia* (Princeton: Princeton University Press, 1990), 92–96.

46. Yun Tae Kim, "Neoliberalism and the Decline of the Developmental State," *Journal of Contemporary Asia* 29:4 (1999).

47. On the development of the private economy see Ross Garnaut, Ligang Song, Yang Yao, Xiaolu Wang, *Private Enterprise in China* (Canberra: Asia Pacific Press; Beijing: China Center for Economic Research, 2001); Zhang Houyi, Ming Lizhi, Liang Zhuanyun, eds., *Bluebook of Private Enterprises, No. 4, 2002* (*zhongguo siying qiye fazhan baogao*) Beijing: Social Sciences Documentation Publishing House, 2002. In comparison to foreign enterprises in China, see Yasheng Huang, *Selling China* (2002).

48. Tun-Jen Cheng, "Political Regimes and Development Strategies: Korea and Taiwan," in Gereffi and Wyman (1990), 142.

49. Gereffi (1990), 98.

50. Yin-Wah Chu, "Labor and Democratization in South Korea and Taiwan," *Journal of Contemporary Asia* 28:2 (1998).

51. Sejin Pak, "Two Forces of Democratization in Korea," *Journal of Contemporary Asia* 28:1 (1998).

52. Tun-Jen Cheng, "Democratizing the Quasi-Leninist Regime in Taiwan," *World Politics* 41 (July 1989). Cheng writes on the social character of the political opposition in Taiwan, "This new political opposition is essentially a middle-class movement, the consequence of rapid economic development. . . . Many of its members are social-science trained intellectuals with professional skills and legal expertise. *Moreover, they are socially connected to small and medium businesses*." Cheng, 474. (emphasis added.)

53. Karl Fields, "Strong States and Business Organization in Korea and Taiwan," in Sylvia Maxfield and Ben Schneider, eds., *Business and the State in Developing Countries,* (Ithaca: Cornell University Press, 1997), 146.

54. On the problem of private entrepreneurs' access to credit see Kellee Tsai, *Back-Alley Banking: Private Entrepreneurs in China* (Ithaca: Cornell University Press, 2002). On other problems facing the private sector see Yasheng Huang, *Selling China: Foreign Direct Investment during the Reform Era* (New York: Cambridge University Press, 2003); Zhangg Houyi, Ming Lizhi, and Liang Zhuanyun, eds., *Bluebook of Private Enterprises, No. 4, 2002* (*zhongguo siying qiye fazhan baogao*) (Beijing: Social Sciences Documentation Publishing House, 2002).

55. On the Three Represents, see James Kynge, "China's Capitalists Get a Party Invitation," *Financial Times,* August 16, 2002; Robert J. Saiget, "Chinese Leader under Fire over Capitalists in Communist Party,"*Agence France Presse,* August 14, 2001. See also Willy Wo-Lap Lam, "China's Struggle for 'Democracy'" www .cnn.com/world; Accessed August 7, 2001.

56. See, for example, James Kynge. "China's Capitalists Get a Party Invitation," *Financial Times,* August 16, 2002.

57. For in-depth analysis of the relatively benign political attitudes and behaviors of China's private entrepreneurs see Bruce Dickson, *Red Capitalists in China: The Party, Private Entrepreneurs, and Prospects for Political Change* (New York: Cambridge University Press, 2003).

58. I am not weighing the relative benefits and disadvantages of continued authoritarianism. In fact, I am overlooking the costs of continued authoritarianism (political repression, human rights violations, arbitrary punishment, torture, and lack of freedom of speech and religion, etc.) The focus here is on what may in fact be happening below the surface of continued political authoritarianism.

59. See Kevin O'Brien, "Rightful Resistance." *World Politics* 49:1 (1996): 31– 55 and essays by Isabelle Thireau and Mary E. Gallagher in Neil J. Diamant, Stanley Lubman, and Kevin O'Brien, eds., *Engaging the Law in China: State, Society, and Possibilities for Justice* (Palo Alto, Calif.: Stanford University Press, 2005). See also Ching Kwan Lee, "From the Specter of Mao to the Spirit of the Law: Labor Insurgency in China." *Theory and Society* 31:2 (April 2002): 189– 228.

60. Many scholars of China's legal development have noted the reliance on foreign laws for the creation of China's domestic laws. Ann Seidman, Robert Seidman, and Janice Payne, *Legislative Drafting for Market Reform: Some Lessons from China* (New York: St. Martin's Press, 1997).

61. Ann Kent, "China, International Organizations and Regimes: The ILO as a Case Study in Organizational Learning, *Pacific Affairs* 70:4 (Winter 1997–98), 517–33; Margaret Pearson, "The Major Multilateral Economic Institutions Engage China," in Alastair Iain Johnston and Robert S. Ross, eds., *Engaging China: The management of an emerging power* (London and New York: Routledge, 1999), 207–34.

62. The Chinese and Soviet reforms both used decentralization and limited marketization as key early reforms. However, Soviet reforms were concentrated in the existing industrial and bureaucratic sectors while Chinese reforms tended to implement the more daring reforms in new sectors, including the foreign-invested sector, or in the rural economy. Reforms that were at first on the margins of the Chinese economy grew in importance over time as they unleashed new competitive pressures on the socialist core. On the Soviet economy and some comparisons with China, see Ed A. Hewett, *Reforming the Soviet Economy* (Washington, D.C.: The Brookings Institution, 1988); "Economic Reform in the USSR, Eastern Europe, and China: The Politics of Economics," *American Economic Review* 79:2 (May 1989); Marshall I. Goldman and Merle Goldman, "Soviet and Chinese Economic Reform," *Foreign Affairs* 66:3 (1988); Janine Ludlam, "Reform and the Redefinition of the Social Contract under Gorbachev," *World Poli-*

tics 43:2 (January 1991). See also Joseph E. Stiglitz, "Whither Reform? Ten Years of the Transition." Keynote address, World Bank Annual Bank Conference on Development Economics, Washington, D.C., April 28–30, 1999.

CHAPTER 3: BLURRING BOUNDARIES

1. Mainland researchers used this phrase to criticize the large-scale acquisitions of state firms by foreign investors, in particular a Hong Kong investment company. China Strategy Investment Corporation (HK) bought out SOEs and then listed the new companies on *foreign* stock exchanges, thus the critical phrase "taking the motherland public" (*bazuguo shangshijizi*), but public in another nation's stock exchange. It aptly demonstrates how in the later stages of reform, foreign acquisition of SOEs has become a major facet of China's privatization. Liu Lisheng et al., eds., *Foreign Capital's Acquisition of State-Owned Enterprises: Analysis and Countermeasures* (*waizi binggou guoyou qiye: shizheng fenxi yu duice yanjiu.*) (Beijing: Zhongguo Jingji Chubanshe, 1997), 328.

2. *Global Development Finance: Analysis and Summary Tables, 1999* (Washington, D.C.: International Bank for Reconstruction and Development/World Bank, 2000), 51.

3. Jiang Xiaojuan, "China's Foreign Direct Investment: Its Contribution to Growth, Structural Upgrading, and Competitiveness," *Social Sciences in China* 24:2 (Summer 2003).

4. Yasheng Huang, "Internal and External Reforms: Experiences and Lessons from China, Part I," www.chinaonline.com, date accessed September 22, 2000.

5. Huang writes that "the extent of China's dependency on FDI is in fact extraordinarily high already. . . . Not only is the absolute size of FDI large, its relative size measured by FDI/capital formation ratio surpassed that of many countries in the world." Ibid.

6. Stark and Bruszt (1998).

7. Huang (2000), 1.

8. "Raking It In: China Ranks as World's Fourth Largest FDI Receiver in 1999," www.chinaonline.com, October 10, 2000; "Foreign Investment in China," U.S.-China Business Council, May 2003, www.uschina.org/china-statistics.html, date accessed August 28, 2004.

9. China's high tariffs have begun to fall due to its accession to the World Trade Organization in December, 2001. FDI inflows are, however, expected to rise as barriers to foreign investment in many sectors are also being dismantled.

10. The importance of separating the two components is demonstrated well in Yasheng Huang, *FDI in China: An Asian Perspective* (Singapore and Hong Kong: Chinese University Press, 1998).

11. Reports of abuse, abysmal working conditions, and horrific accidents appeared in both the domestic and foreign press. "Several Existing Problems in FIEs" (*sanziqiyemuqian cunzai de jige wenti*) *Development Research Centre of the State Council, PRC,* November 7, 1992, 1–13; Wang Hongyi, "Dream of the City: An Examination of the Violation of Workers' Rights in Some FIEs" (*weicheng zhi-*

meng: bufen sanziqiyeqinfan zhigongquanyitoushi) Chinese Worker (zhongguo gongren) 5 (1995), 18–27; "Workers in Foreign-Invested Enterprises," *China Labor Bulletin* (March 1996).

12. Margaret Pearson, *Joint Ventures in the Peoples Republic of China.* (Princeton: Princeton University Press, 1991).

13. Huang (1998), 30; The lack of sufficient legal protection for patents is one reason for the reluctance to transfer technology to Chinese partners. See Tang Zhongshun, "Transfer of Patented Technology to China," in Richard Robinson, ed., *Foreign Capital and Technology in China,* (New York: Praeger Press, 1987), 75–82.

14. For example, Chen Chunlai's summary and analysis of FDI policy evolution argues that the SEZs should be viewed as a "pioneering effort" for the later coastal development strategy, implicitly assuming that SEZs were a planned preparatory stage for much greater liberalization. Chen (1997), 8. The argument presented here argues instead the CDS policy innovation was a result of failures in the SEZ policy and pressure from other regions to extend the preferential policies.

15. These works include Susan Shirk, *The Political Logic of Economic Reform in China* (Berkeley and Los Angeles: University of California, 1993); Barry Naughton, *Growing Out of the Plan: Chinese Economic Reform, 1978–1993* (New York: Cambridge University Press, 1995); and Dali Yang, *Beyond Beijing: Liberalization and the Regions in China* (New York: Routledge, 1997).

16. On the role of ethnic Chinese social networks in China's FDI liberalization see Hongying Wang, *Weak State, Strong Networks: The Institutional Dynamics of Foreign Investment in China* (Hong Kong: Oxford University Press, 2001).

17. Naughton's *Growing out of the Plan* is the best example of this line of argument, covering both urban and rural phenomena. Its publication in 1995 causes Naughton to just miss the FDI boom and subsequent domestic reforms, although he does briefly note the increasing importance of the foreign sector. Barry Naughton (1995), 302–04. See also Kate Xiao Zhou, *How the Farmers Changed China: Power of the People* (Boulder, Colo.: Westview Press, 1996).

18. Yasheng Huang, *Selling China: Foreign Direct Investment during the Reform Era* (New York: Cambridge University Press, 2003).

19. Huang (1998), 29.

20. Ibid, 26.

21. Samuel Ho and Ralph Huenemann *China's Open Door Policy: The Quest for Foreign Technology and Capital* (Vancouver: University of British Columbia Press, 1984); and Pearson (1991).

22. In 1961 half of the Hong Kong workforce was employed in manufacturing; by 1997 this figure had fallen to 15 percent. In neighboring Guangdong Province, by 1998, 5 million Chinese were working in Hong Kong invested factories. "The Ever-Spreading Tentacles of Hong Kong," *Economist,* June 20, 1998, S15. See also Barry Naughton, ed., *The China Circle: Economics and Technology in the PRC, Taiwan, and Hong Kong* (Washington, D.C.: Brookings Institution Press, 1997). For general accounts of trends in FDI from overseas Chinese see articles in Sumner Croix, Michael Plummer, and Keun Lee, eds., *Emerging Patterns of East Asian Investment in China: From Korea, Taiwan, and Hong Kong* (New

York: M. E. Sharpe, 1995); Nomura Research Institute Staff *The New Wave of Foreign Direct Investment in Asia* (Singapore: Institute of Southeast Asian Studies and Nomura Research Institute, 1995).

23. Wei Yuming, "Absorbing Foreign Investment," in *The Open Policy at Work* (Beijing: Beijing Review Publications, 1985), 41.

24. Ibid.

25. For an overall analysis of the Special Economic Zone policy, see Jung-Dong Park, *The Special Economic Zones of China and Their Impact on Its Economic Development* (Westport, Conn.: Praeger Publishers, 1997).

26. Sino-Foreign Equity Joint Venture Law, adopted at the Second Session of the Fifth National People's Congress on July 1, 1979, and revised on April 4, 1990. Herald Translation Services, *Chinalaw Web* http://www.qis.net/chinalaw, date accessed August 28, 2004.

27. Barry Naughton (1995), 11.

28. Ibid.

29. These characteristics are reviewed in chapter 4. In general state firms were bureaucratic, had lax labor discipline, and were not oriented to pursue productivity and efficiency.

30. Barry Naughton, "Economic Policy Reform in the PRC and Taiwan," in *The China Circle: Economics and Technology in the PRC, Taiwan, and Hong Kong* (Washington, D.C.: Brookings Institution Press, 1997), 93.

31. Jamie P. Horsley, "Chinese Labor," *China Business Review* (May-June 1984), 16–25.

32. Barry Naughton (1997), 97.

33. Chen Chunlai, "The Evolution and Main Features of China's Foreign Direct Investment Policies," Chinese Economies Research Centre, University of Adelaide, *Working Paper Series* 97:15 (December 1997).

34. Susan Shirk, *The Political Logic of Economic Reform in China* (Berkeley and Los Angeles: University of California Press, 1993), 50.

35. "Wholly Foreign Owned Enterprise Law of the People's Republic of China." Adopted at the Fourth Session of the Sixth National People's Congress, promulgated by order No. 39 of the President of the People's Republic of China and effective as of April 12, 1986. www.qis.net/chinalaw/prclaw16.htm, date accessed August 28, 2004.

36. Naughton (1997), 100.

37. "Provisions of the State Council Concerning the Encouragement of Investments by Compatriots from Taiwan." Adopted by the Tenth Executive Meeting of the State Council on June 25, 1988 promulgated by Decree no. 7 of the State Council of the People's Republic of China on July 3, 1988, www.qis.net/chinalaw/prclaw13, date accessed August 28, 2004. "Provisions of the State Council Concerning the Encouragement of Investments by Overseas Chinese and Compatriots from Hong Kong and Macao." Promulgated by Decree no. 64 of the State Council of the People's Republic of China on August 19, 1990. www.qis.net/chinalaw/prclaw17, date accessed August 28, 2004.

38. Naughton (1997), 100.

39. Shirk (1993), 48.

40. Dali Yang notes that by the end of 1991 China had only 111 development

zones, including 27 approved by the central government. But by the end of September 1992, there were 1,951 development zones. A later report estimated that including development zones set up at the township level by 1993, there were 8,700 zones nationwide. Yang (1997), 56.

41. Ibid. For an account of the competition that now occurs between the established SEZs on the coast and the new development zones of the inland regions, see "Shenzhen Stays Ahead: Small Economic Zones in Guangdong Pose Competitive Threat to Shenzhen, China." *China Economic Review* 8:7 (July 1998), 17–19.

42. For statistical trends see U.S.-China Business Council Website, which regularly publishes updated information on FDI trends, http://www.uschina.org/statistics/03-01.html, date accessed August 28, 2004. "Wholly Foreign-Invested Enterprises Make Up 39% of Direct Foreign Investment into China," www.chinaonline.com/issues/econ_news, June 1, 2000, date accessed August 28, 2004, Edward Paley, "Mushrooming WFOEs Prove a Marriage of Convenience," *South China Morning Post,* June 21, 1993: 2; "Multinationals in China: Going It Alone," *Economist,* April 19, 1997, 64.

43. Wilfried Vanhonacker (1997),"Entering China: An Unconventional Approach," *Harvard Business Review,* March–April 1997, 130.

44. Interview, deputy personnel manager, Taiwanese WFOE, Shanghai, July, 1997. Interview, Manager, Taiwanese WFOE, Shanghai, July 1997. Two Sino-Japanese general managers also supported this view with their preference for a partner that was not in manufacturing. Interview, general manager, Sino-Japanese JV, Tianjin, July 1997. Interview, personnel manager, Sino-Japanese JV, Shanghai, July 1997, July 1999.

45. Interview, deputy personnel manager, Taiwanese WFOE, Shanghai, July 1997. Interview, Manager, Taiwanese WFOE, July 1997.

46. Ibid.

47. Interview with associate professor of sociology, Beijing Academy of Social Sciences, July 1999.

48. Interview, HR manager, Sino-American JV, Shanghai, October 2003.

49. Trend noted in Paul Delisle, "Salary and Benefit Reforms Prove New Employer Challenge," *South China Morning Post,* April 15, 1994, 2; "Multinationals in China: Going It Alone," *Economist,* April 19, 1997, 64. For the logistics of converting a JV to a WFOE see Daniel C. K. Chow, "Reorganization and Conversion of a Joint Venture into a Wholly Foreign-Owned Enterprise in the People's Republic of China," *Tulane Law Review* (December 1998). The guiding regulations include "Several Regulations Regarding the Change of Ownership Interest of the Investors in Foreign Investment Enterprises," promulgated May 28, 1997 by the Ministry of Foreign Trade and Economic Cooperation and State Administration for Industry and Commerce. http://www.qis.net.chinalaw/prclaw40.htm, date accessed August 28, 2004.

50. Kimberly Silver, "Lessons Learned," *China Business Review* (May–June 1998), 22.

51. Dong Dong Zhang, "Negotiating for a Liberal Economic Regime: The Case of Japanese FDI in China," *Pacific Review* 11:1 (1998): 51–78.

52. Zhu Rongji gave a speech at the Congress later excerpted in the domestic media. Zhu Rongji, "Cut Staff, Increase Profits, Distribute the Laid Off Workers,

Standardize Bankruptcy, Encourage Mergers" (*jianyuan zengxiao, xiagangfenliu, guifanpochan, gulijianbing*). Reprinted in *Jingji Guanli Wenzhai*, March, 1997, 6–7; Kathy Chen, "Chinese President Rachets Up Reforms," *Wall Street Journal,* April 7, 1997, A11.

53. If fully implemented this would have affected over 100,000 small and medium-sized state enterprises. Jean-Francois Huchet, "The 15th Congress and the Reform of Ownership: A Decisive Stage for Chinese State Enterprises," *China Perspectives,* 14 (November–December 1997), 17. Lin and Zhu found that by the summer of 1998 the state retained predominant ownership in over half of the over 40,000 industrial enterprises that were surveyed. Yi-min Lin and Tian Zhu, "Ownership Restructuring in Chinese State Industry: An Analysis of Evidence on Initial Organizational Changes," *China Quarterly* (June 2001).

54. Edward Gu, "Foreign Direct Investment and the Restructuring of Chinese State-Owned Enterprises (1992–1995): A New Institutionalist Perspective," *China Information* 12:3 (1997/98), 47.

55. Ibid, 18.

56. Ibid; Shu-yan Ma, "Foreign Participation in China's Privatization," *Communist Economies and Economic Transformation* 4 (1996); X. L. Ding, "Informal Privatization through Internationalization: The Rise of Nomenklatura Capitalism in China's Offshore Businesses," *British Journal of Political Science* 30 (2000), 121–46.

57. Kathy Chen, "Orient Express: China's Businesses Push for Faster Economic Reform," *Wall Street Journal,* October, 16, 1997.

58. A few examples include Dongshui Su et al., eds., *Research on China's Foreign-Invested Enterprises (Zhongguo Sanzi Qiye Yanjiu)* (Shanghai: Fudan University Press, 1997); Haitao Zhang et al., eds. *Will Foreign Capital Swallow Up China? Where Should National Industry Go? (Waizi Nengfou Tunbing Zhongguo: Minzuqiye ying xiang hechuqu)* (Beijing: Qiye Guanli Chuban She, 1997); and Liu Lisheng, et al., (1997).

59. "The U.S.-China Business Council: Forecast '98," The United States-China Business Council, January 29, 1998.

60. The term "greenfield" refers to production facilities, usually within development zones, that are built from scratch on land previously used for agricultural production. Greenfield development avoids using outdated or dilapidated factories and equipment and has been the favored choice of most investors, especially large companies from the West and Japan. James Harding, "End of the China Goldrush," *Financial Times,* March 25, 1999, 15.

61. Kathy Wilhelm, "Out of Business," *Far Eastern Economic Review,* February 18, 1999, 10–11.

62. Ibid., 11. Similar figures also quoted in Joe Studwell, "Workers Wary over Chinese Buyout Program," *Journal of Commerce,* October 21, 1997, 4A.

63. "China: Fuzhou Forges Ahead," *China Daily,* May 23, 1999, 7. Source: World Reporter—Asia Intelligence Wire.

64. Liu Lisheng et al. (1997), 51.

65. Michael M. Hickman and Julie Bloch Mendelsohn, "China's Laws Now Give Investors More Options," *National Law Journal,* March 2, 1998, C14. They argue that "a foreign investor wishing to invest in China without these start-up

costs may find an acquisition more attractive. An acquisition may also be attractive from the standpoint of a struggling Chinese state-owned enterprise, or SOE. It may enable the SOE to avoid a situation in which its best assets are invested in a new joint venture, leaving it with idle assets and unprofitable holdings."

66. A multiagency government document in 2002 allows the transfer of state-owned shares and legal person shares to foreign investors. This rescinds a 1995 ban on foreign M&A that was prompted in part by China Strategy's acquisition of a large number of SOEs. "Foreign Investment in China," U.S.-China Business Council, May 2003, www.uschina.org, date accessed August 28, 2004.

67. Shu-Yun Ma, "Foreign Participation in China's Privatization," *Communist Economies and Economic Transformation* 8:4 (1996), 539.

68. Gu cites an internal report by an investigation team of the State Planning Commission. That this report was published only internally shows the sensitive political nature of such reform as well as it increases the likelihood that the statistical data is accurate. Gu (1998), 49. Similar figures are given by Liu Lisheng et al. (1997), 51.

69. "China Ranked No. 2 in Absorbing FDI during 1979–99," www .chinaonline.com, October 11, 2000. A report by UNCTAD also pointed to the trend of FDI in the form of M&As, even in developing countries. *World Investment Report: Cross-Border Mergers and Acquisitions and Development* (New York: United Nations Publications, 2000).

70. "Foreign Investment in China."

71. Li Yonghai, "How Could We Reform State-Owned Enterprises by Simply 'Selling Them Off?'" *Renmin Luntan*, December 15, 1998, 8–11. FBIS-CHI-99-009, January 9, 1999, wnc.fedworld.gov/cgi-bin, date accessed September 27, 1999; Wang Xin and Zhou Chunfa, "State Assets Are Important Economic Basis of Socialist System," *Qiushi*, August 16, 1999: 25–27. FBIS-CHI-1999-0915, wnc.fedworld.gov/cgi-bin, date accessed September 27, 1999.

72. Zhang Haitao (1997).

73. Ibid, 135.

74. The conservative critique of the "release the small" policy was published in the journal *Dangdai Sichao* (Contemporary trends). Wang Mingcai, "Across the Board Sales Are Not the Best Way to Reform Small and Medium-Sized Enterprises," *Contemporary Trends* (April 1997) in BBC Worldwide Monitoring, June 28, 1997.

75. Philip Pan, "China Accelerates Privatization, Continuing Shift from Doctrine," *Washington Post,* November 12, 2003, A14. An "international merger and acquisition summit" was held in November 2003 to further encourage foreign investors to participate in M&A activity in China; see www.masummit.org.

76. Under the joint venture law, the foreign partner cannot be legally bound to absorb workers from the Chinese partner, although they often agree to hire some workers as part of the negotiation process. The domestic regulations guiding M&A activity, however, do specify that the acquiring company continue to implement the labor contracts of the employees from the acquired or merged entity. A new regulation in April 2003 finally stipulated that foreign M&As should also provide for worker settlement. See relevant laws and regulations as explained in Dong Baohua, ed., *Legal Information for Older Workers, Two Hundred Questions* (Shanghai: Shanghai Jiaotong University Publishing, 2003).

77. Sheng Hong, Chinese Enterprise Mergers Series, no. 8, "Enterprises' Special Characteristics: Difficulties and Opportunities (*qiyetecheng, kunnan yu jihui*)," *China Business Times,* May 22, 1997, 2.

78. Adam Aston, "State-Owned Enterprises Fail to Attract Foreign Investors," *Journal of Commerce,* October 1, 1998, 1C.

79. Liu Lisheng et al. (1997), 102–3.

80. Ibid.

81. These examples are taken from the appendix Ibid. This appendix supplies detailed case studies of GJVs all over China and involving a variety of investors, including American, French, Filipino, and Japanese firms.

82. "Over 100,000 workers demonstrate in Mianyang City . . ." *Human Rights in China Press Report,* July 16, 1997.

83. For example see Tong Xin, "Unemployment Crisis: Its Significance for the Chinese Working Class," *Social Sciences in China* 24:4 (Winter 2003).

84. Liu Lisheng et al. (1997), 335.

85. Shu-yun Ma (1996), 532.

86. "Number of Shareholding Companies Exceeds 230,000," New China News Agency (*Xinhua*), *BBC Worldwide Monitoring,* August 27, 1999.

87. "Regulations of the State Council on Domestic Listing of Foreign-Oriented Stocks by Share-holding Companies," promulgated by the State Council on December 25, 1995. http://chinalawinfo.com, date accessed August 28, 2004.

88. Ma (1996).

89. See also Carl E. Walter and Fraser J. T. Howe, *Privatizing China: The Stock Markets and Their Role in Coparate Reform* (Singapore: John Wiley and Sons, 2003), 199–200.

90. Ma (1996).

91. See "China's Laws Now Give Investors More Options" and "China May Sell Over 15% of SOE Shares," *China Business Times (zhonghua gongshang shibao),* www.chinaonline.com, September 13, 1999, date accessed August 28, 2004.

92. Lu Ning, "Shanghai Looks Abroad to Market State Assets," *Business Times* (Singapore), September 22, 1998, 8.

93. Anthony Neoh, the then chief adviser to the China Securities Regulatory Commission (and former chairman of the Hong Kong Securities and Futures Commission) announced in September 2000 that the A-share market would be open to foreigners in 2003. In a speech at Princeton University in the spring of 2000, Neoh explained that the opening of the A-share market would create a more competitive environment for inefficient state firms. "The only way to shake the SOEs out of their problems is to make them compete. The SOE sector will be treated the same as other companies in the marketplace." Lester J. Gesteland, "A-Share Market to Open to Foreigners by '03, CSRC's Neoh says," *Chinaonline,* September 19, 2000, www.chinaonline.com, date accessed August 28, 2004. See also Ma (1996), 534.

94. Joe Leahy and Richard McGregor, "China Takes a 'Giant Step' Towards Unified Stock Market: Restrictions Eased on Locals Buying Shares Reserved for Overseas Investors," *Financial Times,* February 20, 2001, A1.

95. Ma (1996), 534.

96. Ching-Ching Ni, "Chinese Abuzz over New Stock Rules," *Los Angeles Times,* February 28, 2001, C1.

97. "China to Allow Overseas Investors Access to Stocks: Reform Following WTO Entry Could Draw Foreign Capital into A Shares and Stabilise Volatile Markets," *Financial Times,* November 6, 2001, 29.

98. Chen, "Chinese President Rachets Up Reforms," April 7, 1997.

99. Ian Johnson, "Entrepreneurs Now Get Some Respect, to Their Surprise," *Wall Street Journal,* October 16, 1997.

100. "New Law to Fuel Privatization," *Laws and Regulations of China,* www .ccpit.org, date accessed April 7, 2000.

101. Gene Linn, "China's Sanction of Private Sector Opens Doors for Investment, Trade," *Journal of Commerce,* May 12, 1999, 7A.

102. "State-Owned Firms to Exit Shenzhen," *Journal of Commerce,* July 12, 1999, 6.

103. Shirk (1993).

104. Yang (1997).

105. China restricts FDI in several sectors, most recently, the restrictions on foreign-invested internet firms have been criticized. See The *New York Times,* November 15, 1999, C1.

106. Naughton (1995).

107. Gu (1996).

108. Mark O'Neill, "New Law 'Not Enough for Private Sector,'" *South China Morning Post,* March 4, 1999, 9.

109. This term is used by Gu (1996).

110. For an example of this debate within academic circles in China see Haitao Zhang (1997) 55–61. Zhang is dismayed at the state of China's national industry and offers comparisons to the West and "even" Korea. On China's automobile industry, he writes, "Shanghai Dazhong (JV with Volkswagon), First Auto's Audi, Beijing Jeep, Tianjin Xiali (JV with Daihatsu). . . . Does China still have its own independent auto factory? For a long time now, China's passenger car industry has become just one big assembly plant for Western car companies!"

111. Interview with Wang Zhongyu, the minister of State Economic and Trade Commission by *Ban Yue Tan* journal; "Economy Minister Outlines Focus of State Enterprise Reform for 1997," *British Broadcasting Corporation,* FE/2909 S1/1, May 3, 1997.

112. Silver (May–June 1998).

113. Philippe Chevalerais, "Investment Strategies in China," *China Perspectives* (September–October 1997), 64–65.

114. *Global Development Finance,* 47.

CHAPTER 4: THE UNMITIGATED MARKET

1. Capitalist labor practices are defined as measures that commodify labor power and marketize the labor relationship (making it amenable to monetization and exchange). In addition, capitalist labor relations are founded on a hierarchical relationship between employer and employee. This hierarchical relationship

entails various modes of control, although there is a wide range of practices among capitalist systems (and indeed between firms within one system) to illicit consent and compliance in the workplace.

2. Jonathan Unger and Anita Chan, "Corporatism in China," in Barrett McCormack and Jonathan Unger, eds., *China after Socialism: In the Footsteps of Eastern Europe or East Asia,* (Armonk, New York: M. E. Sharpe, 1996), 119.

3. Dorothy J. Solinger, "The Chinese Work Unit and Transient Labor in the Transition from Socialism," *Modern China* 21:2 (April 1995): 155–83. For other evidence of converging practices see Anita Chan "Globalization, China's 'Free' (Read Bonded) Labour Market and the Chinese Trade Unions," *Asia Pacific Business Review,* special issue on Globalization and Labor Market Deregulation, 2000; and Minghua Zhao and Theo Nichols, "Management Control of Labour in State-Owned Enterprises: Cases from the Textile Industry," *China Journal* 36 (July 1996), 1–21.

4. See in particular the edited volumes by Suzanne Berger and Ronald Dore, eds., *National Diversity and Global Capitalism* (Ithaca: Cornell University Press, 1996); Colin Crouch and Wolfgang Streeck, *Political Economy of Modern Capitalism: Mapping Convergence and Diversity* (London: Sage Publications, 1997); and Peter Hall and David Soskice, *Varieties of Capitalism: The Institutional Foundations of Comparative Advantage* (New York: Oxford University Press, 2001).

5. For a summary of these debates see David Held, Anthony McGrew, David Goldblatt, and Jonathan Perraton, *Global Transformations: Politics, Economics, and Culture* (Stanford, Calif.: Stanford University Press, 1999), 278–81. See also Dani Rodrik, *Has Globalization Gone Too Far?* (Washington, D.C.: Institute for International Economics, 1997).

6. China has actively examined both German and Japanese labor practices as possible models for its own legislation. These models are not socialist per se, but rather mitigate some of the perceived excesses of free-market capitalism although in different ways. In implementation, however, China's labor policies do not have the intended effects. This is the case for the collective contract system, which is discussed below.

7. Evidence of these effects has also been found in developed countries. For example, Brady and Wallace find inward FDI has negative impacts on U.S. labor and note that "the U.S. states are locked in a 'second war between the states' in which states compete to provide a favorable business climate for the location of business within their borders." David Brady and Michael Wallace, "Spatialization, Foreign Direct Investment, and Labor Outcomes in the American States, 1978–1996," *Social Forces* 79:1 (September 2000) 93.

8. David Zweig *Internationalizing China: Domestic Interests and Global Linkages* (Ithaca: Cornell University Press, 2002).

9. In an article maligning the inflexibility of the Indian investment environment, the *Financial Times* recently compared China and India. Labor flexibility figures prominently in these analyses. It cited a *Global Competitiveness Report* that listed China twenty-third out of seventy-five countries in ease of firing workers. India was listed in seventy-third place. Edward Luce and Martin Wolf, "India's Slowing Growth: Why a Hobbled Economy Cannot Meet the Country's Needs," *Financial Times,* April 4, 2003, 15. In their annual report on foreign investment in

China, the U.S.-China Business Council also noted in 2002, "in vying for investment, localities are looking for ways to minimize business costs for potential investors. Shanghai and Shenzhen have been particularly aggressive on this front."
"Foreign Investment in China," U.S.-China Business Council, May 2003, www
.uschinaorg/china-statistics.html foreign-direct-investment (accessed August 21,
2004).

10. For example, in the development zone in Tianjin municipality, one can find
that advanced human resource practices of American multinationals coexist with
foreign-invested factories that are run like "boot camps." This was reported by a
TEDA official, I was not permitted to visit these "boot camps." Interview, TEDA
Public Relations Department official, May 1997. In Jiangsu, a Taiwanese manager
in a Taiwanese WFOE defined the company's labor practices as "militaristic." Interview, Kunshan, Taiwan WFOE, May 2001.

11. For the important roles played by subcontracting to SOEs and exporting to
foreign markets for TVE growth and survival see Zweig (2002), 120–25. Flemming Christiansen analyzes how the ability of SOEs to subcontract to TVEs allowed internal labor reforms to be delayed even while expanding production capacity. "'Market Transition' in China: The Case of the Jiangsu Labor Market,
1978–1990," *Modern China* 18:1 (January 1992), 72–93.

12. Andrew Walder. "Wage Reform and the Web of Factory Interests." *China
Quarterly* 109 (March 1987); and "Factory and Manager in the Era of Reform."
China Quarterly 118 (June 1989).

13. In 1996 still only a little more than half of China's workforce were employed using labor contracts. In 1997, however, with the renewed impetus to resolve the problems of SOEs, the transformation to the labor contract system was
declared complete. It is highly likely that the implementation of this policy was
haphazard and slapdash. The transition to labor contracts was needed in order to
supply a legal basis for the massive layoffs in SOEs that were beginning to take
place.

14. Interview, SOE manager, Tangshan, July 1997. SOE managers seemed extremely sensitive to the negative feelings conjured up by the introduction of labor
contracts among state-sector workers.

15. Ibid.

16. On the debate over the Chinese adoption of Soviet style one-man management see Stephen Andors, *China's Industrial Revolution: Politics, Planning, and
Management, 1949 to the Present* (New York: Pantheon Books, 1977).

17. Xiaobo Lu and Elizabeth Perry, eds., *Danwei: The Changing Chinese
Workplace in Historical and Comparative Perspective* (New York: M. E. Sharpe,
1997). See also Mark Frazier, *The Making of the Chinese Industrial Workplace:
State, Revolution, and Labor Management.* (New York: Cambridge University
Press, 2002). Joshua H. Howard, *Workers at War: Labor in China's Arsenals,
1937–1953* (Palo Alto, Calif.: Stanford University Press, 2004).

18. Mayfair Mei-hui Yang, "Between State and Society: The Construction of
Corporateness in a Chinese Socialist Factory," *Australian Journal of Chinese Affairs* 22 (July 1989), 31–60.

19. This point is made by Valerie Bunce in *Subversive Institutions: The Design
and the Destruction of Socialism and the State* (New York: Cambridge University

Press, 1999); and in the Chinese context by Xueguang Zhou, "Unorganized Interests and Collective Action in Communist China," *American Sociological Review* 58 (February 1993), 54–73. The degree of social homogenization is probably somewhat exaggerated. In fact, divisions and conflict in Chinese society existed under socialism. Even if there is some hyperbole to this argument, it is true that many urban citizens seem to *remember* the past that way i.e., divisions were fewer, people were poor but were "poor together," inequality and corruption were much less common or better hidden.

20. The seminal work on organized dependence and authority relations in Chinese state-owned enterprises is Andrew Walder, *Communist Neo-Traditionalism: Work and Authority in Chinese Industry* (Berkeley and Los Angeles: University of California Press, 1986).

21. See especially Brantly Womack, "Transfigured Community: Neo-traditionalism and Work-Unit Socialism in China," *China Quarterly* 126 (June 1991): 313–32; Walder's response in the same issue; and Walder, "Factory and Manager in the Era of Reform," *China Quarterly* 118 (June 1989).

22. You Ji, *China's Enterprise Reform: Changing State/Society Relations after Mao* (New York: Routledge Press, 1998).

23. Lee Lai To, *Trade Unions in China, 1949 to the Present* (Singapore: National University of Singapore Press, 1986).

24. This ending date is chosen as a rough division between partial reform and more comprehensive total reform. Some changes began to occur in certain coastal localities in 1992. The "hold the big, release the small" (*zhuada, fangxiao*) policy was first announced in 1994. This policy indicated the state's willingness to let most small-to-medium enterprises go; that is, to be privatized in various ways. At the Fifteenth Party Congress in 1997, this SOE reform policy was reiterated and strengthened. Since then, former Premier Zhu Rongji made SOE reform a central concern during his term in office, openly stating that the large majority of state firms will be privatized. "Turning SOEs around Will Take Privatization, Shareholding Restructuring, Zhu says," www.chinaonline.com, July 3, 2000, date accessed August 28, 2004.

25. The official policy during this period was expressed with the baffling slogan "The manager is the center [*zhongxin*] and the party secretary is the core [*hexin*]." Susan Shirk reported that in "1990–91 economic officials could not keep a straight face when they repeated to me the new official formula for the division of roles." Shirk, *The Political Logic of Economic Reform in China* (Berkeley and Los Angeles: University of California Press, 1993), 46.

26. You Ji (1998), 52.

27. Ellen Salem, "Managers Rule, OK?" *Far Eastern Economic Review* (January 28, 1988), 69.

28. You Ji (1998), 52. See also Andors (1977).

29. Interview, State Owned Enterprise manager, Tianjin, March 1997.

30. A 1996 survey published in *China Business Times* found that 66.1 percent of enterprise managers were concurrently serving as the firm's Communist Party secretary. "Establish Effective Mechanisms of Incentives and Constraints as Quickly as Possible," (*jinkuai jianli youxiao jili yu yueshujizhi*) *China Business Times* (*gongshangshibao*), April 22, 1997, 2.

31. Liu Zhiqiang, "Strengthen and Improve the Political Leadership of the Party in Enterprises" (*jiaqiang he gaishan dang dui qiye de zhengzhilingdao*). *Theoretical Trends* (*lilun dongtai*) (January 25, 1997), 2.

32. Feng Tongqing and Zhao Minghua, "Workers and Trade Unions," *Chinese Sociology and Anthropology* 28 (Spring 1996), 18. See also "Who Will Supervise the SOE Boss?" (*sheilaijiandu guoqi laoban?*), *China Women's News* (April 25, 1997), 2; "Chinese Trade Union: Protecting Rights According to Law Is Difficult" (*zhongguo gonghui: yifa weiquanhaojiannan*), *Guangdong Labor Daily* (July 29, 1996).

33. The irony stems from the fact that management autonomy, while a part of economic restructuring, is also an intensely political act. There is a tendency for authoritarian regimes to tolerate profound economic changes while delaying badly needed political reform because it poses a more overt, immediate threat to their rule. For China this runs the risk of delaying political reform until a point of crisis, when economic reform has widened the wealth and income gap to intolerable levels.

34. Naughton found that even by the early 1990s the changes in the external environment, especially the expansion of the nonstate sector, were putting pressure on state firms. Barry Naughton, "Implications of the State Monopoly over Industry and Its Relaxation," *Modern China* 18:1 (January 1992), 14–41. Naughton focuses on the fiscal consequences of the growing nonstate sector.

35. Walder (1986).

36. Managers were officially granted the right to make personnel decisions, including hiring and firing decisions, in 1992. Malcolm Warner, "China's Labour-Management System Reforms: Breaking the Three Old Irons (1978–1999)," *Asia Pacific Journal of Management* 18 (2001), 315–34. In practice the right to fire or lay off workers was limited due to the fear that widespread layoffs would lead to political instability. These rights of managerial autonomy expanded more quickly after the 1997 decision by the central government to speed up reform of the state sector.

37. In a 1992 survey of 100 enterprises by the Chinese Trade Union Institute, labor mobility from SOEs to FIEs rose 10.4 percent for skilled workers, 8.9 percent for workers, and 7.1 percent for managers over the year before. Feng Tongqing, "Internal Relations and Structure of Chinese Workers under Market Reform" (*zouxiang shichangjingjide zhongguo qiye zhigongneibuguanxi he jiegou*) *Chinese Social Sciences* 3 (May 1993), 103. Economist Barry Naughton found that "labor mobility has been creeping up steadily in China throughout the reform period and has become significant during the 1990s." Barry Naughton "Danwei: The Economic Foundations of a Unique Institution," in Lu and Perry (1997), 184.

38. You Ji, (1998), 141. He quotes official statistics that state 20–25 percent of the urban workforce was engaged in moonlighting in 1991. Despite the state's official disapproval of moonlighting, the moonlighting trend has only increased. In a study that did not break workers down by ownership or break down moonlighting income (rental income vs. personal business income), it was found in 2000 that urban Chinese now get half their income from moonlighting, up from 32.5 percent from 1990. "High Income for Moonlighters and Migrants," *China Staff* (June 2000).

39. It is difficult to find data on the extent of these practices. There are some indications, however, that they are quite common. According to statistics kept by the Hangzhou Employment Management Bureau in 1997 over three-quarters of laid-off workers already had "relatively stable employment" in the nonstate sector. They did not resign their posts from SOEs in order to keep their benefits and subsidies. However, it is possible that these statistics capture primarily workers who had the skills or experience to find work and thus left their firms before the extensive layoffs that began in 1997. It is unlikely that such a high percentage of laid-off workers now find work in the nonstate sector, although this may vary considerably by region. "Why Laid-off Workers Rely on Both Sides," (*xiagangzhe wei he xihuan 'guakaoliangtou*), *Economic Life Daily,* June 6, 1997. Also, many of the new labor disputes involving enterprises under restructuring are disputes involving employees who have long left the *danwei* but have continued to draw benefits. Once the enterprise has restructured, the labor contracts of these employees are no longer in effect, the employees are fired, and their benefits are withdrawn. Many workers have sued the company over the loss of formal employment and benefits. Li Juexin, "Perspective on Difficult Topics in Labor Relations, (*laodong guanxi moca redian toushi*)" *Handling and Research of Labor Disputes* (*laodong zhengyi chuliyuyanjiu*) (September 1998), 9–11; Hu Yimin, "Several Problems That Should Be Carefully Resolved When Dismissing Employees" (*qiyecituizhigong yingdang zhuyi jiejue de jige wenti*). *Handling and Research of Labor Disputes* (August 1998) 12–14. The government finally issued a regulation forbidding the continuation of "*tingxin, liuzhi*" (stop salary, keep post) in 1995, ordering that workers either return to their original danwei and sign a labor contract or resign their posts. "Stop Salary, Keep Post: Unable to Defend Oneself," (*tingxin liuzhi, zishennanbao*) *China Market Economic News,* (November 23, 1996), 3.

40. Interview, State Enterprise personnel manager, Tangshan, May 2001.

41. Warner (2001). Warner quotes the popular expression "*hetonggong gan, gudinggong kan*" (contract workers work, permanent workers look) to express the common belief that contract workers worked harder than workers who retained lifetime employment.

42. "Chinese Ministers Discuss Enterprise Reform and Labor Problems." March 26, 1998 *ChinaOnline,* www.chinaonline.com/issues/social_political/NewsArchive/cs-protected/1998/March/sp_artll.asp, date accessed August 28, 2004.

43. Andrew Walder, "Factory and Manager in the Era of Reform," *China Quarterly* 118 (June 1989), 252.

44. There have been several high profile "*tiaocao*" (job-hopping) cases that involved skilled managers or workers leaving SOEs for foreign companies. One case that allegedly drew the interest of former premier Li Peng was a case involving a Beijing cement company and LaFarge, a large French multinational. The dispute was finally settled in a court settlement with LaFarge agreeing to pay the SOE for economic losses and the training it provided to the manager. Jiang Junlu, "To Stay or Go: Legal Analysis of Employee Resignation in Mainland China," (*zouyuhailiu: zhongguodalu guyuan cizhide falufenxi*) (June 2000), Unpublished paper.

45. You Ji (1998); Wenfang Tang and William Parish *Chinese Urban Life under Reform: The Changing Social Contract* (New York: Cambridge University Press, 2000), 128–62.

46. Articles in the national media as well as more scholarly articles on the problems of reform hammered away at this point of an "unequal playing field" between SOEs and FIEs. These articles focused on the heavy employment burden, the gap in managers' salaries, and the inability of SOEs to retain skilled workers. "Should one take a yearly salary of hundreds of thousand RMB?" (*shubaiwanyuan nianxin gaibugai na*) *Nanfang Zhoumo,* December 20, 1996, 2; "How Can SOEs Retain People?" (*guoqi zenyang liuzhuren*) *Renmin Ribao,* November 19, 1996, 10; (*qiangzhanshichang bixu guimo jingying*) *Zhongguo Gongshang Shibao,* April 22, 1997, 7; "Establish a Consciousness of Talent, Perfect the Two Mechanisms" (*shulirencaiyishi jianquan liangge jizhi*) *Workers Daily,* April 8, 1997, 7. The two mechanisms include the collective contract system (to make it more difficult for workers to leave) and the incentive wage system (to improve skilled workers' wages). "Skilled Workers Call for Policy Help," (*jishugongren huhuan zhengce fuzhu*) *Workers Daily,* December 13, 1996, 3; "Perfect the Adjustment Mechanism for the Distribution of Individual Salaries," (*wanshanqiyegerenshouru fenpei tiaokongjizhi*) *Zhongguo Gongshang Shibao,* May 5, 1997, 3; "The Rights and Interests of Enterprises Must Also Be Protected" (*qiyequanyi yebixu weihu*) *Jingji Ribao,* October 9, 1996.

47. Mary E. Gallagher and Junlu Jiang, "China's Labor Legislation: Introduction and Analysis," *Chinese Law and Government* (November–December 2002), 9.

48. This is often achieved by classifying migrants differently as "labor service workers" (*laowugong*), which denies them the right to a labor contract (*laodong hetong*).

49. See Lee Lai To (1986).

50. The trade union chairman said that pushing short contracts on older workers leads to "unstable thinking" and then to "unstable production." Interview, Trade Union chairman, Tangshan SOE, July, 1999. The different treatment for older workers is the typical "old workers, old system, new workers, new system."

51. This designation means that the worker draws a salary without bonus and generally waits at home or finds a temporary job in the private sector while waiting for a job assignment within the company.

52. On the use of apprenticeship labor in SOEs during the 1950s see Frazier (2002) 198–99.

53. Zhu Shaolu, "Implementation of the 'Rely on the Working Class Policy' Requires Legalization" (*luoshi 'yikao' fangzhen yao fazhihua*), *Workers' Daily,* December 26, 1996, 6.

54. These *tiaocao* (job-hopping) disputes have increased rapidly according to interviews with labor lawyers and firm managers. The problem of retaining skilled staff is a major concern for SOE managers. As one said in a speech on labor disputes, "Presently SOE workers fire the enterprise more than SOEs fire workers." "Speech of Chen Quansheng at the National Conference of Labor Dispute Resolution," *Handling and Research of Labor Disputes* (*laodongzhenghi chuli yu yanjiu*) (January 1996). Some articles criticizing the job-hopping trend: "Job-hopping: Don't Take Secrets with You," (*tiaocao: beidaizou mimi*) *China Youth*

Daily, November 22, 1996, 4; Wang Jiayuan, "Taking Technology: Job-hopping Hits the Law's Gate," (*dai jishu: tiaocao zhuang famen*) *Legal Daily,* October 28, 1996: 2; "Kaifeng Job-Hopping Dispute: One Case Carefully Settled," (*kaifeng tiaocao zhengyi yi an shen shen jie*) *China Youth Daily,* November 20, 1996, 2; Carrie Lee, "Industry Frustrated by Job-Hopping," *South China Morning Post,* August 9, 1997.

55. Interview, former FIE worker, Shanghai, August 2004.

56. Dai Weikang, Li Qi, and Chang Kai, "Multi-level Analysis of Mainland China's Collective Contract System," (*dui zhongguo neidi jitihetong zhidu de jige cengmian de fenxi*), paper presented at The Impact of WTO Membership on Chinese Workers and The Response of the International Trade Union Movement Conference, City University of Hong Kong, Hong Kong, November 29–30, 2003.

57. Interview, labor law professor, Shanghai, December 13, 2002. Disputes with three or more workers are classified as "collective disputes." Collective contract disputes should theoretically be first handled by labor arbitration.

58. A quote by Li Qi in his (2003) presentation.

59. Interview, Kobe City, Japan representative, Tianjin, May 1997; Sino-Japanese JV, personnel manager, July 1999.

60. Peter Sheldon and Ernest Ruan, "Employer Combination among Overseas Multinational Organizations in the PRC: Structuring Local Labour Markets in Response to Skill Shortages," School of Industrial Relations and Organizational Behavior, University of New South Wales, unpublished paper.

61. Chinese labor officials, labor dispute arbitrators, and some judges now openly advocate that the state should recognize the existence of labor relations even in the absence of a written contract. This allows the courts and the state to hear disputes related to employment while a more formalistic reliance on a written contract shuts out many workers from the dispute resolution process. The state's recognition of labor relations in the absence of a labor contract is also a sign that many workers are employed "at will" with very little job security. See Guo Wenlong, "Research on Real Labor Relations," *Shanghai Shenpan Shixian,* September 2002, 12–15; interview, labor lawyer, October 10, 2003.

62. Interview, Sino-Japanese JV, Shanghai, human resource manager, May 1997, May 1999; interview, deputy general manager, November 2003.

63. Interview, SOE personnel manager, May 2001.

64. The practice of "buying out years of service" (*maiduan gongling*) reportedly began in China's northeastern "rust belt" as a way to rid enterprises once and for all of the employment and welfare burdens of employees. In most places workers are paid one month salary for every year worked. This practice is used especially for workers who have long years of tenure prior to the implementation of the labor contract system. The practice remains somewhat controversial; as one Shanghai labor official remarked, "Of course we all do this but we can't really talk about it as 'buying out someone's labor.'" (interview, Shanghai Labor Bureau, December 2002). In late 2003, the Tangshan SOE, which had long resisted using the practice as a way to get rid of unneeded workers, claimed it would begin buying out service in the following year. Interview, SOE personnel manager, November 2003.

65. Local government officials may, however, have key roles in these practices

by allowing them to occur and receiving kickbacks for their silence. A clerk in a Tianjin Sino-Korean joint venture reported in 1997 that she spent much of her time "sending cigarettes and wine" to officials responsible for labor and environmental regulation as a way to ensure protection from inspections and fines. Interview, Korean-contracted SOE worker, March 1997.

66. For a slightly more optimistic analysis of the trade union organization see Feng Chen, "Between the State and Labor: The Conflict of Chinese Trade Unions' Double Identity in the Market Reform," *China Quarterly,* December 2003. Chen may be more optimistic because his analysis focuses on the local level trade union organization, while here it is the firm-level organization that is the major focus. The local level organization is less influenced by the power of management.

67. Anita Chan, "Revolution or Corporatism? Workers and Trade Unions in Post-Mao China," *Australian Journal of Chinese Affairs* (January 1993), 31–61; Jude Howell, "The Impact of China's Open Policy on Labour," *Labour, Capital, and Society* (November 1990), 288–322; Jeanne Wilson, "Labour Policy in China: Reform and Retrogression," *Problems of Communism* 39 (September–October 1990), 44–65; Gordon White, "Chinese Trade Unions in the Transition from Socialism: Towards Corporatism or Civil Society?" *British Journal of Industrial Relations* (September 1996), 433–57.

68. See Wing-yue Leung, *Smashing the Iron Rice Pot: Workers and Unions in China's Market Socialism* (Hong Kong: Asia Monitor Resource Center, 1988), 19–21.

69. Ibid, 33.

70. In a survey of SOE workers in 1993, 46.5 percent believed that "the union doesn't play a large role." Other statements included in the report on workers' attitudes reveal a cynical view of their position in the factory, "Now in reality it is the boss who has the final say." And on the union, "The union is part of the administration, we have no confidence in the union." "A report on the Status of the National Working Class,"(*guanyu quanguo gongren jieji duiwu zhuangkuang de diaocha baogao*) *Trade Union Work Report* (*gonghui gongzuo tongxun*) (1993), 31.

71. Tongqing Feng and Zhao Minghua (1996).

72. Japanese managers, for example, tend to emphasize the "cultural bridge" role that unions in their firms play rather than a more distinct role as an organization to represent workers' interests. Class is deemphasized in what seems to be an intentional attempt to represent labor strife as cultural misunderstanding. Interview, Sino-Japanese JV, general manager, Tianjin, July 1997; Interview, Sino-Japanese JV, human resource manager, Shanghai, May 1997; Interview, Sino-Japanese JV, deputy manager, Shanghai, November 2003.

73. For example, according to the National Labor Law, the trade union must be notified of layoffs in advance, but it has no ability to stop layoffs.

74. White (1996).

75. Pearson, *Joint Ventures in the People's Republic of China* (Princeton: Princeton University Press, 1991), 185–86.

76. Attempts by labor activists to educate and organize workers in these regions were quickly stopped and the activists imprisoned. *Annual Survey of Violations of Trade Union Rights, 1995,* International Confederation of Free Trade Unions, 79.

77. "China Warns of Surge in Strikes in Joint Ventures," *Agence France Presse* (September 28, 1993); Willy Wo-Lap Lam, "China Heading off Labour Unrest," *South China Morning Post* (July 5, 1993), 8.

78. Lau (1996) 58. For a discussion of the unionization process, see Anita Chan, "Labour Relations in Foreign-Funded Ventures, Chinese Trade Unions and the Prospects for Collective Bargaining," in O'Leary (1997).

79. Anne Stevenson-Yang, "Unions and Contracts," *China Business Review* (January–February, 1996).

80. "Research Survey on Shenzhen's Shekou District Union Work," Guangdong Central Union Investigative Bureau (1993), unpublished report.

81. In a survey of 102 Japanese-invested enterprises in China, 74.7 percent of the enterprises had established unions, which is substantially higher than estimates for unionization of overseas Chinese-invested enterprises. Yasumuro Kenichi, ed., *China's Labor-Capital Relations and on the Ground Management (Chugoku no roshikankei to genchi keiei)*. (Tokyo: Hakutoshobo, 1999), 105.

82. Interview, human resources manager, Sino-Japanese JV, Shanghai, May 1997.

83. The Japanese general manager was equally unhappy with the requirement to set up a union and the many other examples of "government interference." Yet the union chairman maintained his position and continued to serve into 1999. Interview, general manager, Sino-Japanese JV, Tianjin, July 1997, July 1999; interview, human resources manager/union chairman, Sino-Japanese JV, Tianjin, July 1997 and July 1999.

84. Interview, TEDA Administrative Committee, July 1999. In October 2003, TEDA's offices in Shanghai were still comparing the welfare and salary requirements of areas in Shanghai and Jiangsu in order to stem the loss of investment from TEDA to those areas. Interview, TEDA Shanghai Development Office, October 2003.

85. It is perhaps significant that there was complete consensus in all interviews about the quality of labor relations in different FIEs. Western firms were rated the highest, Japanese were next, overseas Chinese were second to last, and Koreans came in dead last, usually with comments on the barbarism or militarism of Korean managers.

86. Kiyoshi Kasahara, "Labor Relations a Big Job for Changing China," *Nikkei Weekly*, October 20, 1997: 17

87. Interview, lawyer, Shanghai, July 1997; interview, lawyer, Shanghai, July 1999; Interview, lawyer, Shanghai, July 1999.

88. Dalian EDZ Labor Arbitration Committee and Labor Bureau, "Discussion of Several Problems of Collective Work Stoppages" (*guanyu jiti tinggong ruoganwenti de tantao*), *Handling and Research of Labor Disputes* (April 1997), 13–14. Regulations also reprinted in Yasumuro Kenichi, ed., *Labor Management Relations in China and On-Site Management (Chugoku no roshikankei to genchi keiei)* (Tokyo: Hakutoshobo, 1999), 38.

89. "Discussion of Several Problems of Collective Work Stoppages" (1997), 14.

90. "Multinational Companies in China: Winners and Losers," *Economist Intelligence Unit*, 1997.

91. Ibid.

92. Interview, Japanese lawyer, Shanghai, July 1997, July 1999; interview Chinese labor lawyer, Beijing, July 1997, July 1999.

93. Anne Stevenson-Yang, "Unions and Contracts," *China Business Review* (January–February, 1996), 12. See also Chan (1997).

94. Interview, human resource manager, American WFOE, Beijing, July 1997.

95. One large MNC in footwear now plays an active role in administering union elections in its subcontracted plants, motivated at least in part by consumer pressure in its home markets for better labor conditions in China. This creates a somewhat ironic situation in which a multinational corporation creates a more independent union than is normally realized in China merely through its more assiduous implementation of Chinese labor legislation. (Trade union officials are usually appointed by Communist Party officials or by management.) Alison Maitlind, "Sewing a Seam of Worker Democracy in China," *Financial Times*, December 12, 2002; *Toward Sustainable Code Compliance: Worker Representation in China*, Reebok International Ltd., November 2002 (report issued by Reebok on its union elections in China.)

96. "Investigation on Labor Relations in Public Enterprises Experimentally Run by the People and Countermeasures" *(Dui shixing gongyou minying qiye laodong guanxi de diaocha ji duice)*, *Handling and Research of Labor Disputes* (March 1996). The article notes that these types of enterprise have a high rate of labor disputes.

97. "Cannot Be above the Law" *(bunenglingjia faluzhishang)*, *Workers' Daily*, March 3, 1997; "Chinese Trade Unions: Protecting Rights According to the Law Is Difficult," *(zhongguo gonghui: yifa weiquanhaojiannan) Guangdong Labor Daily*, July 29, 1996.

98. "Ningxia Industrial Union Work is Weakened" *(ningxia chanye gonghui gongzuo shou xueruo")*, *Workers Daily*, March 24, 1997, 5.

99. Unions in coastal Zhejiang Province also report staff reductions and union consolidation. "Warning: Union Cadre Ranks Shrink" *(jingyti: gonghui ganbu duiwu zai weisuo)*, *Baokan Wenzhai*, April 14, 1997, 1; "Who Will Protect Union Property of Bankrupt Enterprises?" *(pochan qiye gonghui zichan sheilai baohu)*, *Workers' Daily*, March 30, 1997; Small SOEs Restructure, What Should the Union Do?" *(guoyou xiaoqiye gaizhi, gonghui zenmaban)*, *Workers' Daily*, March 24, 1997; "Who Will Protect the Rights of Union Cadres?" *(sheilai weihu gonghui ganbu liyi)*, *Jizhai* (July 1995).

100. "Industrial Basic-Level Unions Are According to Law Qualified as Social Organization with Legal Personhood" *(chanye jiceng gonghui yifa juyou shehuituanti ren zige)*, *Workers Daily*, June 5, 1997, 1.

101. "Those That Withhold Union Dues Are Ordered to Pay" *(dui tuoqian gonghui jingfeizhe xiadazhifuling)*, *Workers Daily*, May 21, 1997, 1.

102. Wang Min, "Problems Facing the Handling of Labor Disputes in SOEs and Countermeasures" *(guoyou qiye laodongzhengyi chuli gongzuo mianlin de wenti ji duice)*, *Handling and Research of Labor Disputes*, (June 1997), 5; Interviews with Chinese labor lawyers, Beijing, May, June 1997, July 1999; Also Hong Shou Fang, "Union Chairman, What Is Your Duty?" *(gonghui zhuxi, nide zhize shi shenme?)*, *Handling and Research of Labor Disputes* (May 1996), 26.

103. Yasumuro Kenichi, ed., (1999), 56.

104. Chan (1997), 140.

105. Ibid.

106. Interview, Sino-Japanese JV, Tianjin, July 1997, July 1999; interview, Sino-Japanese JV, Shanghai May 1997, July 1999.

107. In a survey of workers in Zhuhai, Guangdong Province, 80 percent of workers polled believe that the union's role "leaves much to be desired" (*bujinrenyi*) and 62 percent that "after SOEs reform the union is not essential, (we'd) be as well without it." Cheng Zhong, "Analysis of a Survey of Zhuhai Workers' Thinking and Attitude" (*zhuhai qiye zhigong sixiang xiangtai de diaocha fenxi*), *Gongyun Luntan* (December 1996).

108. "The Role of the Union Representative in Protecting Rights during Collective Bargaining: Problems and Countermeasures" (*gonghui daibiao zaijitixieshang tanpanzhong weiquanzuoyong fahuide nandian yu duice*), *Handling and Research of Labor Disputes* (November 1996), 15.

109. Xiang Derong, "Stock-Holding Companies' Board of Directors: Existing Problems and Suggestions" (*gufenzhi qiye dongshihui cunzai de wenti he jianyi*), *Union Theory and Practice* (August 1, 1995), 10.

110. Shenyang City Union Investigative Office, "The Experimental Modern Enterprise System in Shenyang: Union Problems and Countermeasures" (*shenyang Shi xiandaihua qiyezhidu shidianzhong gonghui cunzai de wenti ji duice*) *Union Theory and Practice* (August 1, 1995), 31.

111. Xiang (1995). The central union ideally prefers that the union chairman be a full-time elected position with the right to serve and vote on the board of directors.

112. Interview, trade union chairman, SOE, Tangshan, April 1997.

113. Interview, human resource staff member, American WFOE, Tianjin, November 2003.

114. Sino-American JC, general manager, December 2002, Shanghai.

115. Interview, deputy general manager, Sino-Japanese JV, November 2003.

116. "Workers in Foreign-Invested Enterprises," *China Labor Bulletin* (March 1996).

117. Interview with human resource manager, Taiwanese WFOE, Shanghai, July 1997.

118. The manager indicated that he wished they were a "national joint-venture" as they could then take advantage of preferential policies for FDI. His joint venture with a Beijing university did not earn the company the preferential policies awarded foreign firms. Interview, rural collective, general manager, Tianjin, July 1997.

119. Interview, rural collective, general manager, Tianjin, July 1997.

120. Interview, urban collective, General Affairs office manager, Tianjin, March, 1997.

121. This is not to say that the other firms had no labor disputes, only that the disputes were less incendiary. Disputes in other factories included salary and benefits disputes (Sino-Japanese JV, Tianjin), disputes about health insurance for the children of employees (Taiwanese WFOE, Shanghai), termination (Sino-American JV, Shanghai), and worker compensation (SOE, Tangshan). Health insurance for children is not required by Chinese law but it has become increasingly an issue for companies that employ large numbers of women of child-bearing age.

192 • Notes to Chapter Five

122. Ethnographic research in overseas Chinese-invested enterprises has also uncovered paternalistic, militaristic, and exploitative authority relations. You-Tien Hsing, *Making Capitalism in China: The Taiwan Connection* (New York: Oxford University Press, 1998); Anita Chan (2000); Ching-Kwan Lee "From Organized to Disorganized Despotism: Changing Labor Regimes in Chinese Factories," *China Quarterly* 157 (1999).

123. Interview, Taiwanese WFOE, department manager, Kunshan, May 2001.

124. Interview, Taiwanese WFOE, department manager, Kunshan, May 2001.

125. In December 2002, three clerical employees were interviewed without management's presence. Interviews, Taiwanese WFOE, Kunshan, December 2002.

126. Some analysts of Asian FDI into China divide the flows into two periods. The first period during the 1980s was one of "passive delocalisation" (*beidongxing chuzou*), with firms reacting to higher wages at home. The second period, which began in the 1990s, is called "active delocalisation" (*zhudong chuji*), with firms out to grab up Chinese domestic consumer markets. Firms with more activist plans in China's domestic market also paid greater attention to human resource problems. Philippe Chevalerias, "Investment Strategies in China," *China Perspectives* 13 (September–October 1997), 64.

127. Interview, human resources manager, Taiwanese WFOE, Shanghai, May 1997.

128. Interview, human resources manager, Taiwanese WFOE, Shanghai, May 1997.

129. Akira Hagiwara, "Foreign Investment and Worker-Management Relations in China—The Experience of Taiwanese Firms," *Asian Economic Review* (August 1996), 54.

130. Recent news articles regarding Taiwanese investment in Nicaragua cites strikingly similar examples of Taiwanese investor's aversion to unions, particularly to unions that have a historical connection to communism. The reports also cite similar despotic tactics, such as militaristic punishment, beatings, and various schemes to fragment the workforce. Noah Adams, "All Things Considered," *National Public Radio,* August 18, 2000.

131. Interview, rural collective general manager, July 1997. See also Zhao and Nichols (1996) and Chan (1999).

132. Stephen Crowley and David Ost, eds., *Workers after Workers' States : Labor and Politics in Postcommunist Eastern Europe* (Lanham, Md.: Rowman and Littlefield, 2001).

CHAPTER 5: "USE THE LAW AS YOUR WEAPON!"

1. "Use legal weapons to protect your own rights" (*yong falu wuqi weihu zishen quanyi*), quoted in "The Awakening of Workers' Rights Consciousness"(*laodongzhe quanyi yishi de suxing*), *Workers Daily,* January 2, 1997, 6. Chinese reports of labor unrest are generally circumspect, but allude to large-scale collective disputes and strikes that threaten social stability. External reports are more detailed. Human Rights in China reported that 100,000 workers went on

strike in Mianyang, Sichuan, after their factories were declared bankrupt and their unemployment funds embezzled by the managers. Twenty thousand miners went on strike in April 2000 to protest the redundancy funds distributed after the mines began to close. "Over 100,000 workers demonstrate in Mianyang City . . ." *Human Rights in China Press Report,* July 16, 1997; "Huge Mine Protest in China as Angry Laid-off Workers Vent Anger," April 7, 2000, www.insidechina.com/news; John Pomfret, "Miners' Riot a Symbol of China's New Discontent," *Washington Post,* April 5, 2000, A1. On the large protests in Liaoning Province in the spring of 2002 see "Paying the Price: Worker Unrest in Northeast China," *Human Rights Watch: China* 14:6 (August 2002).

2. These figures are the most conservative measures of disputes, only including disputes that reached the local arbitration level and leaving out disputes that were mediated by the enterprises themselves. Inclusion of mediated disputes and informally negotiated disputes would bring the total in 1999 from 120,191 to 171,669. *China Statistical Yearbook (zhongguo tongjinianjian),* various years (Beijing: China Statistical Publishing House); *(zhongguo laodong tongji nianjian),* various years (Beijing: China Statistical Publishing House).

3. People's Republic of China National Labor Law *(zhonghuarenmingongheguo laodongfa)* was adopted at the Eighth Meeting of the Standing Committee of the Eighth National People's Congress on July 5, 1994, and went into effect on January 1, 1995.

4. Guo Chengdu, "Fujian Province FIEs' Labor Disputes: Special Characteristics and Countermeasures," *(fujianshengsanziqiye laozijiufendetedianjiduice), Research and Suggestions* (1995); Lin Zhengong and Chen Yulin, "Special Characteristics of and Countermeasures for Slowdowns and Strikes in Foreign-Invested Enterprises," *(sanzi qiyegongren daigong bagongde tedian he duice) China Labor Science* 5 (1993), 33–35; Lu Hong, "From Disorder to Order: Analysis of Special Characteristics of Contemporary Labor Disputes," *(cong wuxu dao youxu: xianjieduan laodongzhengyi tezheng fenxi) Journal of Guangzhou Normal University (Social Science Edition)* 20:6 (1998).

5. Interview, Ministry of Labor official, December 12, 2002. For example, see "Where There Is Conflict, They Are There," *(You maodun de difang jiuyou tamen de shenying), Xinmin Evening News,* October 7, 2003, p. 12.

6. Stanley Lubman, *Bird in a Cage: Legal Reform in China after Mao* (Stanford, Calif.: Stanford University Press, 1999) Pitman Potter, "Foreign Investment Law in the People's Republic of China: Dilemmas of State Control," *China Quarterly* (March 1995), 155–85; Karen Turner et al. eds. *The Limits of the Rule of Law in China* (Seattle: University of Washington Press, 2000); Franz Michael, "Law: A Tool of Power," in Yuan-li Wu et al., eds., *Human Rights in the People's Republic of China* (Boulder, Colo.: Westview Press, 1988). Randall Peerenboom is more optimistic about China's development of the rule of law in *China's Long March toward the Rule of Law* (New York: Cambridge University Press, 2002).

7. The concept of "mutual empowerment" was developed in Joel Migdal, Atul Kohli, and Vivienne Shue, eds., *State Power and Social Forces: Domination and Transformation in the Third World* (New York: Cambridge University Press, 1994). Xu Wang argues that rural elections also have mutually empowered peas-

ants and the state apparatus. Xu Wang, "Mutual Empowerment of State and Peasantry: Grassroots Development in Rural China," *World Development,* 25 (1997), 1431–42.

8. Quoted in Albert H. Y. Chen, "Toward a Legal Enlightenment: Discussions in Contemporary China on the Rule of Law," *UCLA Pacific Basin Law Journal* 17:125 (Fall 1999 / Spring 2000), 127.

9. Peerenboom (2002), 239.

10. Zhenmin Wang, "The Developing Rule of Law in China," *Harvard Asia Quarterly* (Autumn 2000).

11. Ching Kwan Lee, "From the Specter of Mao to the Spirit of the Law: Labor Insurgency in China," *Theory and Society* 31 (April 2002), 218.

12. Robert Seidman, Ann Seidman, and Janice Payne, eds. *Legislative Drafting for Market Reform: Some Lessons from China* (New York: St Martin's Press: 1997).

13. Here China may be learning from some of its Southeast Asian neighbors. Singapore and Malaysia have both used legal institutions to suppress dissent and to control opposition parties, often by bankrupting opposition leaders or parties through costly suits.

14. Alan Hunt, Mindie Lazarus-Black and Susan Hirsch, *Contested States: Law, Hegemony, and Resistance* (New York: Routledge, 1994).

15. Ibid.

16. William Alford, "Double-Edged Swords Cut Both Ways: Law and Legitimacy in the People's Republic of China," in Tu Wei-ming, ed., *China in Transformation* (Cambridge: Harvard University Press), 45–69.

17. See Ronald C. Keith and Zhiqiu Lin, *Law and Justice in China's New Marketplace* (New York Palgrave, 2002); Hilary K. Josephs, "Labor Law in a 'Socialist Market Economy': The Case of China," *Columbia Journal of Transnational Law* 33:559 (1995).

18. Margaret Pearson, *Joint Ventures in the People's Republic of China* (Princeton: Princeton University Press, 1991), 105.

19. Pitman B. Potter, "Foreign Investment Law in the People's Republic of China: Dilemmas of State Control," *China Quarterly* (March 1995), 155–85. Potter also finds that due to declining central state capacity and ineffective implementation, the state is not very successful in controlling foreign capital or local governments for that matter.

20. Pearson (1991), 63.

21. "Sino-Foreign Equity Joint Venture Law," adopted at the Fifth National People's Congress on July 1, 1979, and revised at the Third Session of the Seventh National People's Congress, April 4, 1990; "Provisions of the People's Republic of China for Labor Management in Chinese-Foreign Joint Ventures," promulgated by the State Council on and effective as of July 26, 1980. English and Chinese versions of these laws and regulations can be found at www.qis.net/chinalaw/prclaw. Last accessed September 6, 2000.

22. Article 2 of the provisions reads, "The employment dismissal, and resignation of the staff and workers of joint ventures, and their production and work tasks, wages and awards and punishments, work schedules and holidays and paid leaves of absence, labor insurance and welfare benefits, labor protection, labor

discipline and other matters shall be prescribed through the signing of labor contracts."

23. Gordon White, "The Politics of Economic Reform in Chinese Industry: The Introduction of the Labour Contract System," *China Quarterly* 111 (September 1987), 367.

24. "Labour Law of the People's Republic of China" (*zhonghuarenmingonghe-guo laodongfa*) *China Law and Practice* (August 29, 1994), 21–40.

25. Andrew Walder, *Communist Neo-traditionalism: Work and Authority in Chinese Industry.* (Berkeley and Los Angeles: University of California Press, 1986). For a criticism and revision of Walder see Brantly Womack, "Transfigured Community: Neo-traditionalism and Work-Unit Socialism in China," *China Quarterly* (July 1991), 324–32.

26. White (1987); Pat Howard, "Rice Bowls and Job Security: The Urban Contract Labour System," *Australian Journal of Chinese Affairs* 25 (January 1991), 93–114.

27. Chen (1997) 8. Chen Chunlai "The Evolution and Main Features of China's Foreign Direct Investment Policies, Working Paper 97/15, Chinese Economies Research Centre, University of Adelaide, (December 1997).

28. Cycles of reform are discussed in Richard Baum, *Burying Mao* (Princeton: Princeton University Press, 1994).

29. Howard (1991), 95–96.

30. Dorothy Solinger traces the restrictions on rural migration to urban areas over time. She finds that by the early 1960s, stringent measures were in place to control the flow of rural labor and to consolidate a dualistic pattern of employment. *Contesting Citizenship: Peasant Migrants, the State, and the Logic of the Market* (Berkeley and Los Angeles: University of California Press, 1999), 35–36.

31. Elizabeth Perry and Li Xun, *Proletarian Power: Shanghai in the Cultural Revolution* (Boulder, Colo.: Westview Press, 1997).

32. Howard (1991), 96.

33. White (1987), 369–73.

34. Ibid, 381.

35. "Temporary Implementing Regulations for Labor Contracts in State-Run Enterprises" (*guoyingqiye shixinglaodonghetongzhi zhexingguiding*), in Chunhua Dai, *Labor Contracts* (*laodong hetong*) (Beijing: China Politics and Law University Press, 1997), 446.

36. Andrew Walder, "Wage Reform and the Web of Factory Interests," *China Quarterly* 109 (March 1987), 40.

37. Michel Korzec, *Labour and the Failure of Reform in China* (New York: St. Martin's Press, 1992); Gordon White, "State and Market in China's Labour Reforms, *Journal of Development Studies* 24 (July 1988), 180–202.

38. White (1987), 387.

39. Interview, general manager, Sino-HK JV, Tangshan, July 1997 and July 1999.

40. The boom in FDI from China's Asian neighbors happens shortly after the democratization processes in Taiwan and South Korea. Some foreign enterprise managers specifically mentioned problems related to rising wages and rising unionization among their plants in other places as reasons leading to the decision

to open up production locations in the PRC. Interview, Taiwanese WFOE personnel manager, Shanghai, May 1997. Another threatened that his factory would move to Vietnam if similar problems arose in China. Interview, Taiwanese WFOE, general manager, Shanghai, May 1997.

41. Li Xingwen, "How to Interpret and Resolve Labor Problems in FIEs" (*ruhe kandai he jiejue sanziqiyezhong de laogongwenti*), *Theoretical Trends* (lilundongtai), June 20, 1994; "Several Existing Problems in FIEs" (*sanziqiye muqian cunzai de jige wenti*), *Report of the Development Centre of the State Council, PRC* (November 7, 1992); "Report on Chinese Private Enterprise Employment and Labor Relations" (*zhongguo siyingqiye guyongjilaodongguanxi baogao*) in *Social Class and Social Stratum in China's New Era* (*zhongguo xinshiqi jiejijieceng baogao*) (Liaoning: Liaoning People's Publishing House, 1995), 292–333.

42. A study by the Economist Intelligence Unit on foreign firms in China found that human resource problems were on the top of a list of problems for investors. "Multinational Companies in China: Winners and Losers." *Economist Intelligence Unit, 1997;* Keith Goodall and Willem Burgers, "Frequent Fliers: Strong Retention Programs Are the Key to Curbing Chinese Manager Turnover," *China Business Review,* May–June 1998, 50–52; Philippe Chevalerais, "Investing in China: What Taiwan's Businessmen Think," *China Perspectives* 11 (May–June 1997), 42–43; Kimberly Silver, "Lessons Learned," *China Business Review,* (May–June 1988), 20–35; Jamie Horsley, "The Chinese Workforce," *China Business Review* (May–June 1988), 50–55; Jamie Horsley, "Chinese Labor," *China Business Review* (May–June 1984), 16–25.

43. Interview, American WFOE manager, Shanghai, May 1997. This manager complained that after years of frustration in trying to let workers go, the company now just paid some workers to stay home.

44. Some local governments grew more intolerant of migrant hiring as the problem of laid-off workers from the SOE enterprises worsened in the 1990s. Many localities set quotas for the use of migrant labor. "Why Foreign Enterprises' Private Hiring Is Repeatedly Forbidden But Difficult to Stop" (*waiqi sizhao yuanhe lujinnanzhi*), *Workers Daily,* May 15, 1997: 5. Josephine Ma, "FIEs Face New Rules on Labour," *South China Morning Post,* February 28, 1997, 4Business.

45. See chapter 4 for more information on how local governments can intervene in the labor market for migrant workers. In doing so, the local government has more control over migrant labor flows and greater opportunities to collect taxes and fees for migrant employment.

46. Kathy Chen, "China's Brightest Minds Leave State Jobs for Money, Fulfillment in the Private Sector," *Asian Wall Street Journal,* January 31, 1994, 3; Carrie Lee, "Industry Frustrated by Job-Hopping," *South China Morning Post,* August 9, 1994, 4.

47. "When Contracts Come to Term, What Should be Done?" (*hetong daoqi yinggai ruhe*) *Beijing Youth News,* March 9, 1997, 8.

48. In practice, discriminatory treatment toward rural migrants has continued unabated. Some local labor regulations specifically do not include migrant workers in their protections. The National Labor Law laid out a principle of equal treatment that has yet to be realized.

49. Both these attributes are highlighted in Chinese analysis of the law. For example see, Chang Kai, *Labour Relations, Labourers, Labour Rights,* (*laodong guanxi, laodong zhe, laoquan*) (Beijing: China Labor Press, 1995); and Junlu Jiang "Labor Dispute Handling: A System to Guarantee the Implementation of the Labor Law" (*laodong zhengyichuli: laodongfa shixingdebaozhangzhidu*), *Workers Daily,* March 21, 1995. Foreign lawyers in China also paid attention to these aspects. Hiroaki Tsukamoto et al., "Restructuring FIEs in China and Procedures to Cut Staff" (*chugoku niokeru gaisho taishi kigyonoresutora oyobi*) *International Commercial Law Journal* (*kokusai shoji ho*) 27:5 (1999).

50. For analysis of the collective contract system see Malcolm Warner and Ng Sek Hong, "The Ongoing Evolution of Chinese Industrial Relations: The Negotiation of Collective Contracts in the Shenzhen Special Economic Zone," *China Information* (Spring 1998), 1–20. Dai Weikang, Li Qi, and Chang Kai. "Multi-level Analysis of Mainland China's Collective Contract System" (*dui zhongguo neidi jitihetong zhidu de jige cengmian de fenxi*), paper presented at the Impact of WTO Membership on Chinese Workers and the Response of the International Trade Union Movement Conference, City University of Hong Kong, Hong Kong, November 29–30, 2003.

51. Zhang Zuoji, "Labor Legislation in China" (*zhongguo laodong lifa*), *Papers of the 4th Lawasia Labour Law Conference* (*yataifaxie disiju laodongfa taolun huiwen*), 1994, 2.

52. "Workers' Rights Become an Issue," *Financial Times,* Business Law Brief, May 1993.

53. "Workers Strike at Japanese Plant in Zhuhai," *FBIS-CHI-93-095,* May 19, 1993.

54. "Labor-Management Dispute Continues in Factory," *FBIS-CHI-93-099,* May 25, 1993.

55. The original report was published by *Beijing Youth Daily.*

56. "China Warns of Surge in Strikes in Joint Ventures," *Agence France Presse,* September 28, 1993; Willy Wo-Lap Lam, "China Heading off Labour Unrest," *South China Morning Post,* July 5, 1993, 8.

57. Copycat strikes were mentioned by managers of firms in Shanghai and Tianjin as well as by lawyers in Shanghai and Beijing. Interview, general manager Sino-Japanese JV, Tianjin; interview, human resources manager, Sino-Japanese JV, Shanghai, July 1997; interview, Chinese lawyer, Sino-Japanese law firm, Shanghai, May 1997.

58. Jiang Junlu, "The Symbol of Workers' Protection," (*laodongzhe de hushenfu*) *Legal Daily,* December 10, 1994, 1; Cao Min, "Industrial Disputes Framework Established," *China Daily,* July 25, 1997, 2; "The Labor Law: The Constitution of Workers," (*laodong fa: laodongzhe de daxianfa*) *China Economic Times,* July 17, 1997, 4.

59. SOE managers adversely affected by foreign and TVE firm practices called it "disorderly competition" (*luanjingzheng*). The most annoying practices cited were hiring of migrants and abusive labor practices, the evasion of any social welfare burden, and slash-and-burn pricing tactics.

60. "Management Facing the Market," (*mianxiang shichang de guanli*) *China Business Times,* March 20, 1997, 7; Ellen Salem (1988), 69; Minghua Zhao and

Theo Nichols, "Management Control of Labour in State-Owned Enterprises: Cases from the Textile Industry," *China Journal* 36 (July 1996), 1–21.

61. Many articles in the late 1990s focused on the issue of "unequal competition" between state firms and their nonstate counterparts. Issues that were often raised included unfair welfare and pension burdens of SOEs, inability to offer competitive salaries for skilled staff in order to compete with foreign firms, and requests from local governments for SOEs to hire unemployed workers. For example, Gong Yibing and Long Lixin, "SOEs: Faced with a Difficult Challenge," (*guoqi: mianlin kunjingde tiaozhan*) *Chinese Worker* (*zhongguo gongren*), 4–7; "Skilled Workers Call for Helpful Policies" (*jishu gongren huhuanzhengce fuzhu*) *Workers Daily,* December 13, 1996, 3; "SOE Welfare Burdens Hinder Profitability," *China Staff,* www.asialaw.com/cs/prcnews/mar00/soe.htm, accessed August 2, 2000.

62. "China's Labour Legislation to Go Faster in 1997," *China Economic News,* no. 5 (February 3, 1997), 7–8. The delay in supplementary legislation was raised at the annual meeting of the Labor Law Study Association, November 19–20, 2003, Beijing. Many labor law experts have pushed for faster passage of these laws as well as revisions of the 1994 labor law, but this has been resisted by the Ministry of Labor.

63. A considerable number of labor law experts in China believe that the law is so distant from reality that it has become impossible to implement. For example, the law limits overtime to thirty-six hours per month, while some factories in China's coastal development zones run twelve-hour shifts with one day off per week, which equals about 136 hours of overtime per month.

64. "China's Labor Legislation to Go Faster." This bureaucratic wrangling was confirmed in interviews with a labor lawyer in May 2001. Interview, labor lawyer, Beijing, May 2001.

65. The Labor Law was caught in a dispute between the Trade Union, the Ministry of Labor, and various bureaucratic bodies who supported greater enterprise autonomy for state firms. The trade union wanted more of a say in enterprise management through the democratic management system in state firms, while state managers wanted to limit trade union interference in management issues. The AFCTU lost on this issue; the democratic management clause in the Labor Law is very weak. The AFCTU was successful in making the labor law inclusive of all workers and in limiting the legal work week to forty-four hours. Interviews, labor lawyers, Beijing, May 1997, July 1997, July 1999; Murray Scot Tanner, *The Politics of Lawmaking in Post-Mao China* (Oxford: Oxford University Press, 1999), 176.

66. While by no means a controversial point in western labor relations, this recognition that workers are in a weak position vis-à-vis management and capital is a significant reversal of the idea long propagated by the state that Chinese workers are the ruling class and the masters of the factory. Some analysis has openly described the conflict between the workers' real position within the factory and their position in socialist society as "masters" (*zhurenweng*). Chang Kai, *Labour Relations, Labourers, Labour Rights,* (*laodong guanxi, laodong zhe, laoquan*) (Beijing: China Labor Press, 1995), 19–20.

67. Jiang Junlu, "The Handling of Labor Disputes: The Guarantor of the Im-

plementation of the Labor Law" (*laodong zhengyi chuli laodongfa shishi de baozhang zhidu*), *Workers Daily,* March 21, 1995, 1.

68. Ibid.

69. This process is described in Guo Jun et al., eds. *Manual on the Labor Law and Labor Disputes* (*laodongfa yu laodong zhengyi shiyong shouce*) (Beijing: China Procuratorial Publishing House, 1994), 109–20.

70. Lin Feng, "Labour Dispute Resolution," *Employment Report* 2:2, 48–56.

71. Shoichi Ito, "Changes in Labour Markets, Labour Law, and Industrial Relations in Modern China." Paper presented at 1996 Asian Regional Conference on Industrial Relations, 12.

72. The 2001 revised Trade Union Law offers a slightly strengthened union responsibility to workers. Article 6 now reads, "The basic responsibility of the trade union is to safeguard the legal rights of workers. In addition to safeguarding the overall interests of the people of the whole nation, the union should represent and safeguard the legal rights of workers." The first sentence was not in the 1992 Trade Union Law. Article 6 also goes into greater detail specifying how the trade union should achieve its duties: through equal consultation and the collective contract system. Article 6, Trade Union Law of the People's Republic of China, October 27, 2001, and April 3, 1992. Mary E. Gallagher and Junlu Jiang, "China's Labor Legislation," *Chinese Law and Government* 35:6 (Nov.–Dec. 2002).

73. Ibid; Shen Pik-Kwan, "Labour Disputes in China," *Change, Newsletter of the Hong Kong Christian Industrial Committee* (October 1996).

74. The Ministry of Labor translates *zhongcai caijue* as "arbitration lawsuit" but I have used *arbitral judgment* to indicate that this process results in a written judgment, including who was at fault and the amount for compensation.

75. Interviews, labor lawyers, Beijing, March 1997 and May 1997. Labor statistics from *China Statistical Yearbooks, 1994–1998* (*zhongguo tongji nianjian*) (Beijing: China Statistical Publishing House); and *China Labor Statistical Yearbook* (*zhongguo laodong tongjinianjian*) (Beijing: China Statistical Publishing). Also Ito (1996).

76. "People's Court, Procuratorate Present Work Reports to NPC Session," March 11, 2002, BBC Monitoring International Reports. www.lexisnexus.com, date accessed October 12, 2002.

77. Interviews, former Ministry of Labor research, Beijing, December 11, 2002; labor lawyer, Shanghai, December 14, 2002; Tianjin Labor Bureau official, November 20, 2003.

78. The fees required for arbitration and litigation are part of an ongoing debate about access to these procedures. Company representatives and labor officials tend to believe the fees are too low, encouraging frivolous suits. Legal aid advocates and workers believe that these fees are already onerous for poorly paid workers, particularly given the increased need for legal representation due to the complexity of many issues and the use of legal representation by companies. Interview, Tianjin Labor Bureau, November 2003; Interview, Shanghai Higher Court judge, November 2003; interview, Sino-American JV, human resources manager, Shanghai, October 2003; interview, legal aid center employee, Shanghai, October 2003.

79. Jiang Junlu, "Clarify the Position of the Labor Law- Strengthen the Feasi-

bility of the Laws and Regulations (*jinyibu mingque laodongfa diwei zengqiang faluguidingde kexingxing*), *China Labor Newspaper* (*zhongguo laodongbao*), July 6, 1995.

80. The Labor Dispute Arbitration Bureau in Tianjin Economic Development Area also reported that the vast majority of workers preferred arbitration to firm-level mediation. Many workers find a new job first then leave the original company to file suit. This practice protects the worker from extralegal punishment at the hands of management, a common problem for workers involved in disputes with their employer. Interview, TEDA Labor Arbitration Bureau staff member, Tianjin, July 1999. For extralegal punishment, see "Workers Report Problems Only to Have Their Bonuses Deducted," (*zhigongfanying wenti jingbei kouchu jiangjin*), *Workers Daily*; Zhang Xifeng, "Managers Still Choose to Harm Workers' Rights This Way" (*jingli geng xuan zeneng sunhai zhigong quanyi*), *Workers Daily*, February 3, 1997, 5.

81. Various types of legal aid centers have risen up during the 1990s in many Chinese cities. Many of these centers target specific groups, for example, women, workers, and the poor. There are also many workers' hot lines in larger cities that address workers' questions about the Labor Law and other regulations. The Shanghai Trade Union's Labor Law Supervisory Committee set up a hotline and letter box. It received over six hundred responses in the first two weeks of operation. "Going Forward, Protection Is Difficult" (*jubuweinan*), *Workers Daily*, May 26, 1997; Lan Yan, "Discovered through Filing Suits for Workers" (*cong weizhigong daguanci suoxiangdaode*), *Workers Daily*, January 2, 1997: 6; Jiang Junlu, "So Workers May Strive for More Rights" (*weilaodongzhe zhengqu gengduo de quanli*), *Workers Daily*, December 28, 1995.

82. This comparison includes only the labor disputes that reached the arbitration level. Both Taiwan and the PRC have mechanisms to resolve labor disputes through firm-level mediation, but these disputes are not included for either country. In this way we can compare across two relatively similar processes.

83. These themes are discussed in Randall Peerenboom (2002), 27–43; Tsung-fu Chen, "The Rule of Law in Taiwan: Culture, Ideology, and Social Change," in *C. Stephen Hsu, ed., Understanding China's Legal System: Essays in Honor of Jerome A. Cohen* (New York: New York University Press, 2003), 374–410; Hugh T. Scogin, Jr., "Civil 'Law' in Traditional China: History and Theory," in Kathryn Bernhardt and Philip C. C. Huang, eds., *Civil Law in Qing and Republican China* (Stanford, Calif.: Stanford University Press, 1994), 13–41.

84. Sean Cooney, "The New Taiwan and the Old Labour Law: Authoritarian Legislation in a Democratized Society," *Comparative Labor Law Journal* (Fall 1996).

85. Ibid., 5.

86. Interviews, labor lawyers, Beijing, May 1997 and July 1997.

87. Cooney (1996), 7.

88. Ibid., 13.

89. There were 81,524 disputes in urban enterprises and reportedly 153.9 million employees in urban enterprises. *China Statistical Yearbook*, 1999.

90. This is not to ignore problems in China's development of these external institutions. Some of these are discussed in Mary E. Gallagher, "Use the Law as Your

Weapon: Institutional Change and Legal Mobilization in China," in Neil Diamant, Stanley Lubman, Kevin O'Brien, eds., *Engaging Chinese Law* (Stanford, Calif.: Stanford University Press, 2005).

91. Some of these events are detailed by Elizabeth J. Perry, "Labor's Battle for Political Space: The Role of Worker Associations in Contemporary China," in Deborah Davis, Richard Kraus, Barry Naughton, and Elizabeth J. Perry, eds., *Urban Spaces in Contemporary China* (Cambridge: Cambridge University Press, 1995).

92. Dalian Labor Bureau, "Exploration of Problems Related to Collective Work Stoppages," (*guanyu jiti tinggong ruogan wenti de tansuo*) *Laodong zhengyi chuli yu yanjiu* 4 (1997), 13–14.

93. These trends are drawn from the national statistics published by the Chinese government, but interviews at the local level indicated that these trends are also apparent at the local development zone or city level. For example, in the TEDA, the Labor Arbitration Bureau reported a yearly 20 percent increase in the number of disputes, reaching 386 in 1998. The increase in 1999 looked to be significantly higher, with over 515 disputes reported in the first six months. Collective disputes are also increasing. There is also the same general tendency for workers to bypass mediation. The bureau also reported that disputes are most frequent in Taiwanese firms, somewhat frequent in Japanese firms, and rare in American firms. Interview, TEDA Labor Arbitration Bureau staff member, July 1999.

94. The Labor Ministry reported that even though FIEs make up less than 10 percent of all urban firms, over 40 percent of all collective disputes occurred in FIEs in 1994. "Report on the Handling of Labor Disputes in 1994," *Handling and Research of Labor Disputes* (April 1995), 4.

95. "Discussion of the Problems in China's Legislation of Strikes" (*guanyu zhongguo de bagonglifa wenti tantao*), *Handling of Labor Disputes* (July 1999), 12. The author notes that collective disputes have increased nearly 900 percent since 1993.

96. *China Labor Statistical Yearbook, 1996–1998* (Beijing: China Statistical Publishing House).

97. Interview, Taiwanese WFOE, sales manager, Jiangsu, May 2001; interview, Taiwanese WFOE, clerical workers, Jiangsu, December 2002. See also Chan (2001); Lee (1999).

98. *China Statistical Yearbook, 1996–1998*.

99. Information about collective disputes is taken from *China Statistical Yearbook,* 2002.

100. Interview, former Ministry of Labor researcher, December 11, 2002.

101. Mary E. Gallagher, "Providing Legal Clarity: Law and the Shaping of Workers' Grievances." Paper prepared for presentation at the "Reassessing Unrest in China" Conference, December 11–12, 2003, Arlington, Virginia.

102. For the connection between restructuring and a marked rise in disputes see Hu Yimin, "Several Problems to be Resolved in Enterprises' Termination of Employees" (*qiyecituizhigong yingdangzhuyi jiejue de jige wenti*), *Handling and Research of Labor Disputes* (August 1998), 12–14.

103. Li Juexin, "Perspective on Difficult Topics in Labor Relations" (*laodong guanci moca redian toushi*) *Handling and Research of Labor Disputes,* (September 1998), 9.

104. Wu Zhaomin, "Discussion of the Implementation of the Three-Sided Principle in the PRC" (*lun sanfang yuanze zai zhongguo de guanche*), *Handling and Research of Labor Disputes* (September 1996), 23; "The Role of Protecting Rights by Union Representatives: Problems and Countermeasures," *Handling and Research of Labor Disputes* (November 1996), 15–16.

105. Data for the years 1987–93 are taken from Ito (1996). He cites China's Labour and Personnel Management Almanac Editorial Division, *The Labour and Personnel Management Almanac of China (1949/10–1987)* (Beijing: Laodong Renshi Chubanshe, 1989); and Tang Shu-reng and Xi Longsheng, eds., *The Complete Business Works of Labour Law* (Beijing: China Workers Publishing House, 1994).

106. The 1997 proportion of mediated disputes to total disputes was the lowest rate ever. The Ministry of Labor points out that this failure of mediation has much to do with the lack of mediation committees at most foreign, private, and rural enterprises. Fujian Province with its large proportion of nonstate industry, has sought to remedy this problem with the formation of a "floating" meditation committee that can travel to nonstate enterprises and mediate disputes. "Analysis of the Handling of Labor Disputes in 1997" (*yijiujiuqinian laodongzhengyi chuliqingkuangfenxi*), *Handling and Research of Labor Disputes,* (April 1998), 10–14; "Advancement in Local Handling of Labor Disputes" (*gedi laodongzhengyi chuligongzuozai qianjin*), *Handling and Research of Labor Disputes* (June 1998), 9–14.

107. Problems in the Adjustment of Labor Relations Research Group of the Ministry of Labor, "China's Current Work on the Adjustment of Labor Relations (*guanyu woguo xianjieduan laodongguanxi diaozheng gongzuode*), *China Labor Science,* March 20–23, 1994, 13–16.

108. The chain reaction quality (*liansuoxing*) of labor disputes is discussed in Jiang Junlu, "Two Poles Collide," *Legal Daily* (*Fazhi Ribao*), February 18, 1995.

109. Interview, TEDA labor bureau, November 20, 2003.

110. *China Statistical Yearbook,* various years.

111. Jiang Junlu, "To Stay or Go: Legal Analysis of Mainland Employee Resignation" (*zouyuhailiu: zhongguodalu guyongcizhidefalu fenxi*), unpublished paper, June 2000; Cao Min, "China: Law Helps Protect Workers' Rights, *China Daily,* October 11, 1996.

112. *China Statistical Yearbook,* 1996–98.

113. By 2000 Shenzhen's People Court had awarded the highest workers' compensation award. The case involved a worker whose arm was severed in an industrial accident while he was working for a private/foreign company in Dongguan, Guangdong Province. The award for 1.3 million RMB was a great deal higher than the arbitrated award of 115,000 RMB. The case attracted attention for its innovative use of existing laws and regulations to gain a higher award for the worker. Chan Kawai, "The Highest Compensation for Industrial Accident in China," *Change* (July 2000), monthly newsletter of the Hong Kong Christian Industrial Committee.

114. For a discussion of general rights consciousness see Xia Yong, ed., *Toward an Age of Rights* (*zouxiang quanli de shidai*), (Beijing: Chinese Politics and Law University Press, 1995).

115. Chang Kai, *Labour Relations, Labourers, Labour Rights,* (*laodong guanxi, laodong zhe, laoquan*) (Beijing: China Labor Press, 1995), 454.

116. A grafted joint venture (*jiajiehezi*) is a venture between a foreign investor and an existing SOE that usually entails the division of the SOE into profitable and unprofitable halves. Older, more expensive, and less-skilled workers are often left behind in the unprofitable enterprises (which may then go bankrupt), while managers and younger workers will move to the new company.

117. On the large scale strikes in the Northeast in 2002 see "Paying the Price: Worker Unrest in Northeast China," *Human Rights Watch: China* 14:6 (August 2002). See also Michael Sheridan, "China Hit by Wave of Worker Unrest," *Times Newspapers Limited,* October 19, 1997; One report detailed how a "reformist" woman factory head was killed by disgruntled workers, in Wang Jiying, "Can She Become a Martyr?"(*ta neng chengwei lieshi ma*), *China Womens' News,* November s, 1994. In Tianjin the police (Public Security Bureau) announced new measures to protect the areas surrounding factories, many of which were inundated with laid-off workers seeking partial wages. "Tianjin PSB Preserves Factory Safety," (*Tianjin gongan quebao qiye anquan*), *Legal Daily,* July 7, 1997; James Flanigan, "China's Reform: Peril, Promise in the Heartland," *Los Angeles Times,* October 26, 1997, D1. This story details the violent protests that shook an inland province, Sichuan, when an enterprise declared bankruptcy to avoid paying wages and pensions. Managers then quickly restructured the factory and sought out foreign partners.

118. As early as 1994 the Ministry of Labor was publishing reports suggesting legislation be passed on strikes and factory lockouts. By 1999 these suggestions were more detailed and openly supportive of the legalization of strikes. (See below.) Problems in the Adjustment of Labor Relations Research Group of the Ministry of Labor, "China's Current Work on the Adjustment of Labor Relations (*guanyu woguo xianjieduan laodongguanxi diaozheng gongzuode*), *China Labor Science,* March 20–23, 1994, 15.

119. You Quanrong, "Exploration of Several Problems in the Guarantee of Citizen Rights under a Market Economy" (*shichangjingjitiaojianxia gongminquanli jiqibaozhangjigewentitantao*), *Legal Science* (*falu kexue*), 3 (1994), 10–14; Shi Tanjing, "Discussion of the Problems in China's Legislation of Strikes," (*guanyu zhongguo de bagonglifa wenti tantao*), *Handling of Labor Disputes* (July 1999), 12–16; Chang Kai, "China's Strike Legislation," paper presented at the Trade Union Law Research Seminar, Shanghai Normal University, November 11, 2003; Xiao Dechun, "Reflections on Legislation Regarding China's Strike Phenomenon," (*guanyu woguo bagong xianxiang de lifa sikao*), *Research on Finance and Economic Problems* 1:182 (1999).

120. Nearly all of the reasons given to legalize strikes are associated either with the presence of foreign capital on Chinese soil or the need to converge with international practices regarding the right to strike. You Quanrong, "Exploration of Several Problems in the Guarantee of Citizen Rights under a Market Economy" (*shichangjingji tiaojianxia gongminquanli jiqibaozhang jigewentitantao*), *Legal Science* (*falu kexue*) 3 (1994), 10–14.

121. Ibid, 12. The writer avoids the term "foreign capitalist" (*waiguo zibenjia*) with its pre-revolutionary connotation of exploitation and uses the more bland term "foreign businessperson"(*waishang*).

122. The Chinese is *"shangjibumen zuozhu baqiye maigeiwaishang."*

123. There was some speculation in the Hong Kong media prior to the 2001 revision of the Trade Union Law that the right to strike would be reinstated. The 2001 Trade Union Law, however, does not grant a legal right to strike. The only article (27) to mention work actions stipulates, "In the event of a work stoppage or go-slow measures at an enterprise or institution, the trade union shall, on behalf of the workers, enter into consultation with the enterprise, institution, or other interested parties, reflect the views and demands of the workers, and put forward ideas for a solution." This is a slightly more "pro-worker" clause than that of the 1992 Trade Union Law. "Labor law to be revised, allowing workers to strike," Chinaonline, October 4, 2001. www.chinaonline.com:80/issues/social _political/newsarchives. Date accessed October 9, 2001.

124. Interview, Legislation Department, Administrative Commission, TEDA, May 1997 and July 1999.

125. This perception is widely shared by labor researchers in China and foreign investors themselves. Interview, Japanese labor lawyer, Shanghai, July 1999; interview, former Ministry of Labor researcher, December 2002.

126. Zhao Minghua and Theo Nichols, "Management Control of Labor in State-Owned Enterprises: Cases from the Textile Industry," *China Journal* 36 (1996): 1–21. See also Paul Bowles and Gordon White, "Labour Systems in Transitional Economies: An Analysis of China's Township and Village Enterprises," *International Review of Comparative Public Policy* 10 (1998): 245–272.

127. The relatively low rate of labor disputes in SOEs is discussed in greater detail in Mary E. Gallagher, "Use the Law as Your Weapon: Institutional Change and Legal Mobilization in China," in Neil Diamant, Stanley Lubman, Kevin O'Brien, eds., *Engaging Chinese Law* (Stanford, Calif.: Stanford University Press, 2005).

128. Interview, trade union manager, Sino-Japanese JV, Tianjin, July 1997.

129. Interviews, American WFOE, Tianjin, May 1997; Sino-American JV, Shanghai, December 2002; Sino-Japanese JV, Tianjin, July 1997, Sino-Japanese JV, Shanghai, May 1997, July 1999, Sino-Japanese JV, Shanghai, November 2003.

130. Interview, Beijing, November 18, 2003; Ray Cheung, "Scholar Warns against Japan-Bashing; Free Speech could be Hijacked by Ultra-nationalists, Says Top Academic," *South China Morning Post,* January 9, 2004, 8; Robert Marquand, "Japan's War Past Sparks Chinese Rage," *Christian Science Monitor,* November 13, 2003, A1; Ching Cheong, "Chinese Public Speaks Up on Japan Ties," *Straits Times* (Singapore), November 24, 2003.

131. The exact nature and severity of the SOE problem is open to debate. Given the decline in recent years in this sector's size and contributions to output its employment some even wonder if there still is an "SOE problem." Research has found that restructured or privatized SOEs do perform better. However, given that the government's policy since 1997 has been to "grasp" the large SOEs, keeping ownership in the state's control, it is still worrisome that certain problems have not yet been solved, including improving corporate governance, including the selection of managers, and producing globally competitive firms. On these issues see Thomas Rawski, "Is China's State Enterprise Problem Still Important?" Paper prepared for presentation at China's SOE Reform and Privatization Workshop, Uni-

versity of Tokyo, June 25, 2000; Ross Garnaut, Ligang Song, and Yang Yao, "SOE Restructuring in China," credpr.stanford.edu/events/Chinamirror2004/Garnaut _Song_Yao2004.pdf, date accessed August 28, 2004; Weiying Zhang, "China's SOE Reform: A Corporate Governance Perspective," www.gsm.pku.edu/cn/wuan1/ Englishpapers/SIEREF,rtf, date accessed August 28, 2004; and Peter Nolan and Jin Zhang, "The Challenge of Globalization for Large Chinese Firms," *World Development* 30:12 (2002).

CHAPTER 6: FROM STATE-OWNED TO NATIONAL INDUSTRY

1. Robert Gilpin, "The Multinational Corporations and International Production," in Harry F. Dahms, ed., *Transformations of Capitalism: Economy, Society, and the State in Modern Times* (New York: New York University Press, 2000), 364.

2. Chinese Academy of Social Sciences, Institute for Industrial Economics, *China's Industrial Development Report, 2003* (*zhongguo gongye fazhan baogao*) (Beijing: Economic Management Publishing, 2003). See in particular chapter 34 on SOEs in manufacturing, (525–38). Nolan and Wang argue that large SOEs have improved considerably over time often through "institutional innovations" that involved the strategic use of foreign investment and global integration. Peter Nolan and Wang Xiaoqiang, "Beyond Privatization: Institutional Innovation and Growth in China's Large State-Owned Enterprises," *World Development* 27:11 (1999). Nolan and Zhang in a later article find many of the traditional problems persisting in SOEs and threatening their ability to compete globally. Peter Nolan and Jin Zhang, "The Challenge of Globalization for Large Chinese Firms," *World Development* 30:12 (2002).

3. On the foreign sector's contribution to the economy see Jiang Xiaojuan, "China's Foreign Direct Investment: Its Contribution to Growth, Structural Upgrading, and Competitiveness," *Social Sciences in China* 24:2 (Summer 2003). On the development of the private sector see Lan Shiyong, "China's Private Enterprises, 1992–2001," in Zhang Houyi, Ming Lizhi, Liang Zhuanyun, eds., *Bluebook of Private Enteprises, No. 4, 2002* (*zhongguo siyingqiye fazhan baogao*) (Beijing: Social Sciences Documentation Publishing House, 2002).

4. On the debate in China over industrial policy and the creation of "national champions" from large SOEs see Peter Nolan, *China and the Global Economy* (New York: Palgrave Press, 2001).

5. This is not to assert that the Chinese state at present does not have burdens that are related to SOEs. In fact the burdens (obligations to pensioners, state-directed bank funds to keep failing firms afloat, among others) are themselves the cause of the state's change of orientation toward developmentalism and away from socialism. These are the burdens of the past.

6. For example see Marc Blecher and Vivienne Shue, "Into Leather: State-Led Development and the Private Sector in Xinji," *China Quarterly* 166 (June 2001); and Jonathan Unger and Anita Chan, "Inheritors of the Boom: Private Enterprises and the Role of the Local Government in a Rural South China Township," *China Journal* 42 (July 1999): 45–74.

7. China's private sector has developed more quickly since the late 1990s. This later development of the private sector does not contradict the argument here that China's private sector development in relative terms came much later than opening to FDI. Even in 2002 familiar problems continue to dog the development of private industry, including government discrimination, lack of capital and bank credit, and difficulties in expanding in scale or across regions. Some of this is recounted in Yasheng Huang *Selling China: Direct Foreign Investment during the Reform Era* (New York: Cambridge University Press, 2003). See also *Bluebook on China's Private Industry,* no. 4, 2002.

8. Yu Shu'e, "Thoughts on How to Speed Up Development of the Private Economy," (dui jiakuai geti siying jingji fazhan de sikao) *Yanhai Jingji* 8 (2002); Li Min and Niu Ping, "Research on Measures to Develop Heilongjiang's Private Economy after WTO Accession" (*rushihou Heilongjiangsheng geti siying jingji fazhan duice yanjiu*), *zhongguo dangzheng ganbu luntan* 4 (2003); An Hui, "Thoughts on the Promotion of the development of Dalian's Private Economy," (*tuijin dalian geti siying jingji fazhan de sikao*) *Guoji Jingmao* 5 (2002).

9. Yasheng Huang "Internal and External Reform, Parts I and II" September 20, 2000. www.chinaonline.com.

10. Nicholas R. Lardy, *China's Unfinished Economic Revolution* (Washington, D.C.: Brookings Institution Press, 1998).

11. This is a very brief synopsis of the various reform measures undertaken in the 1980s. They are examined in greater detail in chapter 4. The main point is that none of these reforms touched on the ownership structure of the enterprise. The contract-management system has gradually grown closer to ownership reform as contract lengths have lengthened and managers have been given greater control over the enterprise. Although in the end losses of the enterprise are the responsibility of the state, not of the contracted management. Stockholding experiments as well, while nominally changing the structure of the enterprise, generally left the state as the majority stockholder and kept those state stocks as nontransferable. See chapter 3 for changes in the 1990s that have made securitization more akin to privatization.

12. Edward Steinfeld, *Forging Reform in China* (New York: Cambridge University Press, 1998), 22.

13. One notable exception is Haier.

14. Interview, general manager, Tangshan SOE, July 1999; interview, general affairs office manager, urban collective, July 1997.

15. These comparisons ranged from comparisons between Chinese and foreign-invested firms as well as Chinese firms versus foreign multinationals, particularly those from the United States and Japan. For example Li Chengyou, "A Breakthrough Is Needed in Property Rights Reform" (*chanquanzhidu gaige yingyou tupo*), *China Business Times,* March 31, 1997, 2. The author, Li Chengyou, is a Guangdong representative in the National People's Congress and the general manager of a large state-owned conglomerate in Shenzhen. In this speech he presses for deeper reform and justifies it with comparisons to the automotive, electronic, and steel industries of the United States and Japan. Two government researchers interviewed in a separate article in *Workers Daily* also placed reform in the context of an "attack" from imports and foreign capital. "The economy's growth rate

is fast, why is unemployment increasingly severe? Overproduction is the background, structural adjustment is the main cause" (*jingjigaosuzengchang, weiheshiye yujia yansu? zongliang guoshengshibeijing, jiegou diaozhengshi zhuyin*), *Workers Daily,* July 17, 1997, 2.

16. I am not arguing that empirically speaking SOEs had more unfair disadvantages than nonstate firms. In fact SOEs still received ample advantages. Their markets were often protected by bureaucratic fiat, they received bank credit denied to other more efficient sectors, they were bailed out by the government time and time again while nonstate firms went bankrupt, and they had better institutionalized connections with government officials. (Of course from an economic perspective some of these advantages are in truth disadvantages because they strengthen the soft budget constraint and make it hard for an SOE to be good.) The debate about what was wrong with SOEs in the 1990s focused on the disadvantages of SOEs vis-à-vis other sectors. Often this argument was put forward by reformists who wanted to reform SOEs more totally, remove the soft budget constraint, and in letting them fail, allow the best to survive. It was also put forward by managers of SOEs, some who wanted more rational management and some who needed a scapegoat for their own ineptitude, corruption, or bad luck.

17. On national champions see Nolan (2001). On the adoption of piece rates and mimetic processes of adaptation see Lisa A. Keister, "Adapting to Radical Change: Strategy and Environment in Piece-Rate Adoption during China's Transition," *Organization Science* 13:5 (September–October 2002), 459–74. See also Douglas Guthrie, *Dragon in a Three-Piece Suit: The Emergence of Capitalism in China* (Princeton: Princeton University Press, 1998). On the adoption of wage systems from foreign enterprises see "On the Adoption of 'Secret Wages' in Some Shanghai SOEs" (*guanyu shanghaishi bufen guoyouqiye shixing gongzi baomi fangfa*), *Inside Labor* (*Laonei*) 17 (November 1994).

18. Guthrie (1998), 3.

19. Jiang Zemin's report to the Fifteenth National Communist Party Congress, quoted in "On Reemployment of Laid-Off SOE Workers," FBIS-CHI-98-267, wnc.fedworld.gov. Date accessed November 5, 1998.

20. Dennis Woodward, "Reforming China's State-Owned Enterprises," in Zhang Yuezhou et al., eds., *Chinese Economy toward the 21st Century* (Sydney: University of Sydney, 1999), 193.

21. Joseph Kahn, "Major Chinese Firms Are Modeling Themselves on Japanese Conglomerates in their Expansion," *Asian Wall Street Journal,* June 26, 1995, 2; Shawn Shieh, "Is Bigger Better? A Conglomerate Case Study," *China Business Review,* May 1, 1999. Lessons from the Korean model are delineated by the Chinese ministers of Labor and the vice minister of State Economic and Trade Commission in "Chinese Ministers Discuss Enterprise Reform and Labour Problems," www.chinaonline.com/issues/social. Date accessed March 2, 2000. Some Chinese leaders opposed the emphasis placed on large, diversified enterprises and continued to press for government support to small and medium sized business. "Wu Jinglian on Small, Medium Businesses," *Qiushi,* July 16, 1999. In FBIS-CHI-1999-0803, wnc.fedworld.gov. Date accessed September 27, 1999.

22. Joseph Fewsmith *China after Tiananman* (New York: Cambridge University Press, 2001), 203.

23. Jiang Zemin, "Hold High the Great Banner of Deng Xiaoping Theory . . ." Speech delivered at the Fifteenth National Congress of the Communist Party of China. Quoted in Woodward (1999), 194.

24. Interviews at the Tangshan SOE also demonstrated that SOE management had also been made aware of the problems of the Korean model even as they pursued it. Responses to my questions about problems with the Korean chaebol system were detailed defenses of the model in general with some acceptance of the pitfalls.

25. Ren Rongwei and Liu Xiaochan, "The General Trading Company Analyzed," *Problems in International Trade (guoji maoyi wenti),* April 6, 1999: 20–24. FBIS-CHI-1999, wnc.fedworld.gov/cgi. Date accessed September 27, 1999.

26. The merger between Tangshan and QX Cement is introduced here in this section on the central level because as a "key" state enterprise of Hebei Province, Tangshan was one of the SOEs to remain state-owned and to receive the full attention of the state as a potential chaebol-style firm. Tangshan managers mentioned the Korean system frequently in their interviews as a model for their expansion. Interviews, general manager, company group business manager, Tangshan SOE, July 1999. By 2003, however, the company resisted government-run mergers, preferring instead to look for new opportunities in other provinces. These opportunities emerged out of personal ties, not government fiat. Interview, SOE deputy general manager, Tangshan, November 2003.

27. Zhu Rongji, "Cut Staff, Increase Profits, Distribute the Laid Off Workers, Standardize Bankruptcy, Encourage Mergers" *(jianyuan zengxiao, xiagangfenliu, guifanpochan, gulijianbing),* reprinted in *Jingji guanli wenzhai,* March 1997, 6–7.

28. The older SOE had a workforce that was 25 percent larger than the Tangshan SOE but its annual output was only one-third that of Tangshan SOEs. Interview, company group business manager, Tangshan SOE, July 1999.

29. "Report Predicts Merger, Acquisition Wave in China," *Beijing Xinhua,* March 2, 2000. In FBIS-CHI-2000-0302, www.fedworld.gov/cgi-bin. Date accessed May 17, 2000.

30. Interview, company group business manager, Tangshan SOE, July 1999.

31. Tangshan managers mentioned the recent investments of large Taiwanese cement companies as well as that of LaFarge, a French multinational. Interview, Tangshan SOE, deputy general manager, November 2003. See also "France's Lafarge sees China as Growth Area Despite Difficult Market Conditions," *AFX News Limited,* October 23, 2003.

32. One-time severance payments became very widespread by 2003. The *China Daily,* China's official English newspaper even ran a special report on them. Fu Jing, "For Workers, Parting is Painful," *China Daily,* February 2, 2004, 5.

33. "New Exploration of Using Foreign Investment to Spur Revision of an Industry," (a report by the State Development Planning Commission) *Renmin Ribao,* August 10, 1999, 2. FBIS-CHI-1999-0826, date accessed May 17, 2000.

34. No doubt the chairmen and presidents of the multinationals who increasingly invest in China in order to reach its domestic consumer market have quite different ideas about the future of foreign firms in China. As the chairman of Proctor and Gamble stated at *Fortune* magazine's Global Forum, held in Shanghai in

1999, "I believe a more open and prosperous China is sure to provide even bigger room for us." "On World Economic Giants Interests in PRC," *Beijing Xinhua*, September 26, 1999. FBIS-CHI-1999-0926, wnc.fedworld.gov/cgi-bin, date accessed May 17, 2000.

35. "Kodak Snaps Up Lucky Stake," October 24, 2003, *http://englishl.people.com.cn/200310/24/eng20031024_126772.shtml*, date accessed August 25, 2004.

36. Quoted in James Kynge, "Remove the Iron Rice Bowl," *Financial Times*, May 26, 1998.

37. Some analysts of this problem pointed to Taiwan's developmental trajectory in addition to Japan's and Korea's to show that Chinese large firms do better when they are government-run, thus adding an efficiency argument to the argument that China needed to build competitive industries owned by the state, not by private domestic entrepreneurs. They argued that Taiwan's economic structure was made up of many small to medium-sized entrepreneurial firms with the larger, strategic industries kept in government control. They seemed not to notice that Taiwanese small-to-medium business owners did not have to compete with large numbers of foreign-invested firms since most Taiwanese firms were linked to foreign capital indirectly through subcontracting agreements, not equity ownership. Xu Ming, ed. "The State-Owned Enterprise Problem: China Does Not Have Entrepreneurs," *The Critical Moment of Modern China: Twenty-Seven Problems that Need to be Earnestly Resolved* (*guanjianshike dangdai zhongguo jidaijiejuede ershiqqigewenti*) (Beijing: Contemporary China Publishing House, 1997), 208–211.

38. Kynge (1998).

39. Interview with Gai Ruyin, deputy mayor of Shenyang, quoted in James Kynge, "Two-Speed China: State Factories Are Shut or Sold," *Financial Times*, June 16, 1998.

40. You Ji, *China's Enterprise Reform: Changing State-Society Relations after Mao* (New York and London: Routledge Press, 1998), 168.

41. "Xinhua Analyzes Liaoning's SOE Reform," *Xinhua Domestic Service*, March 7, 2000. FBIS-CHI-2000-0307, date accessed May 17, 2000. "Jiangsu's New Policy on State Enterprise Reform," *Nanjing Xinhua Ribao*, February 7, 2000. FBIS-CHI-2000-0223, date accessed May 17, 2000. "On Enlivening Small State Enterprises" (Hunan Province reforms), *Renmin Ribao*, January 13, 2000. FBIS-CHI-2000-0208; Bruce Gilley, "Model Privatization: Guangdong Leads China's State-Enterprise Sell-Off," *FEER*, October 9, 1997: 73; Fan Jun, "State Enterprise Reform Takes Difficult First Step" (Shandong Province reforms), *Openings* 1:1997, 13–16.

42. Clay Chandler, "WTO Membership Imperils China's Industrial Dinosaurs," *Washington Post*, March 30, 2000: A1.

43. Kynge, "Two Speed China." The article quotes a one-time sum of 10,000 RMB.

44. Access to foreign capital varies widely across different regions. Shenyang and other northern cities were more aggressive in their marketing tactics (i.e., going to Europe) because these areas lacked the dynamic nonstate economies that had already grown up on the coast. Fujian, Guangdong Shanghai, Shandong, and

other provinces on the coast all enjoyed a "critical mass" of foreign and private investors to draw from locally. It is, unfortunately, extremely difficult to find data on the number of sales, auctions, mergers, and grafted joint ventures that have occurred. Despite this problem, however, the argument can be made that some of the restructuring precedes the arrival of a buyer. Most local officials and SOE managers are fully aware of the drawbacks to SOEs and make attempts to cut the workforce and boost productivity as a selling point. Recent data on the percentages of FDI that are mergers and acquisitions demonstrate that this trend of foreign acquisition is real. In 1999 Chinaonline stated that 60 percent of China's FDI (or $21 billion) went to mergers and acquisitions. "China ranked No. 2 in absorbing FDI during 1979–99," www.chinaonline.com, October 11, 2000. However it is not clear how this figure was determined as it cannot possibly include only formal M&As, which were still restricted by the government. Other estimates for formal M&As are much lower, about 10% of all FDI in 2002.

45. The notion of an "unequal playing field" is discussed in greater detail in chapter 4.

46. "SOE Welfare Burden Hinders Profitability," *ChinaStaff,* March 2000. www.asialaw.com/cc/prcnews, date accessed August 2, 2000.

47. Labor Science Research Institute, "The Influence of China's Enterprise Reform on the Labor and Social Security Field," Unpublished research paper, November 1998, 5. Interview, researcher, Labor Science Research Institute, Beijing, July 1999.

48. A manager at an urban collective firm in Tianjin noted that when a foreign investors invests in a company owned by the collective, they (the managers at the central office) defer immediately to foreign management practices. Interview, urban collective manager, May 1997.

49. Chinese managers in JVs particularly those with a joint position as a trade union official often spoke of their role in this way. They communicated the production goals and corporate policies of the company to the workforce but they also relayed to management which policies would be most difficult for Chinese workers to accept. This role is most relevant when a large number of workers have been transferred from the Chinese partner. With the rise in popularity of WFOEs this role has become less important. Interview, personnel manager, Sino-Japanese JV, Shanghai, July 1999; Interview, trade union chairman, Sino-American JV, Shanghai, December 2002.

50. Yasheng Huang (2000).

51. Douglas Guthrie *Dragon in a Three-Piece Suit* (Princeton: Princeton University Press, 1998), 216.

52. Reinhard Bendix, *Work and Authority in Industry: Ideologies of Management in the Course of Industrialization* (New York: John Wiley and Sons, Inc., 1956).

53. Ibid., xxi.

54. For example, a typical article in 1996 touting the deepening of state enterprise reform and the establishment of a "modern enterprise" stated that "the most important trait of a correct outlook on honor has collectivism as the foundation. The first demand is that the worker place the state's and the enterprise's honor before his individual honor." "Several Problems in the Establishment of a Modern

Enterprise" (*xiandaiqiye jianshezhong de jigewenti*), *Workers Daily,* November 25, 1996, 2.

55. Blecher found that workers in Tianjin tended to accept the ideas referred to here regarding the market and workers' own fallibility in failing to adjust quickly enough to the demands of a market for labor. Marc Blecher, "Hegemony and Workers' Politics in China," *China Quarterly* (June 2002).

56. Interview, general affairs office manager, urban collective, Tianjin, March 1997.

57. *Waidi dagong yunji lixiang ben xian, xiagang gong zuo dengshoulao, Workers Daily,* October 11, 1997; "Would You Rather Lose Face or Your Rice Bowl" (*Qiudiao mianzi duanqi fanwan*), *Workers Daily,* October 11, 1997. "Where Are the Difficulties in Reemployment" (*zaijiuye nanzaihe chu*), *China Business Times,* March 3, 1997. These were typical articles arguing that laid-off workers must change their mindset regarding employment and go to work for rich peasants in the suburbs.

58. "State Circular on Helping Laid-Off Workers," *Beijing Xinhua,* July 3, 1998, in FBIS-CHI-98-184, wnc.fedworld.gov/cgi-bin. Date accessed December 3, 1998.

59. "Facing Up to Unemployment, What Should Chinese Workers Do?" (*mianduishiye, zhongguo gongrenying zenmaban*), *Shenyang Daily,* March 12, 1997, 2.

60. "Workers, What Kind of Employment Outlook Should You Have?" (*laodongzhe, gaiyou zeyangdejiuyeguan?*), *Workers Daily,* July 18, 1997, 1.

61. Interview, personnel manager, Tangshan SOE, May 1997.

62. The Sino-HK JV had the most apparent Taylorist labor practices, organized around spinning wheels for plastic threads. The managers showed how workers had to stand a certain way in order to operate as many wheels as possible at one time. They had recently changed the pattern to increase the number of wheels per worker, thus increasing the intensity of the work. The productivity of the workers doubled, allowing a large increase in profits with hardly any increase in labor costs. Interview, Sino-HK joint venture general manager, Tangshan, May 1999, November 2003. Minghua Zhao and Theo Nichols found extensive use of "Taylorism" in state-owned textile factories as well as Japanese production methods like lean production and the "full-load work method," a practice intended to utilize every bit of labor productivity in order to cut costs and boost productivity. Zhao and Nichols (1996), 78–80.

63. Interview, General Manager, Tangshan SOE, July 1999.

64. The policy was part of general nationwide campaign to turn workers into "civilized employees" (*wenming zhigong*). Infractions listed above would remove the worker's status as civilized. The "civilized bonus" was 30 percent of the worker's annual salary at this particular SOE. Interview, personnel manager, Tangshan SOE, May 1997.

65. Interview, general affairs office manager, urban collective, Tianjin, March 1997.

66. Firms in Tianjin and Shanghai both reported informal practices of wage setting between firms owned by the same nationality, in particular Japanese and Taiwanese firms through their respective business associations. United States firms in Beijing met monthly with the U.S.-China Business Council to discuss labor and

human resource problems. Japanese companies in a Shanghai development zone circulated surveys of workers' wages and benefits to neighboring factories in an attempt to restrain increases.

67. "Regarding the Experimental Implementation of the Confidential Wage System in Shanghai SOEs" (*guanyu shanghai shi bufen guoyouqiye shixing gongzibaomi fafang*), *Laonei,* November 1994, Report #17.

68. Bendix (1956), 436.

69. Ziya Onis, "Logic of the Developmental State," *Comparative Politics* 24:1 (October 1991), 117.

70. On Japan see T. J. Pempel and Keichi Tsunekawa, "Corporatism without Labor? The Japanese Anomaly," in Philippe Schmitter and Gerhard Lehmbruch, eds., *Trends toward Corporatist Intermediation* (Beverly Hills, Calif.: Sage, 1979), 231–70. See also Frederick Deyo, *Beneath the Miracle: Labor Subordination in the New Asian Industrialism* (Berkeley and Los Angeles: University of California, 1989) and his edited volume *The Political Economy of the New Asian Industrialism* (Ithaca: Cornell University Press, 1987).

CONCLUSION

1. Haitao Zhang et al., eds. *Will Foreign Capital Swallow Up China: Where Should National Industry Go?* (*Waizi Nengfou Tunbing Zhongguo: Minzuqiye ying xiang hechuqu*), (Beijing: Qiye Guanli Chuban She, 1997), 9.

2. Lawrence Lau, Yingyi Qian, and Gerald Roland, "Reform without Losers: An Interpretation of China's Dual-Track Approach to Transition." *Journal of Political Economy* 108 (February 2000), 120.

3. See "Merger, Acquisition of SOEs by Private, Foreign Enterprises Encouraged: Official," *People's Daily Online,* November 19, 2003, http://english.people.com.cn/200311/19/eng20031119_128569.shtml, date accessed August 28, 2004; "Chances and Challenges of M&A of SOEs for foreign capital," *People's Daily Online,* August 17, 2004, http://english.people.com.cn/200408/17/eng20040817_153442.html, date accessed August 28, 2004. An example of the continuous effort by local governments to entice FDI into the restructuring process is Shanghai's publication of new liberalized regulations for foreign investment. They include two important measures (1) "encouraging foreign investors to acquire state-owned enterprises"; and (2) "promoting use of capital markets in setting up joint ventures." The second measure will allow foreign investors to buy up shares of SOEs that were previously limited to domestic investors. "Shanghai Unveils Regs to Lure Foreign Investment," www.chinaonline.com, October 19, 2000.

4. A recent study by Chinese Academy of Social Sciences argued that if the "SOE's welfare payments were brought in line with private or foreign-invested enterprises, many more would be profitable." "SOE Welfare Burden Hinders Profitability," *China Staff* (March 2000).

5. China's private sector has long suffered from discrimination due to the leadership's ideological inclination to favor industry owned by the state or collectives; also because China's banking system has long funneled money to state firms with good political connections over firms with favorable performance indicators,

China's private industry has had difficulty raising money for investment. As one analyst recently commented, "If state-owned enterprises can't perform and there isn't a viable domestic private sector, the economy will by default become mostly foreign-owned." Quoted in Craig Smith, "Private Business in China: A Tough, Tortuous Road," *New York Times* (July 12, 2000). See also Karby Leggett, "Foreign Investment: Not a Panacea," *Wall Street Journal,* January 14, 2002, A1.

6. Yasumuro Kenichi, ed. *China's Labor-Capital Relations and on the Ground Management* (1999) 32; Li Juexin, "Perspectives on the Hotspots of Labor Relations Friction," (*laodongguanxi mocarediantoushi*) *Handling and Research on Labor Disputes* (*laodong zhengyi chuli yu yanjiu*) (September 1998), 9–11.

7. Elizabeth Rosenthal, "Factory Closings in China Arouse Workers to Fury," *New York Times,* August 29, 2000: A1; "Labor Unrest Erupts as Chinese Firms Get Trimmer," *Straits Times* (Singapore), August 26, 2000.

8. See, for example, Tong Xin's account of a Thai acquisition of a SOE in Guangxi Province in "Unemployment Crisis: Its Significance for the Chinese Working Class," *Social Sciences in China* (Winter 2003).

9. T. J. Pempel, "The Developmental Regime in a Changing World Economy," in Meredith Woo-Cumings, ed., *The Developmental State* (Ithaca: Cornell University Press, 1999), 130.

10. Meredith Woo-Cumings, "Introduction: Chalmers Johnson and the Politics of Nationalism and Development," in *The Developmental State* (Ithaca: Cornell University Press, 1999), 1.

11. Frederic C. Deyo, *Beneath the Miracle: Labor Subordination in the New Asian Industrialism* (Berkeley and Los Angeles: University of California Press, 1989).

12. Ronald Dore, *British Factory—Japanese Factory* (Berkeley and Los Angeles: University of California Press, 1974); Price (1997).

13. Deyo (1989); Ping-Chun Hsiung (1996). Ping-Chun Hsiung, *Living Rooms as Factories: Class, Gender, and the Satellite Factory System in Taiwan* (Philadelphia: Temple University Press, 1996).

14. Jang Jip Choi (1989); Hagen Koo in Perry, ed. (1996). Jang Jip Choi, *Labor and the Authoritarian State: Labor Unions in South Korean Manufacturing Industries, 1961–1980* (Seoul: Korea University Press, 1989); Hagen Koo, "Work, Culture, and Consciousness of the Korean Working Class," in Elizabeth J. Perry, ed., *Putting Class in Its Place: Worker Identities in East Asia* (Berkeley and Los Angeles: University of California Press, 1996).

15. Peter Nolan *China Global Economy* (New York: Palgrave, 2001), 217.

16. As is clear from the example above, workers also resort to force and the threat of violence to oppose restructuring. However, my point here still stands. The workers at Meite in Tianjin took the managers hostage because they believed that the layoff decision was in violation of their labor contracts.

17. On "tinkering" see Janos Kornai, *The Socialist System: The Political Economy of Communism* (Princeton: Princeton University Press, 1992).

18. Kevin O'Brien, "Rightful Resistance" *World Politics* 49:1 (1996), 31–55.

Bibliography

BOOKS AND ARTICLES

"Advancement in Local Handling of Labor Disputes" (*gedi laodongzhengyi chuli-gongzuozai qianjin*). *Handling and Research of Labor Disputes* (June 1998): 9–14.

Alford, William. "Double-Edged Swords Cut Both Ways: Law and Legitimacy in the People's Republic of China." In Tu Wei-ming, ed., *China in Transformation*, pp. 45–69. Cambridge: Harvard University Press.

Amsden, Alice. *Asia's Next Giant: South Korea and Late Industrialization*. New York: Oxford University Press, 1989.

"Analysis of the Handling of Labor Disputes in 1997" (*yijiujiuqinian laodong-zhengyi chuliqingkuangfenxi*). *Handling and Research of Labor Disputes* (April 1998): 10–14.

Andors, Stephen. *China's Industrial Revolution: Politics, Planning, and Management, 1949 to the Present*. New York: Pantheon Books, 1977.

An, Hui. "Thoughts on the Promotion of the Development of Dalian's Private Economy" (*tuijin dalian geti siying jingji fazhan de sikao.*) *Guoji Jingmao* 5 (2002).

Annual Survey of Violations of Trade Union Rights, 1995. International Confederation of Free Trade Unions.

Apter, David. *The Politics of Modernization*. Chicago: University of Chicago Press, 1965.

Aslund, Anders. *Gorbachev's Struggle for Economic Reform*. London: Pinter Publishers, 1991.

———. *How Russia Became a Market Economy*. Washington, D.C.: Brookings Institution, 1995.

Aston, Adam. "State-Owned Enterprises Fail to Attract Foreign Investors," *Journal of Commerce*, October 1, 1998, 1C.

Baran, Paul. "On the Political Economy of Backwardness." *Manchester School* (January 1952): 66–84.

Barrett, Richard, and Martin Whyte. "Dependency Theory and Taiwan: Analysis of a Deviant Case." *American Journal of Sociology* (5:87): 1064–89.

Baum, Richard. *Burying Mao*. Princeton: Princeton University Press, 1994.

Bendix, Reinhard. *Work and Authority in Industry: Ideologies of Management in the Course of Industrialization*. New York: John Wiley and Sons, 1956.

Berger, Suzanne, and Ronald Dore, eds. *National Diversity and Global Capitalism*. Ithaca: Cornell University Press, 1996.

Bienefeld, M. "The Significance of the Newly Industrializing Countries for the Development Debate." *Studies in Political Economy* 25 (Spring 1988): 7–39.

Biersteker, Thomas. *Multinationals, the State, and Control of the Nigerian Economy* Princeton: Princeton University Press, 1987.

Binder, Leonard, et al., eds. *Crises and Sequences in Political Development.* Princeton: Princeton University Press, 1971.

Blecher, Marc. "Developmental State, Entrepreneurial State: The Political Economy of Socialist Reform in Xinji Municipality and Guanghan County." In Gordon White, ed. *The Road to Crisis: The Chinese State in the Era of Economic Reform,* London: Macmillan, 1991.

———. "Hegemony and Workers' Politics in China." *China Quarterly* 170 (June 2002): 284–303.

Blecher, Marc and Vivienne Shue. *Tethered Deer: Government and Economy in a Chinese County.* Stanford, Calif: Stanford University Press, 1996.

———. "Into Leather: State-Led Development and the Private Sector in Xinji." *China Quarterly* 166 (June 2001): 369–93.

Brady, David, and Michael Wallace. "Spatialization, Foreign Direct Investment, and Labor Outcomes in the American States, 1978–1996." *Social Forces* 79:1 (September 2000).

Bunce, Valerie. *Subversive Institutions: The Design and Destruction of Socialism and the State.* New York: Cambridge University Press, 1999.

Burawoy, Michael. *The Politics of Production.* London: Verso, 1985.

Byrd, William, and Lin Qingsong. *China's Rural Industry: Structure, Development, and Reform.* Oxford: Oxford University Press, 1990.

Cardoso, Fernando, and Enzo Faletto. *Dependency and Development in Latin America.* Trans. Marjory Mattingly Urquidi. Berkeley and Los Angeles: University of California Press, 1979.

Chan, Anita. "Revolution or Corporatism? Workers and Trade Unions in Post-Mao China," *Australian Journal of Chinese Affairs* (January 1993) 31–61.

———. "Globalization, China's 'Free' (Read Bonded) Labour Market and the Chinese Trade Unions," *Asia Pacific Business Review* 6:3 (Spring 2000), special issue on Globalization and Labor Market Deregulation, 2000.

———. *Chinese Workers under Assault: The Exploitation of Labor in a Globalizing Economy.* New York: M. E. Sharpe, 2001.

Chan, Kawai. "The Highest Compensation for Industrial Accident in China." *Change* (July 2000) (monthly newsletter of the Hong Kong Christian Industrial Committee).

Chang, Kai. *Labour Relations, Labourers, Labour Rights (laodong guanxi, laodong zhe, laoquan).* Beijing: China Labor Press, 1995.

———. "China's Strike Legislation." Paper presented at the Trade Union Law Research Seminar, Shanghai Normal University, November 11, 2003.

Chen, Albert H. Y. "Toward a Legal Enlightenment: Discussions in Contemporary China on the Rule of Law." *UCLA Pacific Basin Law Journal* 17:125 (Fall 1999/Spring, 2000).

Chen, Chunlai. "The Evolution and Main Features of China's Foreign Direct Investment Policies." Chinese Economies Research Centre, University of Adelaide, Working Paper Series 97:15 (December 1997).

Chen, Feng. "Between the State and Labor: The Conflict of Chinese Trade Unions' Double Identity in the Market Reform," *China Quarterly* (December 2003).

Chen, Jiagui. Research on the Development of China's State-Owned Enterprise

Reform (*zhongguo guoyou qiye gaige fazhan yanjiu*). Beijing: Economic Management Press, 2000.

Chen, Tsung-fu. "The Rule of Law in Taiwan: Culture, Ideology, and Social Change." In C. Stephen Hsu, ed., *Understanding China's Legal System: Essays in Honor of Jerome A. Cohen*. New York: New York University Press, 2003: 374–410.

Cheng, Zhong. "Analysis of a Survey of Zhuhai Workers' Thinking and Attitude" (*zhuhai qiye zhigong sixiang xiangtai de diaocha fenxi*). *Gongyun Luntan* (December 1996).

Cheng, Tun-Jen. "Democratizing the Quasi-Leninist Regime in Taiwan," *World Politics* 41 (July 1989).

Chevalerais, Philippe. "Investing in China: What Taiwan's Businessmen Think." *China Perspectives* 11 (May–June 1997): 42–43.

———. "Investment Strategies in China." *China Perspectives* 13 (September–October 1997): 63–67.

China Labor Statistics Yearbook (*zhongguo laodong tongji nianjian*). Beijing: China Statistical Publishing House, various years.

China Statistical Yearbook (*zhongguo tongjinianjian*), Beijing: China Statistical Publishing House, various years.

Chinese Academy of Social Sciences, Institute for Industrial Economics. *China's Industrial Development Report, 2003* (*zhongguo gongye fazhan baogao*). Beijing: Economic Management Publishing, 2003.

Choi, Jang Jip. *Labor and the Authoritarian State: Labor Unions in South Korean Manufacturing Industries, 1961–1980*. Seoul: Korea University Press, 1989.

Chow, Daniel C. K. "Reorganization and Conversion of a Joint Venture into a Wholly Foreign-Owned Enterprise in the People's Republic of China." *Tulane Law Review* (December 1998).

Christiansen, Flemming. "Market Transition in China: The Case of the Jiangsu Labor Market, 1978–1990." *Modern China* 18:1 (January 1992), 72–93.

Chu, Yin-wah. "Labor and Democratization in South Korea and Taiwan." *Journal of Contemporary Asia* 28:2 (1998).

Collier, Ruth Berns, and David Collier. *Shaping the Political Arena: Critical Junctures, the Labor Movement, and Regime Dynamics in Latin America*. Princeton: Princeton University Press, 1991.

Cooney, Sean. "The New Taiwan and the Old Labour Law: Authoritarian Legislation in a Democratized Society." *Comparative Labor Law Journal* (Fall 1996).

Croix, Sumner, Michael Plummer, and Keun Lee, eds. *Emerging Patterns of East Asian Investment in China: From Korea, Taiwan, and Hong Kong*. New York: M. E. Sharpe, 1995.

Crouch, Colin, and Wolfgang Streeck. *Political Economy of Modern Capitalism: Mapping Convergence and Diversity*. London: Sage Publications, 1997.

Crowley, Stephen, and David Ost, eds. *Workers after Workers' States : Labor and Politics in Postcommunist Eastern Europe* . Lanham, Md.: Rowman and Littlefield, 2001.

Cumings, Bruce. "The Legacy of Japanese Colonialism in Korea." In Ramon

Myers and Mark Peattie, eds., *The Japanese Colonial Empire, 1895–1945,* Princeton: Princeton University Press, 1984.

Dahms, Harry, ed. *Transformations of Capitalism: Economy, Society, and the State in Modern Times.* New York: New York University Press, 2000.

Dai, Chunhua. *Labor Contracts (laodong hetong).* Beijing: China Politics and Law University Press, 1997.

Dai, Weikang, Li Qi, and Chang Kai. "Multi-level Analysis of Mainland China's Collective Contract System" *(dui zhongguo neidi jitihetong zhidu de jige cengmian de fenxi).* Paper presented at the Impact of WTO Membership on Chinese Workers and the Response of the International Trade Union Movement Conference, City University of Hong Kong, Hong Kong, November 29–30, 2003.

Dalian EDZ Labor Arbitration Committee and Labor Bureau. "Discussion of Several Problems of Collective Work Stoppages" *(guanyu jiti tinggong ruoganwenti de tantao). Handling and Research of Labor Disputes* (April 1997): 13–14.

Deyo, Frederick. *Beneath the Miracle: Labor Subordination in the New Asian Industrialism.* Berkeley and Los Angeles: University of California Press, 1989.

———, ed. *The Political Economy of the New Asian Industrialism.* Ithaca: Cornell University Press, 1987.

Diamant, Neil J., Stanley Lubman, and Kevin J. O'Brien, eds. *Engaging the Law in China: State, Society, and Possibilities for Justice.* Palo Alto, Calif.: Stanford University Press, 2005.

Dickson, Bruce. *Red Capitalists in China: The Party, Private Entrepreneurs, and Prospects for Political Change.* New York: Cambridge University Press, 2003.

Ding, X. L. "The Illicit Asset Stripping of Chinese State Firms." *China Journal* 43 (January 2000).

———. "Informal Privatization through Internationalization: The Rise of Nomenklatura Capitalism in China's Offshore Businesses," *British Journal of Political Science* 30 (2000): 121–46

"Discussion of the Problems in China's Legislation of Strikes" *(guanyu zhongguo de bagonglifa wenti tantao). Handling and Research of Labor Disputes* (July 1999).

Dong, Baohua, ed. *Legal Information for Older Workers: Two Hundred Questions.* Shanghai: Shanghai Jiaotong University Publishing House, 2003.

Dong, Xiao-yuan, and Louis Putterman. "China's State Owned-Enterprises in the First Reform Decade: an Analysis of a Declining Monopsony." *Economics of Planning* 35 (2002): 109–39.

Dore, Ronald. *British Factory—Japanese Factory.* Berkeley and Los Angeles: University of California Press, 1974.

The East Asian Miracle: Economic Growth and Public Policy (A World Bank Policy Research Report). New York: Oxford University Press, 1993.

Evans, Peter. *Dependent Development: The Alliance of Multinational, State, and Local Capital.* Princeton: Princeton University Press, 1979.

———. *Embedded Autonomy: States and Industrial Transformation.* Princeton: Princeton University Press, 1995.

———. "The Eclipse of the State? Reflections on Stateness in an Era of Globalization," *World Politics* 50:1 (1997).

Fang, Hong Shou. "Union Chairman, What Is Your Duty?" (*gonghui zhuxi, nide zhize shi shenme?*). *Handling and Research of Labor Disputes* (May 1996).

Felker, Greg. "Globalization and the State in Late Industrialization: The Malaysian and Thai Cases." Paper prepared for delivery at the 1998 Annual Meeting of the American Political Science Association, Boston, September 3–6, 1998.

Feng, Lin. "Labour Dispute Resolution." *Employment Report* 2:2: 48–56.

Feng, Tongqing. "Internal Relations and Structure of Chinese Workers under Market Reform" (*zouxiang shichangjingjide zhongguo qiye zhigongneibuguanxi he jiegou*). *Chinese Social Sciences* 3 (May 1993).

Feng, Tongqing, and Zhao Minghua. "Workers and Trade Unions." *Chinese Sociology and Anthropology* 28 (Spring 1996).

Fewsmith, Joseph. *China after Tiananmen: The Politics of Transition.* New York: Cambridge University Press, 2001.

Fields, Karl. "Strong States and Business Organization in Korea and Taiwan." In Sylvia Maxfield and Ben Schneider, eds., *Business and the State in Developing Countries* (Ithaca: Cornell University Press, 1997).

Frank, Andre Gunder. *Capitalism and Underdevelopment in Latin America: Historical Studies of Chile and Brazil.* New York: Monthly Review Press, 1967.

Frazier, Mark W. *The Making of the Chinese Industrial Workplace: State, Revolution, and Labor Management.* New York: Cambridge University Press, 2002.

From Plan to Market: World Development Report, 1996. Washington, D.C.: International Bank for Reconstruction and Development/World Bank. Oxford University Press, 1996.

Gallagher, Mary E. "Providing Legal Clarity:' Law and the Shaping of Workers' Grievances." Paper prepared for presentation at the "Reassessing Unrest in China" Conference, December 11–12, 2003, Arlington, Virginia.

———. "Reform and Openness: Why China's Economic Reforms Have Delayed Democracy." *World Politics* 54:3 (April 2002).

———. "Use the Law as Your Weapon: Institutional Change and Legal Mobilization in China." In *Engaging Chinese Law,* ed. Neil Diamant, Stanley Lubman, Kevin O'Brien. Stanford, Calif.: Stanford University Press, 2005.

Gallagher, Mary E. and Junlu Jiang. "China's Labor Legislation: Introduction and Analysis." *Chinese Law and Government* (November–December 2002).

Gallagher, Mary. "Why Labor Laws Fail to Protect Workers." *China Rights Forum* (Summer 1997): 12–15.

Garnaut, Ross, Ligang Song, and Yang Yao. "SOE Restructuring in China." Paper posted at www.credpr.stanford.edu/events/Chinamirror2004/Garnaut_Song _Ydate accessed August 28, 2004.

Garnaut, Ross, Ligang Song, Yang Yao, and Xiaolu Wang. *Private Enterprise in China.* Canberra: Asia Pacific Press; Beijing: China Center for Economic Research, 2001.

Gereffi, Gary, and Donald Wyman, eds. *Manufacturing Miracles: Paths of Industrialization in Latin America and East Asia.* Princeton: Princeton University Press, 1990.

Global Development Finance: Analysis and Summary Tables, 1999. Washington, D.C.: International Bank for Reconstruction and Development/World Bank.

Gold, Thomas. *State and Society in the Taiwan Miracle*. New York: M. E. Sharpe, 1986.

Goldman, Marshall I., and Merle Goldman. "Soviet and Chinese Economic Reform." *Foreign Affairs* 66:3 (1988).

Goldstone, Jack A. "The Coming Chinese Collapse." *Foreign Policy* (Summer 1995): 35–53.

Goodall, Keith, and Willem Burgers. "Frequent Fliers: Strong Retention Programs Are the Key to Curbing Chinese Manager Turnover." *China Business Review* (May–June 1998): 50–52.

Goodman, David S. G., and Gerald Segal, eds. *China Deconstructs: Politics, Trade, Regionalism*. New York and London: Routledge Press, 1994.

Gu, Edward. "Foreign Direct Investment and the Restructuring of Chinese State-Owned Enterprises, 1992–1995: A New Institutionalist Perspective." *China Information* 12:3): 46–71.

Guo, Chengdu, "Fujian Province FIEs' Labor Disputes: Special Characteristics and Countermeasures"*(fujianshengsanziqiye laozijiufendetedianjiduice)*. *Research and Suggestions, 1995*.

Guo, Jun, et al., eds. *Manual on the Labor Law and Labor Disputes (laodongfa yu laodong zhengyi shiyong shouce)*. Beijing: China Procuratorial Publishing House, 1994.

Guo, Wenlong. "Research on Real Labor Relations." *Shanghai Shenpan Shixian* (September 2002): 12–15.

Guthrie, Doug. "The Declining Significance of *Guanxi* in China's Economic Transformation." *China Quarterly* (June 1998).

———. *Dragon in a Three-Piece Suit: The Emergence of Capitalism in China*. Princeton: Princeton University Press, 1998.

———. "Transition to a Market Economy: The Transformation of Labor Relations in China's Global Economy." Paper presented at the Annual Conference of the Association of Asian Studies, Chicago, March 2001.

Haggard, Stephan. *Pathways from the Periphery: The Politics of Growth in the Newly Industrializing Countries*. Ithaca: Cornell University Press, 1990.

Haggard, Stephan, and Robert Kaufman, eds. *The Politics of Economic Adjustment* Princeton: Princeton University Press, 1992.

Hagiwara, Akira. "Foreign Investment and Worker-Management Relations in China—The Experience of Taiwanese Firms." *Asian Economic Review* (August 1996).

Hall, Peter, and David Soskice. *Varieties of Capitalism: The Institutional Foundations of Comparative Advantage*. New York: Oxford University Press, 2001.

Held, David, Anthony McGrew, David Goldblatt, and Jonathan Perraton. *Global Transformations: Politics, Economics, and Culture*. Stanford, Calif.: Stanford University Press, 2001.

Hellman, Joel. "Winners Take All: The Politics of Partial Reform in Post-communist Transitions," *World Politics* 50:2 (1998): 203–35.

Hewett, Ed A. "Economic Reform in the USSR, Eastern Europe, and China: The Politics of Economics." *American Economic Review* 79:2 (May 1989).

———. *Reforming the Soviet Economy*. Washington, D.C.: Brookings Institution, 1988.

Hickman, Michael M., and Julie Bloch Mendelsohn. "China's Laws Now Give Investors More Options." *National Law Journal,* March 2, 1998, C14.

"High Income for Moonlighters and Migrants." *China Staff* (June 2000). www.asialaw.com/cs/prcnews/jun00/high.htm.

Ho, Samuel, and Ralph Huenemann. *China's Open Door Policy: The Quest for Foreign Technology and Capital.* Vancouver: University of British Columbia Press, 1984.

Hofheinz, R., and Kent Calder. *The Eastasian Edge.* New York: Basic Books, 1982.

Horsley, Jamie P. "Chinese Labor." *China Business Review* (May–June 1984): 16–25.

———. "The Chinese Workforce." *China Business Review* (May–June 1988): 50–55.

Howard, Pat. "Rice Bowls and Job Security: The Urban Contract Labour System." *Australian Journal of Chinese Affairs* 25 (January 1991): 93–114.

Howell, Jude. *China Opens Its Doors: The Politics of Economic Transition* (Boulder, Colo.: Lynne Reinner Publishers, 1993.

———. "The Impact of China's Open Policy on Labour." *Labour, Capital, and Society* (November 1990): 288–322.

Hsing, You-Tien. *Making Capitalism in China: The Taiwan Connection.* New York: Oxford University Press, 1998.

Hsiung Ping-Chun. *Living Rooms as Factories: Class, Gender, and the Satellite Factory System in Taiwan* Philadelphia: Temple University Press, 1996.

Hu, Yimin. "Several Problems to be Resolved in Enterprises' Termination of Employees" (*qiyecituizhigong yingdangzhuyi jiejue de jige wenti*). *Handling and Research of Labor Disputes* (August 1998): 12–14.

Huang, Yasheng. *FDI in China: An Asian Perspective.* Hong Kong: Chinese University Press, 1998.

———. "Internal and External Reforms: Experiences and Lessons from China, Parts I and II." September 20, 2000. www.chinaonline.com.

———. *Selling China: Foreign Direct Investment during the Reform Era.* New York: Cambridge University Press, 2003.

———. "Why China Will Not Collapse." *Foreign Policy* (Summer 1995): 54–69.

Huchet, Jean-Francois. "The 15th Congress and the Reform of Ownership: A Decisive Stage for Chinese State Enterprises." *China Perspectives* (November–December 1997.

Hunt, Alan, Mindie Lazarus-Black, and Susan Hirsch. *Contested States: Law, Hegemony, and Resistance.* New York: Routledge, 1994.

"Investigation on Labor Relations in Public Enterprises Experimentally Run by the People and Countermeasures" *(Dui shixing gongyou minying qiye laodong guanxi de diaocha ji duice). Handling and Research of Labor Disputes* (March 1996).

Ito, Shoichi. "Changes in Labour Markets, Labour Law, and Industrial Relations in Modern China." Paper presented at 1996 Asian Regional Conference on Industrial Relations (Tokyo, Japan, March 14–15, 1996).

Jefferson, Gary, and Inderjit Singh. *Enterprise Reform in China: Ownership, Transition, and Performance.* New York: Oxford University Press, 1999.

Ji, You. *China's Enterprise Reform: Changing State/Society Relations after Mao.* New York: Routledge Press, 1998.

Jiang, Junlu. "To Stay or Go: Legal Analysis of Employee Resignation in Mainland China" (*zouyuhailiu: zhongguodalu guyuan cizhide falufenxi*). (June 2000) Unpublished paper.

Jiang, Xiaojuan. "China's Foreign Direct Investment: Its Contribution to Growth, Structural Upgrading, and Competitiveness." *Social Sciences in China* 24:2 (Summer 2003).

Johnson, Chalmers. *MITI and the Japanese Miracle: The Growth of Industrial Policy, 1925–1975.* Stanford, Calif.: Stanford University Press, 1982.

Josephs, Hilary K. "Labor Law in a 'Socialist Market Economy': The Case of China," *Columbia Journal of Transnational Law* 33:559 (1995).

Kaple, Deborah. *Dream of a Red Factory: The Legacy of High Stalinism in China.* New York: Oxford University Press, 1994.

Keith, Ronald C., and Zhiqiu Lin. *Law and Justice in China's New Marketplace.* New York: Palgrave, 2002.

Keohane, Robert, and Helen Milner, eds. *Internationalization and Domestic Politics* New York: Cambridge University Press, 1996.

Keister, Lisa A. "Adapting to Radical Change: Strategy and Environment in Piece-Rate Adoption during China's Transition." *Organization Science* 13:5 (September–October 2002): 459–74.

Kent, Ann. "China, International Organizations and Regimes: The ILO as a Case Study in Organizational Learning." *Pacific Affairs* 70:4 (Winter 1997–98): 517–33.

Kim, Yun Tae. "Neoliberalism and the Decline of the Developmental State." *Journal of Contemporary Asia* 29:4 (1999).

Kohli, Atul. "Where Do High-Growth Political Economies Come From? The Japanese Lineage of Korea's 'Developmental State,'" *World Development* 22: 9 (1994): 1269–93.

Kornai, Janos. *The Socialist System: The Political Economy of Communism.* Princeton: Princeton University Press, 1992.

Korzec, Michael. "Contract Labor, the Right to Work, and New Labor Laws in the People's Republic of China." *Comparative Economic Studies* 30:2 (Summer 1988): 117–49.

———. *Labour and the Failure of Reform in China.* New York: St. Martin's Press, 1992.

Krup, Barbara, and Hans Hendrischke. "China Incorporated: Property Rights, Networks, and the Emergence of a Private Business Sector in China." *Managerial Finance* 29:12 (2003).

Labor Management. New York: Cambridge University Press, 2002.

Lan, Shiyong. "China's Private Enterprises, 1992–2001." In Zhang Houyi, Ming Lizhi, Liang Zhuanyun, eds., *Bluebook of Private Enterprises, No. 4, 2002* (*zhongguo siying qiye fazhan baogao*). Beijing: Social Sciences Documentation Publishing House, 2002.

Lardy, Nicholas R. "Economic Engine? Foreign Trade and Investment in China." *Brookings Review* 14:1 (Winter 1996).

—————. *China's Unfinished Economic Revolution*. Washington, D.C.: Brookings Institution, 1998.

Lau, Lawrence, Yingyi Qian, and Gerald Roland. "Reform without Losers: An Interpretation of China's Dual-Track Approach to Transition." *Journal of Political Economy* 108 (February 2000).

Lee, Ching Kwan. "From Organized Dependence to Disorganized Despotism: Changing Labour Regimes in Chinese Factories." *China Quarterly* 157 (1999).

—————. "From the Specter of Mao to the Spirit of the Law: Labor Insurgency in China," *Theory and Society* 31 (2002): 189–228.

—————. *Gender and the South China Miracle: Two Worlds of Factory Women.* Berkeley and Los Angeles: University of California Press, 1998.

Leung, Wing-yue. *Smashing the Iron Rice Pot: Workers and Trade Unions in China's Market Socialism.* Hong Kong: Asia Monitor Resource Centre, 1988.

Li, Juexin. "Perspective on Difficult Topics in Labor Relations" (*laodong guanxi moca redian toushi*). *Handling and Research of Labor Disputes* (*laodong zhengyi chuli yu yanjiu*). (September 1998): 9–11.

Li, Min, and Niu Ping, "Research on Measures to Develop Heilongjiang's Private Economy after WTO Accession" (*rushihou Heilongjiangsheng geti siying jingji fazhan duice yanjiu*). *Zhongguo Dangzheng Ganbu Luntan* 4 (2003).

Li, Shaomin, Shuhe Li, and Weiying Zhang, "The Road to Capitalism: Competition and Institutional Change in China." *Journal of Comparative Economics* 28 (June 2000): 269–92.

Li, Xingwen. "How to Interpret and Resolve Labor Problems in FIEs" (*ruhe kandai he jiejue sanziqiyezhong de laogongwenti*). *Theoretical Trends* (*lilundongtai*) (June 20, 1994).

Lin, Yi-min, and Tian Zhu. "Ownership Restructuring in Chinese State Industry: An Analysis of Evidence on Initial Organizational Changes." *China Quarterly* (June 2001).

Lin, Zhengong and Chen Yulin. "Special Characteristics of and Countermeasures for Slowdowns and Strikes in Foreign-Invested Enterprises" (*sanzi qiye gongren daigong bagong de tedian he duice*). *China Labor Science* 5 (1993): 33–35.

Linn, Gene. "China's Sanction of Private Sector Opens Doors for Investment, Trade." *Journal of Commerce,* May 12, 1999, 7A.

Lipset, Seymour Martin. "Some Social Requisites of Democracy: Economic Development and Political Legitimacy." *American Political Science Review* 53 (March 1959).

Liu, Lisheng, et al., eds. "*Foreign Capital's Acquisition of State-Owned Enterprises: Analysis and Countermeasures*" (*waizi Binggou Guoyou Qiye: Shizheng fenxi yu duice yanjiu.*) Beijing: Zhongguo Jingji Chubanshe, 1997.

Liu, Zhiqiang. "Strengthen and Improve the Political Leadership of the Party in Enterprises." (*jiaqiang he gaishan dang dui qiye de zhengzhilingdao*) *Theoretical Trends* (*lilun dongtai*) (January 25, 1997).

Lu, Hong. "From Disorder to Order: Analysis of Special Characteristics of Contemporary Labor Disputes" (*cong wuxu dao youxu: xianjieduan laodong zhengyi tezheng fenxi*). *Journal of Guangzhou Normal University* (Social Science Edition) 20:6 (1998).

Lu, Xiaobo, and Elizabeth Perry eds. *Danwei: The Changing Chinese Workplace in Historical and Comparative perspective*. New York: M. E. Sharpe, 1997.

Lubman, Stanley. *Bird in a Cage: Legal Reform in China after Mao*. Stanford, Calif.: Stanford University Press, 1999.

Ludlam, Janine. "Reform and the Redefinition of the Social Contract under Gorbachev." *World Politics* 43:2 (January 1991).

Ma, Shu-Yun. "Foreign Participation in China's Privatization." *Communist Economies and Economic Transformation* 8:4 (1996).

Mardon, Russell. "The State and Effective Control of Foreign Capital: The Case of South Korea." *World Politics* 1:43 (1990): 111–38.

Maurer-Fazio, Margaret. "Labor Reform in China: Crossing the River by Feeling the Stones." *Comparative Economic Studies* 37:4 (Winter 1995): 111–23.

McKinnon, Ronald. "Gradual versus Rapid Liberalization in Socialist Economies: The Problems of Macroeconomic Control." In Michael Bruno and Boris Pleskovic, eds., *Proceedings of the World Bank Annual Conference on Development Economics, 1993*. Washington, D.C.: World Bank, 1994.

McMillan, John, and Barry Naughton. "How to Reform a Planned Economy: Lessons from China." *Oxford Review of Economic Policy* 8 (Spring 1992).

Michael, Franz. "Law: A Tool of Power." In Yuan-li Wu et al., eds., *Human Rights in the People's Republic of China*. Boulder, Colo.: Westview Press, 1988.

Migdal, Joel, Atul Kohli, and Vivienne Shue, eds. *State Power and Social Forces: Domination and Transformation in the Third World*. New York: Cambridge University Press, 1994.

Montinola, Gabriella, Yingyi Qian, and Barry Weingast. "Federalism, Chinese Style: The Political Basis for Economic Success." *World Politics* 48:1 (1996): 50–81.

"Multinational Companies in China: Winners and Losers." *Economist Intelligence Unit* (1997).

Naughton, Barry. *Growing Out of the Plan: Chinese Economic Reform, 1978–1993*. New York: Cambridge University Press, 1995.

———. "Implications of the State Monopoly over Industry and Its Relaxation." *Modern China* 18:1 (January 1992): 14–41.

———, ed. *The China Circle: Economics and Technology in the PRC, Taiwan, and Hong Kong*. Washington, D.C.: Brookings Institution Press, 1997.

Nelson, Joan, ed. *Economic Crisis and Policy Choice: The Politics of Adjustment in the Third World*. Princeton: Princeton University Press, 1990.

The New Wave of Foreign Direct Investment in Asia. Singapore: Institute of Southeast Asian Studies, 1995.

Nolan, Peter. *China and the Global Economy*. New York: Palgrave Press, 2001.

Nolan, Peter, and Wang Xiaoqiang. "Beyond Privatization: Institutional Innovation and Growth in China's Large State-Owned Enterprises." *World Development* 27:11 (1999).

Nolan, Peter, and Jin Zhang. "The Challenge of Globalization for Large Chinese Firms." *World Development* 30:12 (2002).

O'Brien, Kevin. "Rightful Resistance." *World Politics* 49:1 (1996): 31–55.

Oi, Jean. *Rural China Takes Off: Institutional Foundations of Economic Reform*. Berkeley and Los Angeles: University of California Press, 1999.

O'Leary, Greg, ed. *Adjusting to Capitalism: Chinese Workers and the State.* Armonk, N.Y.: M. E. Sharpe, 1997.

"On the Adoption of 'Secret Wages' in Some Shanghai SOEs" (*guanyu shanghaishi bufen guoyouqiye shixing gongzi baomi fangfa*). *Inside Labor* (*Laonei*) 17 (November 1994).

Onis, Ziya. "Logic of the Developmental State." *Comparative Politics* 24:1 (October 1991): 109–26.

"Over 100,000 workers demonstrate in Mianyang City . . ." *Human Rights in China Press Report,* July 16, 1997.

Pak, Sejin. "Two Forces of Democratization in Korea." *Journal of Contemporary Asia* 28:1 (1998).

Park, Jung-Dong. *The Special Economic Zones of China and Their Impact on Its Economic Development.* Westport, Conn.: Praeger Publishers, 1997.

Pearson, Margaret. *Joint Ventures in the People's Republic of China: The Control of Foreign Direct Investment under Socialism.* Princeton: Princeton University Press, 1991.

———. "The Major Multilateral Economic Institutions Engage China." In Alastair Iain Johnston and Robert S. Ross, eds., *Engaging China: The Management of an Emerging Power.* London: Routledge, 1999, 207–34.

Peerenboom, Randall. *China's Long March toward the Rule of Law.* New York: Cambridge University Press, 2002.

Pempel, T. J., and Keichi Tsunekawa. "Corporatism without Labor? The Japanese Anomaly." In Philippe Schmitter and Gerhard Lehmbruch, eds., *Trends toward Corporatist Intermediation.* Beverly Hills, Calif.: Sage, 1979, 231–70.

"People's Republic of China, Labour Law." *China Law and Practice* (August 29, 1994): 21–40.

Perry, Elizabeth J. "Labor's Battle for Political Space: The Role of Workers' Associations in Contemporary China." In Deborah Davis, Richard Kraus, Barry Naughton, and Elizabeth Perry, eds., *Urban Spaces in Contemporary China.* Cambridge: Cambridge University Press, 1995.

Perry, Elizabeth J., ed. *Putting Class in Its Place: Worker Identities in East Asia* Berkeley and Los Angeles: University of California Press, 1996.

Perry, Elizabeth J., and Li Xun. *Proletarian Power: Shanghai in the Cultural Revolution.* Boulder, Colo.: Westview Press, 1997.

Potter, Pitman. "Foreign Investment Law in the People's Republic of China: Dilemmas of State Control." *China Quarterly* (March 1995): 155–85.

Pravda, Alex. "East-West Interdependence and the Social Compact in Eastern Europe." In Morris Bornstein, Zvi Gitelman, and William Zimmerman, eds., *East-West Relations and the Future of Eastern Europe,* London: Allen and Unwin, 1981.

Price, John. *Japan Works: Power and Paradox in Postwar Industrial Relations.* Ithaca: Cornell University Press, 1997.

Problems in the Adjustment of Labor Relations Research Group of the Ministry of Labor. "China's Current Work on the Adjustment of Labor Relations" (*guanyu woguo xianjieduan laodongguanxi diaozheng gongzuode*). *China Labor Science,* March 20–23, 1994: 13–16.

Przeworski, Adam, and Fernando Limongi. "Modernization: Theories and Facts." *World Politics* 49 (January 1997).

Przeworski, Adam, Michael Alvarez, Jose Antonio Cheibub, and Fernando Limongi. *Democracy and Development: Political Institutions and Well-Being in the World, 1950–1990.* New York: Cambridge University Press, 2000.

Rawski, Thomas. "Is China's State Enterprise Problem Still Important?" Paper prepared for presentation at China's SOE Reform and Privatization Workshop, University of Tokyo, June 25, 2000.

Remmer, Karen. "Theoretical Decay and Theoretical Development: The Resurgence of Institutional Analysis." *World Politics* 50:1 (1997).

Ren, Rongwei, and Liu Xiaochan. "The General Trading Company Analyzed." *Guoji Maoyi Wenti,* April 6, 1999, 20–24. FBIS-CHI-1999, wnc.fedworld,gov/cgi. Date accessed September 27, 1999.

"Regarding the Experimental Implementation of the Confidential Wage System in Shanghai SOEs" (*guanyu shanghai shi bufen guoyouqiye shixing gongzibaomi fafang*). *Laonei,* November 1994, report no. 17.

"Report on Chinese Private Enterprise Employment and Labor Relations" (*zhongguo siyingqiye guyongjilaodongguanxi baogao*). In *Social Class and Social Stratum in China's New Era* (*zhongguo xinshiqi jiejijieceng baogao*). Liaoning: Liaoning People's Publishing House, 1995: 292–333.

"Report on the Handling of Labor Disputes in 1994." *Handling and Research of Labor Disputes* (April 1995).

"A Report on the Status of the National Working Class" (*guanyu quanguo gongren jieji duiwu zhuangkuang de diaocha baogao*). *Trade Union Work Report* (*gonghui gongzuo tongxun*) (1993).

"Research Survey on Shenzhen's Shekou District Union Work." Guangdong Central Union Investigative Bureau, 1993. Unpublished report.

Robinson, Richard, ed. *Foreign Capital and Technology in China.* New York: Praeger Press, 1987.

Rodrik, Dani. *Has Globalization Gone Too Far?* Washington, D.C.: Institute of International Economics, 1997.

"The Role of Protecting Rights by Union Representatives: Problems and Countermeasures." *Handling and Research of Labor Disputes* (November 1996): 15–16.

"The Role of the Union Representative in Protecting Rights during Collective Bargaining: Problems and Countermeasures" (*gonghui daibiao zaijitixieshang tanpanzhong weiquanzuoyong fahuide nandian yu duice*). *Handling and Research of Labor Disputes* (November 1996).

Rona-Tas, Akos. "The Second Economy as a Subversive Force." In Andrew Walder, ed., *The Waning of the Communist State: Economic Origins of Political Decline in China and Hungary.* Berkeley and Los Angeles: University of California, 1995.

Sabin, Lora. "New Bosses in the Workers' State: The Growth of Non-state Sector Employment in China." *China Quarterly* (December 1994).

Salem, Ellen. "Managers Rule, OK?" *Far Eastern Economic Review* (January 28, 1988).

Santoro, Michael. *Profits and Principles: Global Capitalism and Human Rights in China.* Ithaca: Cornell University Press, 2000.

Schmitter, Philippe. "Still the Century of Corporatism." In Frederick Pike and Thomas Strich eds., *The New Corporatism: Social-Political Structures in the Iberian World*. Indiana: University of Notre Dame Press, 1974.

Schumpter, Joseph A. "Capitalism in the Postwar World (1943)." In Harry F. Dahms, ed. *Transformations of Capitalism: Economy, Society, and the State in Modern Times*. New York: New York University Press, 2000.

Scogin, Hugh T., Jr. "Civil 'Law' in Traditional China: History and Theory." In Kathryn Bernhardt and Philip C. C. Huang, eds., *Civil Law in Qing and Republican China*. Stanford, Calif.: Stanford University Press, 1994: 13–41.

Seidman, Robert, Ann Seidman, and Janice Payne, eds. *Legislative Drafting for Market Reform: Some Lessons from China*. New York: St Martin's Press: 1997.

"Several Existing Problems in FIEs" (*sanziqiye muqian cunzai de jige wenti*). *Report of the Development Centre of the State Council*, PRC (November 7, 1992).

Sheldon, Peter and Ernest Ruan. "Employer Combination among Overseas Multinational Organizations in the PRC: Structuring Local Labour Markets in Response to Skill Shortages." Paper presented at the School of Industrial Relations and Organizational Behavior, University of New South Wales.

Shen, Pik-Kwan. "Labour Disputes in China." *Change: Newsletter of the Hong Kong Christian Industrial Committee* (October 1996).

Shenyang City Union Investigative Office. "The Experimental Modern Enterprise System in Shenyang: Union Problems and Countermeasures" (*shenyang Shi xiandaihua qiyezhidu shidianzhong gonghui cunzai de wenti ji duice*). *Union Theory and Practice* (August 1, 1995).

"Shenzhen Stays Ahead: Small Economic Zones in Guangdong Pose Competitive Threat to Shenzhen, China." *China Economic Review* 8:7 (July 1998): 17–19.

Shi Meixia, ed. *Collective Contracts and Collective Bargaining* (*jitihetong hititanpan*). Beijing: Legal Publishing House, 1996.

Shi, Tanjing. "Discussion of the Problems in China's Legislation of Strikes" (*guanyu zhongguo de bagonglifa wenti tantao*). *Handling of Labor Disputes* (July 1999): 12–16.

Shieh, Shawn. "Is Bigger Better? A Conglomerate Case Study." *China Business Review*, May 1, 1999.

Shirk, Susan. *The Political Logic of Economic Reform in China*. Berkeley and Los Angeles: University of California, 1993.

Sikkink, Kathryn. *Ideas and Institutions: Developmentalism in Brazil and Argentina*. Ithaca: Cornell University Press, 1991.

Silver, Kimberly. "Lessons Learned." *China Business Review* (May–June 1998).

"SOE welfare burden hinders profitability." *China Staff* (March 2000). www.asialaw.com/cs/prcnews/mar00/soe.htm.

Solinger, Dorothy J. "The Chinese Work Unit and Transient Labor in the Transition from Socialism." *Modern China* 21:2 (April 1995): 155–83.

———. *Contesting Citizenship in China: Peasant Migrants, the State, and the Logic of the Market*. Berkeley and Los Angeles: University of California Press, 1999.

"Speech of Chen Quansheng at the National Conference of Labor Dispute Resolution." *Handling and Research of Labor Disputes* (*laodongzhenghi chuli yu yanjiu*). (January 1996).

Stallings, Barbara, ed. *Global Change, Regional Response: The New International Context of Development.* New York: Cambridge University Press, 1995.

Stark, David, and Laszlo Bruszt. *Postsocialist Pathways: Transforming Politics and Property in East Central Europe.* New York: Cambridge University Press, 1998.

"State-Owned Firms to Exit Shenzhen." *Journal of Commerce,* July 12, 1999, 6.

Steinfeld, Edward. *Forging Reform in China: The Fate of State-Owned Industry.* New York: Cambridge University Press, 1998.

Stevenson-Yang, Anne. "Unions and Contracts." *China Business Review* (January–February 1996).

Strange, Susan. "The Defective State." *Daedalus* 124 (Spring 1995).

———. *The Retreat of the State: The Diffusion of Power in the World Economy.* Cambridge: Cambridge University Press, 1996.

Studwell, Joe. "Workers Wary over Chinese Buyout Program." *Journal of Commerce,* October 21, 1997, 4A.

Sturgeon, Timothy J. "How Do We Define Value Chains and Production Networks?" Background paper for Bellagio Value Chains Workshop. September 25–October 1, 2000, Bellagio, Italy. http://www.ids.ac.uk/ids/global/bella.html.

Su, Dongshui, et al., eds. *Research on China's Foreign-Invested Enterprises (zhongguo Sanzi Qiye Yanjiu).* Shanghai: Fudan University Press, 1997.

Tang, Rengshu, and Xi Longsheng, eds. *The Complete Business Works of Labour Law.* Beijing: China Workers Publishing House, 1994.

Tang, Wenfang, and William Parish. *Chinese Urban Life under Reform: The Changing Social Contract.* New York: Cambridge University Press, 2000.

Tanner, Murray Scot. *The Politics of Lawmaking in Post-Mao China.* Oxford: Oxford University Press, 1999.

To, Lee Lai. *Trade Unions in China, 1949 to the Present.* Singapore: National University of Singapore Press, 1986.

Tong, Xin. "Unemployment Crisis: Its Significance for the Chinese Working Class." *Social Sciences in China* (Winter 2003).

Toward Sustainable Code Compliance: Worker Representation in China, Reebok International Ltd., November 2002.

Tsai, Kellee. *Back-Alley Banking: Private Entrepreneurs in China.* Ithaca: Cornell University Press, 2002.

Tsukamoto, Hiroaki, et al. "Restructuring FIEs in China and Procedures to Cut Staff" (*chugoku niokeru gaisho taishi kigyonoresutora oyobi*). *International Commercial Law Journal (kokusai shoji ho)* 5 (1999).

Turner, Karen, et al., eds. *The Limits of the Rule of Law in China.* Seattle: University of Washington Press, 2000.

Unger, Jonathan, and Anita Chan. "Corporatism in China." In Barrett McCormack and Jonathan Unger, eds., *China after Socialism: In the Footsteps of Eastern Europe or East Asia,* Armonk, N.Y.: M. E. Sharpe, 1996.

———. "Inheritors of the Boom: Private Enterprises and the Role of the Local Government in a Rural South China Township." *China Journal* 42 (July 1999): 45–74.

"The U.S.-China Business Council: Forecast '98," The United States–China Business Council, January 29, 1998.

Vanhonacker, Wilfried. "Entering China: An Unconventional Approach." *Harvard Business Review* (March–April 1997).

Wade, Robert. *Governing the Market: Economic Theory and the Role of the Government in East Asian Industrialization.* Princeton: Princeton University Press, 1990.

Walder, Andrew. *Communist Neo-traditionalism: Work and Authority in Chinese Industry.* Berkeley and Los Angeles: University of California Press, 1986.

———. "Factory and Manager in the Era of Reform." *China Quarterly* 118 (June 1989): 242–64.

———. "Wage Reform and the Web of Factory Interests." *China Quarterly* 109 (March 1987).

———. ed. *The Waning of the Communist State: Economic Origins of Political Decline in China and Hungary.* Berkeley and Los Angeles: University of California, 1995.

Walter, Carl E., and Fraser J. T. Howe. *Privatizing China: The Stock Markets and their Role in Corporate Reform.* Singapore: John Wiley and Sons (Asia), 2003.

Wang, Fengzhi, ed. *Theory and Practice of Labor Law.* Beijing: China Legal Publishing House, 1995.

Wang, Hongyi. "Dream of the Encircled City: An Examination of the Violation of Workers' Rights in Some FIEs" (*weicheng zhimeng: bufen sanziqiyeqinfan zhigongquanyitoushi*). *Chinese Worker (zhongguo gongren)* 5 (1995): 18–27.

Wang, Hongying. *Weak State, Strong Networks: The Institutional Dynamics of Foreign Investment in China.* Hong Kong: Oxford University Press, 2001.

Wang, Min. "Problems Facing the Handling of Labor Disputes in SOEs and Countermeasures" (*guoyou qiye laodongzhengyi chuli gongzuo mianlin de wenti ji duice*). *Handling and Research of Labor Disputes* (June 1997).

Wang, Mingcai. "Across the Board Sales Are Not the Best Way to Reform Small and Medium-Sized Enterprises." *Contemporary Trends* (April 1997). In BBC Worldwide Monitoring, June 28, 1997.

Wang, Xu. "Mutual Empowerment of State and Peasantry: Grassroots Development in Rural China." *World Development* 25 (1997): 1431–42.

Wang, Zhen Quan. *Foreign Investment and Economic Development in Hungary and China.* Aldershot: Ashgate Publishing, 1995.

Wang, Zhenmin. "The Developing Rule of Law in China." *Harvard Asia Quarterly* (Autumn 2000).

Wank, David. *Commodifying Communism.* New York: Cambridge University Press, 1998.

Warner, Malcolm. "China's Labour-Management System Reforms: Breaking the Three Old Irons (1978–1999)." *Asia Pacific Journal of Management* 18 (2001) 315–34.

Warner, Malcolm, and Ng Sek Hong. "The Ongoing Evolution of Chinese Industrial Relations: The Negotiation of Collective Contracts in the Shenzhen Special Economic Zone." *China Information* (Spring 1998): 1–20.

Waterbury, John. *Exposed to Innumerable Delusions: Public Enterprise and State*

Power in Egypt, India, Mexico, and Turkey. New York: Cambridge University Press, 1993.

Wei, Yuming. "Absorbing Foreign Investment." In *The Open Policy at Work*. Beijing: Beijing Review Publications, 1985.

Weller, Robert, and Jiansheng Li. "From State-Owned Enterprise to Joint Venture: A Case Study of the Crisis in Urban Social Services." *China Journal* 43 (January 2000): 83–99.

White, Gordon. "Chinese Trade Unions in the Transition from Socialism: Towards Corporatism or Civil Society." *British Journal of Industrial Relations* (September 1996): 433–57.

———. "The Politics of Economic Reform in Chinese Industry: The Introduction of the Labour Contract System." *China Quarterly* 111 (September 1987).

———. "State and Market in China's Labour Reforms." *Journal of Development Studies* 24 (July 1988): 180–202.

White, Gordon, ed. *Developmental States in East Asia.* New York: St. Martin's Press, 1988.

Whiting, Susan H. *Power and Wealth in Rural China: The Political Economy of Institutional Change.* New York: Cambridge University Press, 2001.

"Wholly Foreign-Invested Enterprises Make Up 39% of Direct Foreign Investment into China." ChinaOnline, www.chinaonline.com/issues/econ_news, 6/21/00.

Wilson, Jeanne. "Labour Policy in China: Reform and Retrogression." *Problems of Communism* 39 (September–October 1990): 44–65.

Winkler, Edwin, ed. *Transition from Communism in China: Institutional and Comparative Analysis.* Boulder, Colo.: Lynne Rienner, 1999.

Womack, Brantly. "Transfigured Community: Neo-traditionalism and Work-Unit Socialism in China." *China Quarterly* 126 (June 1991): 313–32.

Woo, Wing Thye, Stephen Parker, and Jeffrey Sachs, eds. *Economies in Transition: Comparing Asia and Eastern Europe.* Cambridge: MIT Press, 1997.

Woo-Cumings, Meredith, ed. *The Developmental State.* Ithaca: Cornell University Press, 1999.

Woodward, Dennis. "Reforming China's State-Owned Enterprises." In Zhang Yuezhou et al., eds., *Chinese Economy Towards the 21st Century.* Sydney: University of Sydney, 1999.

"Workers in Foreign-Invested Enterprises." *China Labor Bulletin* (March 1996).

World Bank. *Bureaucrats in Business: The Economics and Politics of Government Ownership.* New York: Oxford University Press, 1995.

World Investment Report: Cross-Border Mergers and Acquisitions and Development (New York: United Nations Publications, 2000).

"Wu Jinglian on Small, Medium Businesses," *Qiushi,* July 16, 1999. In FBIS-CHI-1999-0803, wnc.fedworld.gov. Date accessed September 27, 1999.

Wu, Yanrui. *Foreign Direct Investment and Economic Growth in China.* Cheltenham, UK: Edward Elgar, 1999.

Wu, Zhaomin. "Discussion of the Implementation of the Three-Sided Principle in the PRC" (*lun sanfang yuanze zai Zhongguo de guanche*). *Handling and Research of Labor Disputes* (September 1996).

Xia Yong, ed., *Toward an Age of Rights (zouxiang quanli de shidai)*. Beijing: Chinese Politics and Law University Press, 1995.

Xiang, Derong. "Stockholding Companies' Board of Directors: Existing Problems and Suggestions" (*gufenzhi qiye dongshihui cunzai de wenti he jianyi*). *Union Theory and Practice* (August 1, 1995).

Xu, Ming, ed. *The Critical Moment of Modern China: Twenty-Seven Problems that Need to be Earnestly Resolved (guanjianshike dangdai zhongguo jidaijiejuede ershiqqigewenti)*. Beijing: Contemporary China Publishing House, 1997.

Yang, Dali. *Beyond Beijing: Liberalization and the Regions in China*. New York: Routledge, 1997.

Yang, Mayfair Mei-hui. "Between State and Society: The Construction of Corporateness in a Chinese Socialist Factory." *Australian Journal of Chinese Affairs* 22 (July 1989): 31–60.

Yasumuro, Kenichi, ed. *China's Labor-Capital Relations and On the Ground Management (Chugoku no roshikankei to genchi keiei)*. Tokyo: Hakutoshobo, 1999.

You, Quanrong. "Exploration of Several Problems in the Guarantee of Citizen Rights under a Market Economy" (*shichangjingjitiaojianxia gongminquanli jiqibaozhangjigewentitantao*). *Legal Science (falu kexue)* 3 (1994): 10–14.

Yu, Shue. "Thoughts on How to Speed up Development of the Private Economy" (*dui jiakuai geti siying jingji fazhan de sikao*). *Yanhai Jingji* 8 (2002).

Yuan-li, Wu, et al., eds. *Human Rights in the People's Republic of China*. Boulder, Colo.: Westview Press, 1988.

Zhang, Dong Dong. "Negotiating for a Liberal Economic Regime: The Case of Japanese FDI in China." *Pacific Review* 11:1 (1998): 51–78.

Zhang, Haitao, et al., eds. *Will Foreign Capital Swallow Up China? Where Should National Industry Go? (waizi nengfou unbing zhongguo: minzuqiye ying xiang hechuqu)*. Beijing: Qiye Guanli Chuban She, 1997.

Zhang, Houyi, Ming Lizhi, and Liang Zhuanyun, eds. *Bluebook of Private Enteprises, No. 4, 2002 (zhongguo siyingqiye fazhan baogao)*. Beijing: Social Sciences Documentation Publishing House, 2002.

Zhang, Weiying. "China's SOE Reform: A Corporate Governance Perspective." Paper posted at www.gsm.pku.edu/cn/wuan1/Englishpapers/SOEREF.rtf, date accessed August 28, 2004.

Zhang, Zuoji. "Labor Legislation in China." (*zhongguo laodong lifa*) *Papers of the 4h Lawasia Labour Law Conference (yataifaxie disiju laodongfa taolun huiwen)*. 1994.

Zhao, Minghua, and Theo Nichols. "Management Control of Labour in State-Owned Enterprises: Cases from the Textile Industry." *China Journal* 36 (July 1996): 1–21.

Zheng, Yongnian. "From Rule by Law to Rule of Law? A Realistic View of China's Legal Development." *EAI Working Paper no. 1*. Singapore: National University of Singapore, 1998.

Zhou, Xueguang. "Unorganized Interests and Collective Action in Communist China." *American Sociological Review* 58 (February 1993): 54–73.

Zhu, Rongji. "Cut Staff, Increase Profits, Distribute the Laid Off Workers, Standardize Bankruptcy, Encourage Mergers" (*jianyuan zengxiao, xiagangfenliu, guifanpochan, gulijianbing*). Reprinted in *Jingji Guanli Wenzhai,* March 1997, 6–7.

Zweig, David. *Internationalizing China: Domestic Interests and Global Linkages.* Ithaca: Cornell University Press, 2002.

NEWSPAPERS, NEWS MAGAZINES, WIRE SERVICES, AND ONLINE RESOURCES

Agence France Presse

Asian Wall Street Journal

Baokan Wenzhai

BBC Worldwide Monitoring

Beijing Qingnian Bao (Beijing Youth Daily)

Beijing Xinhua Wire Service

Center for Legal Information of Peking University (www.lib.umich.edu)

China Daily

China News Analysis

The Economist

Far Eastern Economic Review

Fazhi Ribao (Legal Daily)

Financial Times

Gongren Ribao (Workers Daily)

Guangdong Laodongbao (Guangdong Labor Daily)

Jiefang Ribao (Liberation Daily)

Los Angeles Times

Nanfang Zhoumo (Southern Weekend)

The New York Times

Shenyang Daily

South China Morning Post

Washington Post

World News Connection (FBIS)

www.chinaonline.com

Zhongguo Gongshang Shibao (China Business Times)

Zhongguo Jingji Shibao (China Economic Times)

Zhongguo Laodong Bao (China Labor)

Zhongguo Qingnian Bao (China Youth Daily)

Index

ACFTU. *See* All-China Federation of Trade
Unions
All-China Federation of Trade Unions
(ACFTU): Chinese Communist Party
and, 78, 83–84; historic weakness of,
78, 83–84; legal unionization requirements, 44, 76; managerial dominance
despite organizational presence of,
65; National Labor Law, impact on,
198n.65; structure and history of, 82–
84
Aslund, Anders, 164n.17, 170n.36

Beijing Light Bus, 53
Bendix, Reinhard, 147–48, 153
Blecher, Marc, 211n.55
Brady, David, 181n.7
Brazil, 30
Bruszt, Laszlo, 167n.14

capitalism: emergence of in China and
labor relations, 65 (*see also* labor rela-
tions); foreign investment (*see* foreign di-
rect investment); globalization and varieties of, 63 (*see also* globalization);
laboratories for (*see* laboratories for
change)
CCP. *See* Chinese Communist Party
CDS. *See* Coastal Development Strategy
Chan, Anita, 62, 164n.7
change, economic. *See* economic development; laboratories for change
Cheng, Tun-Jen, 171n.52
Chen, Quansheng, 169n.29
Chiang, Ching-kuo, 26
China, Republic of. *See* Taiwan
China Strategy Co., Ltd. (CS), 50–52
China Strategy Investment Corporation,
173n.1
Chinese Communist Party (CCP): decline
in power in firms 1978–1992, 70–71;
domestic private enterprise, divisive de-
bate regarding support for, 27; domi-
nance of organizational structure in pre-

1978 firms, 68–70; Fifteenth Congress,
46, 55, 102, 134, 140, 183n.24; foreign
direct investment and, 157–58; foreign-
invested enterprises, role in, 92–93; the
rule of law and, 101–2; the trade union
and, 78, 83–84
Chinese Enterprise Managers Association, 3
Christiansen, Fleming, 182n.11
Chunlai, Chen, 174n.14
Coastal Development Strategy (CDS), 39–
42
competitive liberalization: competitive
pressure through foreign direct investment, contribution to, 11; effects of, 56–
61; firms, impact on, 13–14; regional
competition and, 11–12
competitive pressure: competition for
skilled labor and, 14; foreign direct investment and, 6, 10–14, 56; ownership
liberalization and, 12–14; regional competition, promotion of, 11–12
confidential wage system, 151–52
convergence of firms: competition as force
promoting, 14; labor disputes and, 18,
112–13, 130; market pressures and, 89–
90
Cooney, Sean, 118
CS. *See* China Strategy Co., Ltd.

decentralization, competitive pressure and,
11–12
democratization: China, Korea, and Taiwan compared, 25–27; economic development and, 10, 165n.19
Deng, Xiaoping: preferential policies promoted by, 12; rule of law, support for,
102; slogan lauded by, 4; southern
China, 1992 visit to, 21, 42, 72, 108
developmentalism. *See* ideology
disarticulation, 14, 169n.14
disorderly competition, 140, 142, 197n.59

East Asian development model, 6–7,
165n.22

into global economy, 11, 24–27; national developmentalist ideology and, 155–56; political and economic impacts of, 10; state capacity and, 9–10
gradualism: growth and, 9; regional competition and, 12
grafted joint ventures (GJV): controversy surrounding, 49–51; defined, 203n.116; increase in, 46–47; joint ventures, distinguished from, 48–49; labor and, 50–52; popularity of, 49
greenfields, 2, 177n.60
Gu, Edward, 46, 49, 58, 178n.68
Guthrie, Douglas, 140, 147, 164n.7

Held, David, 167n. 10
Hickman, Michael M., 177–78n.65
Hong Kong, 174n.22
Huang, Yasheng, 36, 137, 163n.4, 173n.4
Human Resources Club of Electronics Companies in Suzhou Industrial Park, 81
Hungary, 22–23

ideology: developmentalism and foreign direct investment, contradictions between, 7, 135, 153; developmentalism and managerial, 148–53; developmentalism in practice, 139–53; foreign direct investment and, 10, 18–19; globalization and national developmentalism, contradiction between, 155–56; managerial, 147–53; from socialism to developmentalism, 6–7, 136–39; from state-owned to national industry, 133–36
India, 181n.9
iron rice bowl, 1, 13, 15, 163n.3
Isuzu Motor, 53
Itochu, 53

Japan, 24, 188n.72
Jiangling Auto Company, 52
Jiang, Zemin, 1, 140, 144
joint ventures (JV): control of, struggle for, 59–60; diversification of, 42, 45; grafted (see grafted joint ventures); grafted joint venture, distinguished from, 48–49; labor relations in, 94; unionization in, 44–45
JV. See joint ventures

KMT. See Kuomintang
Korea: foreign direct investment, amount of, 30; foreign direct investment and integration into the global economy, comparison to China regarding, 24–27; labor relations in, 156; top ten firms, percentage of GDP by, 171n.45
Kornai, Janos, 19, 166n.5
Kuomintang (KMT), 117–18

Labor Arbitration Committees (LAC), 115
laboratories for change: foreign direct investment and, 6, 10, 14–18; regional competition and, 12; Special Economic Zones as, 106
labor contract system (LCS), 105–10
labor disputes: in China compared to Taiwan, 116–21; collective, trends in, 121–24; fees for arbitration and litigation, 199n.78; firm ownership and, 123–25; foreign investment and, 130–31; increasing numbers of, 98–100; legal institutions and, 98–101, 103, 131–32; mediation, failure of, 125–27, 202n.106; the National Labor Law and, 110–13; rise of, 16, 18; in the 1990s, 114–16; strikes, 128–29, 192–93n.1; trends in, 121–29; worker-initiated, 128; workers' compensation, highest award for, 202n.113
Labor Law. See National Labor Law
labor relations: buying out years of service, 187n.64; capitalism in China and, 62–65, 96–97; capitalist, definition of, 180–81n.1; Chinese Communist Party and, 69, 92–93; confidential wage system, 151–52; conflict in (see labor disputes); contract as foundation of, 64–65; contracts and employment insecurity, 76–82; develomentalist managerial ideology and, 148–53 (see also ideology); the developmentalist state and, 156; domination/suppression of worker organizations, 82–96; downsizing/restructuring of firms and, 89–90; firing workers, ease of, 181n.9; foreign direct investment and the transformation of, 32–33; in foreign-invested enterprises, 85–86, 189n.85; German and Japanese practices, examination of, 181n.6; globalization and, 63, 96; grafted joint ventures

11, 13–14; foreign direct investment and, 6, 19–20; ideological change and, 18–19; pattern of, 11; restructuring and downsizing following, 89. *See also* convergence of firms; foreign-invested enterprises

Pearson, Margaret, 4, 85
Potter, Pitman B., 104, 194n.19
privatization: avoidance of shock-therapy style, 13; grafted joint ventures and, 48–49; nationalist developmentalism and, 18–19, 134–35, 138–39; promotion of by central leadership, 140; sale of state-owned enterprises, 46–47
Proctor and Gamble, 51
Przeworski, Adam, 167n. 9

QX Cement, 141–42

recombinant property, 13, 167n.14
Rona-Tas, Akos, 23
Russia, 30

Schumpeter, Joseph A., 9
segmented deregulation, 12, 167n.13. *See also* competitive liberalization
SEZs. *See* Special Economic Zones
shareholding enterprises (SHEs), 52
Shirk, Susan, 183n.25
Singapore, 194n.13
Solinger, Dorothy, 62, 195n.30
South Korea. *See* Korea
Soviet Union, 20–22. *See also* Russia
Special Economic Zones (SEZs): decision to form, 166n.5; inauguration and problems with, 38–39; as laboratory for change, 14–15, 106; labor contract system, introduction of, 106; as preparation for liberalization, 174n.14; state-owned enterprises and, 55; unionization in, 86–87
Stark, David, 167n.14
state capacity, globalization and, 9–10
state-owned enterprise (SOE): advantages and disadvantages faced by, 207n.16; burdens related to, 205n.5; collective labor disputes in, 121–22; competition for skilled labor, difficulties of, 14, 75, 169n.29, 185n.44, 186n.54; contracts, use of short-term, 78–80; "disorderly

competition" faced by, 197n.59; foreign acquisition of, 173n.1; foreign competition and investment, impact of, 3–4; ideological change and privatization, implications of, 18–19; ideology and reform of, 133–37, 139–43, 146–48; inefficiency, causes of, 169n.32; joint posting in, 90–91; labor disputes, management initiation of, 128; labor relations, reform of, 66, 109–10, 131–32; level playing field and, 14, 16–17, 132, 168n.26, 186n.46; reform and labor relations, 72–75, 89–90; reform of, 20–22, 32, 166n.5; reform of, foreign participation in, 45–56, 58–59; unequal competition faced by, 198n.61; unionization in, 84–86, 188n.70
stock markets, Chinese, foreign participation in, 47–48, 52–55

Taiwan: economic structure of ownership in, 209n.37; foreign direct investment, amount of, 30; foreign direct investment and globalization, comparison to China regarding, 24–27; labor disputes compared to China, 116–21; top ten firms, percentage of GDP by, 171n.45
technology transfer, patent protection and reluctance regarding, 174n.13
Thailand, 30
Tiananmen Square, demonstrations at, 20
township-village enterprises (TVEs), 40, 65, 139–40
Trade Union Law of 2001, 115, 199n.72, 204n.123
TVEs. *See* township-village enterprises

Unger, Jonathan, 62
U.S.-China Business Council, 46–47, 49, 182n.9
USSR. *See* Soviet Union

Wade, Robert, 7
Walder, Andrew, 68, 78
Wallace, Michael, 181n.7
Wang, Xiaoqiang, 205n.2
Wang, Zhongyu, 59
Warner, Malcolm, 74, 185n.41
Wei, Yuming, 38
Wenzhou model, 166n.5